Prog₁ Business Plan for a Health Care Staffing Agency

Health Care Staffing Agency
Business Plan

_____ (date)

Business Name: _____

Plan Time Period: 2017 - 2019

Founding Directors:

Name: _____

Name: _____

Contact Information:

Owner: _____

Address: _____

City/State/Zip: _____

Phone: _____

Cell: _____

Fax: _____

Website: _____

Email: _____

Submitted to: _____

Date: _____

Contact Info: _____

NON-DISCLOSURE AGREEMENT

_____ (Company)., and _____ (Person Name), agrees:

_____ (Company) Corp. may from time to time disclose to _____ (Person Name) certain confidential information or trade secrets generally regarding Business plan and financials of _____ (Company) corp.

_____ (Person Name) agrees that it shall not disclose the information so conveyed, unless in conformity with this agreement. _____ (Person Name) shall limit disclosure to the officers and employees of _____ (Person Name) with a reasonable "need to know" the information, and shall protect the same from disclosure with reasonable diligence.

As to all information which _____ (Company) Corp. claims is confidential, _____ (Company) Corp. shall reduce the same to writing prior to disclosure and shall conspicuously mark the same as "confidential," "not to be disclosed" or with other clear indication of its status. If the information which _____ (Company) Corp. is disclosing is not in written form, for example, a machine or device, _____ (Company) Corp. shall be required prior to or at the same time that the disclosure is made to provide written notice of the secrecy claimed by _____ (Company) Corp.. _____ (Person Name) agrees upon reasonable notice to return the confidential tangible material provided by it by _____ (Company) Corp. upon reasonable request.

The obligation of non-disclosure shall terminate when if any of the following occurs:
(a) The confidential information becomes known to the public without the fault of _____ (Person Name), or;
(b) The information is disclosed publicly by _____ (Company) Corp., or ;
(c) a period of 12 months passes from the disclosure, or;
(d) the information loses its status as confidential through no fault of _____ (Person Name).

In any event, the obligation of non-disclosure shall not apply to information which was known to _____ (Person Name) prior to the execution of this agreement.

Dated: _____

_____
_____ (Company) Corp.
_____(Person Name)

Business and Marketing Plan Instructions

1. If you purchased this Business Plan Book via Amazon's Print-on-Demand System, please send proof-of-purchase to Probusconsult2@Yahoo.com and we will email you the file.

2. Complete the Executive Summary section, as your final step, after you have completed the entire plan.

3. Feel free to edit the plan and make it more relevant to your strategic goals, objectives and business vision.

4. We have provided all of the formulas needed to prepare the financial plan. Just plug in the numbers that are based on your particular situation. Excel spreadsheets for the financials are available on the microsoft.com website and www.simplebizplanning.com/forms.htm
    http://office.microsoft.com/en-us/templates/

5. Throughout the plan, we have provided prompts or suggestions as to what values to enter into blank spaces, but use your best judgment and then delete the suggested values (?).

6. The plan also includes some separate worksheets for additional assistance in expanding some of the sections, if desired.

7. Additionally, some sections offer multiple choices and the word 'select' appears as a prompt to edit the contents of the plan.

8. Your feedback, referrals and business are always very much appreciated.

Thank you

Nat Chiaffarano, MBA
Progressive Business Consulting, Inc.
Pembroke Pines, FL 33027
ProBusConsult2@yahoo.com

Health Care Staffing Agency Business Plan: Table of Contents

Section	Description	Page
1.0	**Executive Summary**	____
1.1.0	Tactical Objectives	____
1.1.1	Strategic Objectives	____
1.2	Mission Statement	____
1.2.1	Core Values Statement	____
1.3	Vision Statement	____
1.4	Keys to Success	____
2.0	**Company Summary**	____
2.1	Company Ownership	____
2.2	Company Licensing and Liability Protection	____
2.3	Start-up To-do Checklist	____
2.4.0	Company Location	____
2.4.1	Company Facilities	____
2.5.0	Start-up Summary	____
2.5.1	Inventory	____
2.5.2	Supply Sourcing	____
2.6	Start-up Requirements	____
2.7	SBA Loan Key Requirements	____
2.7.1	Other Financing Options	____
3.0	**Products and Services**	____
3.1	Service Descriptions	____
3.1.1	Product Descriptions	____
3.2	Alternate Revenue Streams	____
3.3	Production of Products and Services	____
3.4	Competitive Comparison	____
3.5	Sale Literature	____
3.6	Fulfillment	____
3.7	Technology	____
3.8	Future Products and Services	____
4.0	**Market Analysis Summary**	____
4.1.0	Secondary Market Research	____
4.1.1	Primary Market Research	____
4.2	Market Segmentation	____
4.3	Target Market Segment Strategy	____
4.3.1	Market Needs	____
4.4	Buying Patterns	____
4.5	Market Growth	____

Section	Description	Page
4.6	Service Business Analysis	____
4.7	Barrier to Entry	____
4.8	Competitive Analysis	____
4.9	Market Revenue Projections	____
5.0	**Industry Analysis**	____
5.1	Industry Leaders	____
5.2	Industry Statistics	____
5.3	Industry Trends	____
5.4	Industry Key Terms	____
6.0	**Strategy and Implementation Summary**	____
6.1.0	Promotion Strategy	____
6.1.1	Grand Opening	____
6.1.2	Value Proposition	____
6.1.3	Positioning Statement	____
6.1.4	Distribution Strategy	____
6.2	Competitive Advantage	____
6.2.1	Branding Strategy	____
6.3	Business SWOT Analysis	____
6.4.0	Marketing Strategy	____
6.4.1	Strategic Alliances	____
6.4.2	Monitoring Marketing Results	____
6.4.3	Word-of-Mouth Marketing	____
6.5	Sales Strategy	____
6.5.1	Customer Retention Strategy	____
6.5.2	Sales Forecast	____
6.5.3	Sales Program	____
6.6	Merchandising Strategy	____
6.7	Pricing Strategy	____
6.8	Differentiation Strategies	____
6.9	Milestone Tracking	____
7.0	**Website Plan Summary**	____
7.1	Website Marketing Strategy	____
7.2	Development Requirements	____
7.3	Sample Frequently Asked Questions	____
8.0	**Operations**	____
8.1	Security Measures	____
9.0	**Management Summary**	____
9.1	Owner Personal History	____

Section	Description	Page

Section	Description	Page
9.2	Management Team Gaps	_____
9.2.1	Management Matrix	_____
9.2.2	Outsourcing Matrix	_____
9.3	Employee Requirements	_____
9.4	Job Descriptions	_____
9.4.1	Job Description Format	_____
9.5	Personnel Plan	_____
9.6	Staffing Plan	_____
10.0	**Business Risk Factors**	_____
10.1	Business Risk Reduction Strategies	_____
10.2	Reduce Customer Perceived Risk Strategies	_____
11.0	**Financial Plan**	_____
11.1	Important Assumptions	_____
11.2	Break-even Analysis	_____
11.3	Projected Profit and Loss	_____
11.4	Projected Cash Flow	_____
11.5	Projected Balance Sheet	_____
11.6	Business Ratios	_____
12.0	**Business Plan Summary**	_____
13.0	**Potential Exit Strategies**	_____
	Appendix	_____
	Helpful Resources	_____

"Progressive Business Plan for a Health Care Staffing Agency"

1.0 Executive Summary

Industry Overview

Along with a growing aging population, there is an increasing amount of ailments. With all those extra health issues, we need as many Medical professionals as we can get. But 2006 projections from the Bureau of Labor Statistics showed an expected shortfall of more than 1 million nurses by 2020. That's a clear call for staffing professionals to step into the health-care realm and help companies deal with the shortage. There is also a growing demand in pharmacy staffing and preventive Medical and disease management.

Medical Staffing agencies play a significant role in for businesses and workers alike. America's staffing companies employed an average of 2.96 million temporary and contract workers per day in 2007, which is more than any other year according to the American Staffing Association's quarterly employment and sales survey. The U.S. Bureau of Labor Statistics estimates that the U.S. staffing industry will grow faster and add more new jobs than most industries over the next decade. The staffing industry has been growing faster than the economy because of the flexibility provided to businesses and medical professionals. Jobs, flexibility, bridge to permanent employment, choice of alternative employment arrangements, and training are the benefits staffing firms offer to workers. Flexibility and access to talent are the benefits that staffing firms bring to businesses.

Medical staffing companies supply health care professionals, such as nurses and therapists, to health care organizations, such as hospitals or nursing home facilities. For the employee, working for a medical staffing company offers flexibility in choosing assignments and work hours. The organization seeking staffing does not have to screen employees, provide health insurance, benefits or paychecks. Starting a medical staffing company may require significant funding but payback is likely for those agencies that hire quality employees and cost-effectively market their services.

Hospitals, nursing homes, private practices and clinics use temporary medical staffing to hire transcriptionists, certified nursing professionals, and other temporary support staff to fill vacation voids, take up the slack during staff shortages and cover unexpected peaks in admissions. Many healthcare institutions have turned to outside staffing agencies for all of their employee needs, turning over the recruitment and human resource duties to the contractor. The temporary staffing industry continues to expand, with yearly double-digit growth being commonplace. Companies find it convenient and cost-effective to work with a temporary staffing agency to fulfill unforeseen demand, fill short-term vacancies, and assist with changing workloads due to restructuring or mergers. Additionally, employers are like the idea of "test driving" new employees to minimize risk and ensure a good match for permanent positions.

As the industry continues to grow and change, more facilities will be turning to a Health Care Staffing Agency for employees. Agencies must look into the needs of the community that they intend to serve and find out which organizations regularly utilize outside contractors for their staffing needs. Agencies must consider employment trends and average salaries for the types of professionals they plan to recruit and decide which specialties might be most needed. Specialty staffing agencies, such as those for registered nurses, can direct marketing and recruiting efforts to a designated population. Agencies with a broader scope that include aides, office workers and physicians will require a vast network to fulfill the needs of the business.

Resource: http://www.ibisworld.com/industry/healthcare-staff-recruitment-agencies.html

Business Overview

_____ will be a diversified leader in Medical staffing services offering a comprehensive suite of staffing and outsourcing services to the Medical market that include nurse and allied staffing, physician staffing, clinical trials services and other human capital management services.

By leveraging extensive professional recruiting experience, direct knowledge of the Medical industry and a strategic network of recruiters and agents, _____ (company name) is positioned to address the growing critical need for Registered Nurses and other Medical professionals. The company will work with end users to fulfill their Medical staffing requirements or may work on a brokered basis, with other recruiting firms. Main revenues will come from percentage or hourly recruiting commissions, earned on permanent placements or temporary contracts.

On a company-wide basis, _____ (company name) expects to procure approximately _____ (#) contracts with hospitals and Medical facilities, pharmaceutical and biotechnology clients, and other Medical organizations to provide our Medical staffing and outsourcing solutions, in its first year of operations.

_____ (company name) will find and arrange placements for _____ (Medical Professionals) who are registered with it. The agency takes details of job vacancies from clients and aims to match the requirements of the job to the most suitable applicant, either by selecting from its candidate database or by advertising. The agency recruits, interviews, filters and screens potential candidates and provides clients with a shortlist from which they can choose who they want to interview. It then organizes the placement, administers the paperwork and carries out background checks, including Criminal Records Bureau checks. It also advises clients and careers on issues such as statutory requirements and wages.

The agency charges the clients a fee for finding and securing the services of a Medical Professional. The agency will then pay the professional directly for the service they provide. As a Health Care Staffing Agency, we will be an employment service that is licensed by the state department of labor.

As a quality Health Care Staffing Agency, we will verify references and conduct background checks, and may even require applicants to have a physical and a TB test. Our Health Care Staffing Agency will be staffed with licensed employment counselors and recruiters.

_____ (company name) _____ was formed on _____ (date) to be a full-service Health Care Staffing Agency in ____ (city), _____ (state). It will distinguish itself from the competition and capture market share by developing a reputation for absolute trustworthiness. It will follow the best practices of Medical Professional Staffing Agencies, with particular emphasis on excellent customer service, convenient 24/7 hours, a deep selection of pre-screened Medical Professional candidates, in-house skills development programs, a knowledgeable staff and competitive pricing.

The Health Care Staffing Agency will compete on the following basis:
1. Superior level of reliable service.
2. Wraparound services, including home Medical service support.
3. Unique ability to help identify and match the needs and goals of each client with the 'right' Medical Professional.
4. The most selective, thorough and detailed Medical Professional screening service.

We believe that we can become the Health Care Staffing Agency of choice in the _____ area for the following reasons:
1. We will develop a training program to create a competent staff, dedicated to continuously improving their skill sets to better assist our clients in making informed Medical Professional contract arrangements.
2. We will develop a questionnaire to survey changing customer needs and wants, build a customer preference profile and enable clients to express their level of satisfaction.
3. We will become a one-stop destination for clients in need of domestic services, including tutoring, housekeeping and babysitting.
4. We will offer quality services, using the latest profiling and matching software.

In order to succeed, _____ (company name) will have to do the following:
1. Conduct extensive market research to demonstrate that there is a demand for a Health Care Staffing Agency with our aforementioned differentiation strategy.
2. Make superior customer service our number one priority.
3. Stay abreast of developments in the Health Care Staffing Agency industry.
4. Precisely assess and then exceed the expectations of all clients.
5. Form long-term, trust-based relationships with clients to secure profitable repeat business and referrals.
6. Develop process efficiencies to achieve and maintain profitability.
7. Thoroughly understand the client's need for highly qualified, expertly trained medical professionals.
8. Work with medical professionals to find medical jobs and employment opportunities that fit their personality and their needs.

Business Model
Our business model will incorporate a combination of per-diem staffing, travel nursing, and private-duty home care to capitalize on the operational and top line synergies of the

various staffing models, while also broadening the universe of potential acquisitions. After acquiring a base of operations, either per-diem registry or a specialized staffing firm, in a given market, we will augment local staff with the addition of travel nurses and foreign recruits, and provide additional services through our other divisions. This strategy is aimed at building the company's available supply of nurses and other licensed personnel to service its diversified client base in its target markets. Organic growth through acquisition will be accelerated through efficient integration practices and the deployment of additional products and services, such as private-duty home care in an acquired operating market.

Services

_____ (company name) will be initially a regional provider of temporary and permanent employment solutions for nurses/doctors/Medical technicians that work in clinics, hospitals, assisted living facilities, and outpatient centers. The Company will also have the ability to easily source other Medical Professionals, such as physical therapists, speech pathologists, pharmacists, X-ray technicians, imaging equipment specialists, dentists, and other allied health professionals. There are a number of other related Medical staffing services that are in strong demand among the Company's potential clients. Once the Health Care Staffing Agency establishes is initial revenue streams, the business will easily expand into the following types of medical staffing placement services:

1.	Short term/long term temps	2.	Per Diem staffing
3.	Local contracts	4.	Travelers
5.	Physician staffing	6.	Direct Hire
7.	Permanent placement	8.	Executive search

Market

The present demand for _____ (Registered Nurses/Physicians?) exceeds the supply by about _____ (150,000) positions and by _____ (2019?), the shortage is expected to increase to _____ (500,000) positions. In 2017, the recruiting market for _____ (Registered Nurses?) is _____ ($3.5Billion) and by _____ (2019), this figure will grow to about _____ ($5.0 Billion), an average annual growth rate of _____ %.

Marketing Strategy

The foundation for this plan is a combination of primary and secondary research, upon which the marketing strategies are built. Discussions and interviews were held with a variety of individuals and other agencies to develop financial and proforma detail. We consulted census data, county business patterns, and other directories to develop the market potential and competitive situation. We will make appointments with local Medical facilities to talk with the heads of human resource departments, office managers and recruiters. We will introduce our company and its services through these meetings and hand out brochures highlighting the availability of our staff and specialties. We will set up a phone line to handle the requests for staff on a 24-hour basis and consider buying software that is designed for Medical staffing agencies that can help track staff, record hours and payroll and client requests. We will also create a website that clients can use to enter staffing requests and learn more about our company. Our market strategy will be based on a cost effective approach to reach this defined target market. The basic approach to promote our services will be through establishing relationships with key influencers in the community and then through referral activities, once a significant client base has been established.

_____ (company name) will focus on developing loyal client relationships by offering Medical Professional matching services based on the customer's need for time-saving convenience, selection recommendation support and value. The newest service offerings, staff accessibility and value-based pricing will all serve to differentiate our company from the other providers in the area. With the help of an aggressive marketing plan, _____ (company name) expects to experience steady growth.

_____ (company name) also plans to attract its job candidates through the use of the following recruiting methods:

1.	Internet recruiting	2.	Online classifieds
3.	Direct emails	4.	Newsletter
5.	Online job sites	6.	Ezine Advertising
7.	Direct Mailers	8.	Telephone Recruiting
9.	Job Fairs	10.	Word Of Mouth Recruiting (WOM)
11.	Specialty Magazines	12.	Local Newspaper Ads
13.	Industry Specific Journals	14.	Flyers
15.	Press Releases	15.	Website

Resource: www.staffingrobot.com/2013/01/the-top-10-marketing-strategies-for-staffing-firms-in-2013.html

Mission Statement   (optional)
Our Mission is to address the following customer pain points or unmet needs and wants, which will define the opportunity for our business: _____
In order to satisfy these unmet needs and wants, we will propose the following unique solutions, which will create better value for our clients:

_____

Critical Risks
Management recognizes there are several internal and external risks inherent in our business concept. Customer service quality, selection, value pricing and online convenience will be key factors in the consumers' decision to utilize our staffing services. Consumers must be willing to accept our one-stop services and become repeat and referral clients in order for the agency to meet its sales projections. Building a loyal and trusting relationship with our clients and referral partners is a key component to the success of _____ (company name).

Customer Service
We will take every opportunity to help the customer, regardless of what the revenue might be. We will outshine our competition by doing something "extra" and offering added-value services in a timely manner. We will take a long-term perspective and focus on the client's possible lifetime value to our business. By giving careful consideration to customer responsiveness, _____ (company name) goal will be to meet and exceed every

service expectation. Quality service, and quick and informed responsiveness will be the philosophy guiding a customer-centric approach to our Health Care Staffing Agency. By encouraging our employees to provide unparalleled customer service, our staffing business will be rewarded by lasting customer loyalty.

Business Plan Objectives

This business plan serves to detail the direction, vision, and planning necessary to achieve our goal of providing a superior Medical staffing service. The purpose of this document is to provide a strategic business plan for our company and to support a request for a $ _____ ($100,000), five year bank loan to purchase computer equipment, software and supplies, as part of the financing for a start-up Health Care Staffing Agency. The plan has been adjusted to reflect the particular strengths and weaknesses of _____ (company name). Actual financial performance will be tracked closely and the business plan will be adjusted when necessary to ensure that full profit potential and loan repayment is realized on schedule. The plan will also help us to identify and quantify objectives, track and direct growth and create benchmarks for measuring success.

The Company

The business _____ (will be/was) incorporated on _____ (date) in the state of _____, as a _____ (Corporation/LLC), and intends to register for Sub-chapter 'S' status for federal tax purposes. This will effectively shield the owner(s) from personal liability and double taxation. _____ (Company Name) is a _____ (state) based corporation that will provide outsourced HR management and employment solutions for clinics, hospitals, and related Medical facilities in its targeted market. The Company was founded in ___ (year) by _____ -.

Business Goals

Our business goal is to continue to develop the _____ (company name) brand name. To do so, we plan to execute on the following:
1.   Offer Medical Professional matching services and continuing customer support.
2.   Focus on quality controls and ongoing operational excellence.
3.   Recruit and train the very best ethical candidates.
4.   Create a marketing campaign with a consistent look and message content.

Location

_____ (company name) will be located in the ___ (complex name) on _____ (address) in ___ (city), ___ (state). The ___ (purchased/leased) space is easily accessible and provides ample parking for ___ (#) clients and staff. The location is attractive due to proximity to several _____ (hospitals) and _____ (private practices).

Marketing Plan

The foundation for this plan is a combination of primary and secondary research, upon which the marketing strategies are built. Discussions and interviews were held with a variety of Medical professionals and area Medical private practice owners to develop financial and proforma detail. We consulted census data, county business patterns, and other directories to develop the market potential and competitive situation. The marketing plan will rely on an aggressive multi-media marketing campaign and a robust R&D program.

Resource:
www.thestaffingstream.com/2014/01/06/marketing-secrets-of-successful-staffing-and-recruiting-companies/

Competitive Edge

_____ (company name) will compete well in our market by offering competitive prices on an expanded line of pres-screened position candidates, knowledgeable and approachable staff, and by using the latest software to match candidates to clients, and enable convenient online application submissions. Furthermore, we will maintain an excellent reputation for trustworthiness and integrity with the community we serve.

Differentiation Strategy

We will differentiate our staffing agency from other healthcare staffing agencies through comprehensive on-boarding processes, service delivery speed, candidate branding programs, generous incentives, the utmost professional integrity, a dedication to excellence, our expertise in staffing, and a commitment innovations in medical staffing technologies. We will also incorporate new data sets into the analysis and mining of industry job information at scale to allow our firm to differentiate on value, delivering more targeted candidates and ultimately greater insight to clients.

Resources:
http://hiring.monster.com/hr/hr-best-practices/recruiting-hiring-advice/strategic-workforce-planning/staffing-services2.aspx
http://www.bullhorn.com/blog/2014/05/big-data-in-the-staffing-industry/

We will offer the following additional courtesies:
1. A++ Occurrence Malpractice (No tail purchased needed)
2. Next Day and Weekly Payroll for Locum Physicians
3. CAQH Credentialing Standards
4. 24/7 Customer Support
5. Onsite Licensure Department
6. Travel Department

The Management Team

_____ (company name) will be lead by _____ (owner name) and _____ (co-owner name). _____ (owner name) has a _____ degree from _____ (institution name) and a _____ background within the Medical industry, having spent _____ (#) years with _____ (former employer name or type of business). During this tenure, ___ (he/she) helped grow the business from $_____ in yearly revenue to over $___. _____ (co-owner name) has a ___ background, and while employed by ___ was able to increase operating profit by ___ percent. These acquired recruiting skills, work experiences and educational backgrounds will play a big role in the success of our Health Care Staffing Agency. Additionally, our president, _____ (name), has an extensive knowledge of the

_____ area and has identified a niche market retail opportunity to make this venture highly successful, combining his ___ (#) years of work experience in a variety of businesses. _____ (owner name) will manage all aspects of the business and service development to ensure effective customer responsiveness while monitoring day-to-day operations. Qualified and trained clerks personally trained by _____ (owner name) in customer service skills will provide additional support services. Support staff will be added as seasonal or extended hours mandate.

Past Successful Accomplishments
_____ (company name) is uniquely qualified to succeed due to the following past successes:

1.   **Entrepreneurial Track Record**: The owners and management team have helped to launch numerous successful ventures, including a _____.

2.   **Key Milestones Achieved**: The founders have invested $___ to-date to staff the company, build the core technology, acquire starting inventory, test market the _____ (product/service), realize sales of $_____ and launch the website.

Start-up Funding
_____ (owner name) will financially back the new business venture with an initial investment of $_____, and will be the principal owner. Additional funding in the amount of $_____ will be sought from _____, a local commercial bank, with a SBA loan guarantee. This money will be needed to start the company.   This loan will provide start-up capital, financing for a selected site lease, office remodeling, inventory purchases, pay for permits and licensing, staff training and certification, equipment expenditures, contingent cash reserves and working capital to cover expenses during the first year of operation. This cash infusion will result in a dramatic revenue and income growth, during the 3 year planning period, and position the company to expand its recruiting services throughout the United States.

Financial Projections
We plan to open for business on ___(date). __ (company name) is forecasted to gross in excess of $___ in sales in its first year of operation, ending ___ (month/ year). Profit margins are forecasted to be at about __ percent. Second year operations will produce a net profit of $__. This will be generated from an investment of $__ in initial capital. It is expected that payback of our total invested capital will be realized in less than __ (#) months of operation. It is further forecasted that cash flow becomes positive from operations in year __ (one?). We project that our net profits will increase from $___ to over $ __ over the next three years.

Financial Profile Summary

Key Indicator	2017	2018	2019
Total Revenue			
Expenses			
Gross Margin			

Operating Income	_____
Net Income	_____
EBITDA	_____

EBITDA = Revenue - Expenses (excluding tax, interest, depreciation and amortization)
EBITDA is essentially net income with interest, taxes, depreciation, and amortization added back to it, and can be used to analyze and compare profitability between companies and industries because it eliminates the effects of financing and accounting decisions.

Gross Margin (%) = (Revenue - Cost of Goods Sold) / Revenue

Net Income = Total revenue - Cost of sales - Other expenses - Tax

Risk Assessment

_____ (company name) is positioned to exploit the critical long term shortage of _____ (Registered Nurses). Successful financing, strategic alliance forming, effective marketing, interactive website development and continued expansion are viewed as highly achievable.

Exit Strategy

If the business is very successful, _____ (owner name) may seek to sell the business to a third party for a significant earnings multiple. Most likely, the Company will hire a qualified business broker to sell the business on behalf of _____ (company name). Based on historical numbers, the business could generate a sales premium of up to __(#) times earnings.

Summary

Through a combination of a proven business model and a strong management team to guide the organization, _____ (company name) will be a long lasting, profitable business. We believe our ability to create future product opportunities and growth will only be limited by our imagination and our ability to attract talented people who understand the concept of branding.

1.1.0   Tactical Objectives   (select 3)

The following tactical objectives will specify quantifiable results and involve activities that can be easily tracked. They will also be realistic, tied to specific marketing strategies and serve as a good benchmark to evaluate our marketing plan success. (Select Choices)

1.   Earn and maintain a rating as one of the best Medical staffing agencies in the ___ (city).
2.   Establish and maintain ___ % minimum gross profit margins.
3.   Achieve a profitable return on investment within _____ (one?) year.
4.   Earn a _____ (15?)% internal rate of return for investors over the life of the lease.

5. Recruit a talented and motivated staff of __ (#) people by _____ (date).
6. Offer our clients superior services, at an affordable price.
7. Create a company whose primary goal is to exceed customer expectations.
8. To develop a cash flow that is capable of paying all salaries , as well as grow the business, by the end of the _____ (first?) year.
9. To be an active networking participant and productive member of the community by _____ (date).
10. Create over _____ (30?) % of business revenues from repeat clients by _____ (date).
11. Achieve an overall customer satisfaction rate of ____ (98?) % by _____ (date).
12. Get a business website designed, built and operational by _____ (date), which will include an online shopping cart.
13. Achieve total sales revenues of $_____ in _____ (year).
14. Achieve net income more than ___ percent of net sales by the ____ (#) year.
15. Increase overall sales by _____ (20?) percent from prior year through superior service and word-of-mouth referrals.
16. Reduce the cost of new customer acquisition by ___ % to $ ___ by _____ (date).
17. Provide employees with continuing training, benefits and incentives to reduce the employee turnover rate to _____%.
18. To pursue a growth rate of ____ (20?) % per year for the first ____ (#) years.
19. Enable the owner to draw a salary of $ _____ by the end of year ____ (one?).
20. To reach cash break-even by the end of year ____ (one?).
21. Increase the number of account executives by at least ____ (one?) per year.

1.1.1 Strategic Objectives

We will seek to work toward the accomplishment of the following strategic objectives, which relate back to our Mission and Vision Statements:
1. Improve the overall quality of our Medical Professional matching services.
2. Make the recruiting experience better, faster and more client friendly.
3. Strengthen personal relationships with clients.
4. Enhance affordability, responsiveness, match accuracy and accessibility.
5. Foster a spirit of technological innovation.

1.2.0 Mission Statement   (select)

Our Mission Statement is a written statement that spells out our organization's overall goal, provides a sense of direction and acts as a guide to decision making for all levels of management. In developing the following mission statement we will encourage input from employees, volunteers, and other stakeholders, and publicize it broadly in our website and other marketing materials.

Our mission is to become the recognized leader in its targeted market for outsourced employment solutions for Medical services businesses. To objectively evaluate, report, and educate individuals regarding their duties and roles while providing superior patient care in accordance with professional standards, applicable laws, policies, procedures, and regulations. This will be achieved through a system that encourages teamwork, partnership, and respect for others. Each individual representing the compliance team is committed to the highest ethical standards and integrity, which is reflected in our actions.

_____ (company name) is committed to excellence in providing compassionate and personalized health services to our client's and their patients through innovative staffing solutions. Our mission is to provide our clients with significant assistance in managing their profitability by giving them a high degree of control in managing their labor costs without sacrificing clinical expertise. In addition, working on a per diem or short-term contract basis allows our healthcare professionals substantial flexibility in balancing their careers with their lifestyle objectives.

Our on-going goal is to continually raise our standards of interviewing, screening, and service, in order to provide our clients with highly qualified applicants who are at the top of their respective fields. We work with our clients in assessing their job requirements so they can hire and retain the most viable employees possible. Our goal is to set ourselves apart from the competition by making customer satisfaction our number one priority and to provide customer service that is responsive, informed and respectful.

Our Corporate Goals:
1. To build a company whose strength is rooted in the values of service, integrity, creativity, and in our commitment to place the interests of our clients and their patients ahead of personal interests and never compromise our values.
2. To reach and maintain a reputation, which is recognized in the industry as providing true benefits to our clients and as providing staffing services that are realistic, practical, and can be implemented promptly and economically.
3. To foster and empower our clients to be innovative when creating new goals, to be strategic thinkers, and to hold fast to a philosophy of continuous improvement.
4. To guard as confidential, all information concerning the affairs of a client that is gathered during the course of a professional assignment.
5. To develop solutions that are resourceful, innovative, and that can be implemented swiftly, and cost-effectively.

1.2.1   Mantra

We will create a mantra for our organization that is three or four words long. Its purpose will be to help employees truly understand why the organization exists. Our mantra will serve as a framework through which to make decisions about product and business direction. It will boil the key drivers of our company down to a sentence that defines our most important areas of focus and resemble a statement of purpose or significance.
Our Mantra is _____

1.2.2   Core Values Statement

The following Core Values will help to define our organization, guide our behavior, underpin operational activity and shape the strategies we will pursue in the face of various challenges and opportunities:

Being respectful and ethical to our clients and employees.

Building enduring relationships with clients.

Seeking innovation in our industry.

Practicing accountability to our colleagues and stakeholders.

Pursuing continuous improvement as individuals and as a business entity.

Performing tasks on time to satisfy the needs of our internal and external clients.

Taking active part in the organization to meet the objectives and the establishment of continuous and lasting relationships.

Offering professional treatment to our clients, employees, shareholders, and the community.

Continuing pursuit of new technologies for the development of the projects that add value for our clients, employees, shareholders, and the community.

Personal and professional improvement through education.

Teamwork to achieve our goals.

Honesty and integrity in all areas of our professional relationships.

Loyalty to the team and dedication to achieving our mission.

1.3 Vision Statement   (select)

The following Vision Statement will communicate both the purpose and values of our organization. For employees, it will give direction about how they are expected to behave and inspires them to give their best. Shared with clients, it will shape clients' understanding of why they should work with our organization.

_____ (company name) will strive to become one of the most respected and favored Medical Staffing Agencies in the _____ area.

To set the standard for Medical Staffing in the _____ area and beyond.
It is our desire to become a landmark business in _____ (city), ____ (state), and become known not only for the quality of our Health Care Staffing Agency Services, but also for our community and charity involvement.

_____ (company name) is dedicated to operating with a constant enthusiasm for learning about the Health Care Staffing Agency business, being receptive to implementing new ideas, and maintaining a willingness to adapt to changing customer needs and wants.

To be an active and vocal member of the community, and to provide continual reinvestment through participation in community activities and financial contributions. To incorporate the use of more state-of-the-art technologies to provide high-quality staffing services, and thereby improve the effectiveness, efficiency and competitiveness of the business.

1.4   Keys to Success

In broad terms, the success factors relate to providing what our clients want, and doing what is necessary to be better than our competitors. The following critical success factors are areas in which our organization must excel in order to operate successfully and achieve our objectives:

1. Because it is common for associates to be paid by the agency before the agency is paid by the client, an account must be maintained with sufficient funds to cover payroll costs until bills are paid by the clients.
2. Personal service, attention to detail, ethical values, and an expert knowledge of the Health Care Staffing Agency business.
3. Securing regular and ongoing client feedback
4. Ability to fill the needs for virtually any nursing specialty or assignment length.
5. Maintain an excellent sales force, practice good customer service and supply quality healthcare professionals.
6. Launch a website to showcase our services and customer testimonials, provide helpful information, and facilitate online resume posting and talent searching.
7. Local community involvement to form strategic business partnerships.
8. Conduct a targeted and cost-effective marketing campaign that seeks to differentiate our one-stop heath care staffing services from competitor offerings.
9. Institute a pay-for-performance component to the employee compensation plan.
10. Control costs and manage budgets at all times in accordance with company goals.
11. Institute management processes and controls to insure the consistent replication of operations.
12. Recruit screened Medical professionals with a passion for delivering exceptional service.
13. Institute an employee training to insure the best techniques are consistently practiced.
14. Network aggressively within the Medical community, as word of mouth will be our most powerful advertising asset.
15. Retain clients to generate repeat purchases and initiate referrals.
16. Competitive pricing in conjunction with a differentiated service business model.
17. Build our brand awareness, which will drive clients to increase their usage of our services and make referrals.
18. Business planning with the flexibility to make changes based on gaining new insightful perspectives as we proceed.

19. Build trust by circulating to our Code of Ethics and Service Guarantee.
20. Growing a good reputation for supplying quality Medical Professionals.

21. Good people skills and the ability to recognize a good match after interviewing prospective Medical professions.

22. Must do the necessary groundwork when it comes to background checks and police clearances.

23. A well-researched, forward-looking business plan with multiple revenue streams.

24. A cost-effective and well-directed marketing campaign directed at quickly building a valuable reputation within the local operating area.

25. Branch into niches such as temporary Medical staffing or technical fields to allow recruiters to build a pool of highly-educated, trained, and experienced associates who are able to provide the best service to clients within a particular industry. (This confidence also helps associates to command better wages than they might otherwise receive through a general-service temporary staffing agency.)

26. Develop well-designed, database software to facilitate the process of matching qualified associates with appropriate job openings.

27. Promote research and development of new services and markets.

28. Optimize operating processes to maximize efficiency and customer satisfaction.

29. Demand for excellence in Medical recruitment, retention, and customer care.

30. Must ensure references are checked, ensure that the people are qualified for the positions they seek, have the necessary experience and do not have questionable backgrounds.

31. Accuracy in placement matches due to thoroughness of screening process.

32. Predicting future employer needs.

33. Provide clients with the flexibility to deal with the peaks and valleys in their businesses.

34. Consider factoring accounts receivable to provide the business with the cash needed to pay employees and bills on time. Resource: PRN Funding

35. Eliminate the red tape and make the hiring process smooth, efficient, fast and to the point.

36. Keep the recruits satisfied, so that they will in turn act as money saving recruiters.

37. Make good judgment calls on the employees doing what is needed, because

sending poor quality workers out will damage the credibility of the agency.

38. Practice good organizational skills to know where workers are and what jobs businesses need filled.

39. The contract signed with a client should spell out the flat fee to be paid to the agency in the event that a client decides to permanently hire an associate.

41. Use an inexpensive and well-directed marketing campaign to quickly build a valuable reputation within the local operating region of the startup agency.

42. Branch into niches, such as temporary medical staffing, to allow recruiters to build a pool of highly-educated, trained, and experienced associates who are able to provide the best service to clients within a particular industry.

43. Use well-designed database software to ease the process of matching qualified associates with appropriate job openings.

44. Create competency tests for specific medical positions to determine if a potential employee is capable of completing all required duties for the position.

45. Maintain the right mix of personal interaction with clients and the latest in IT systems and services.

46. Develop a physician and employee online portal that enables direct access to business intelligence and other information to help them work more efficiently and effectively.

47. Take advantage of the cloud-computing environment to create an easier method for communication and collaboration.

48. Initially consider outsourcing back office operations to be able to focus on revenue generating activities and instead of getting absorbed with administrative concerns.

49. Persistence and relationship building are required to develop a consistent client base.

50. Responsiveness and customer service, for clients and employees, are key to retaining them.

51. Stand out from competitors by creating a niche specialty and focusing on a specific market for which the agency and its staff have extensive experience finding candidates, developing skill sets and filling openings.
Source: www.factorfinders.com/5-tips-for-staffing-agency-success

52. Automate the job entry and job distribution from and to multiple systems to better understand the staffing business and place more candidates into new opportunities.

53. Provide Travelers with proper training and continued resources.
     Source: www.staffingindustry.com/Research-Publications/Publications/Staffing-Industry-Review/September-2014/10-Tips-Your-Healthcare-Staffing-Firm-Can-Use-to-Ensure-Quality-and-Value-to-Hospitals-White-Paper

54. Have in place and regularly update strong contract language to decisively handle and parse the changing employment issues, laws and regulations related to staffing agencies.
     Source: www.go-cdl.com/uncategorized/legal-trends-in-staffing-and-leased-labor-aca-unemployment-wc-and-more/

55. LinkedIn's user base continues to grow at a steady rate and is continually adding improved solutions for employers to brand, source and maintain communications with talent.
     Source: http://blog.ckrinteractive.com/top-10-projections-for-the-recruitment-industry-in-2013-2/

56. Take the necessary steps to be able to pay employees in an accurate and timely manner to reduce potential liability and increase staff morale.
     Resource: www.apihealthcare.com/blog/healthcare-staffing-best-practices/strategies-for-a-successful-merger-or-acquisition-focus-on-payroll

57. Automate the healthcare staffing credentialing process to reduce the risks of non-compliance and reduce costs..
     Resource: http://info.whatisbluesky.com/blog/bid/282884/Three-Tips-to-Automate-Healthcare-Staffing-Credentialing

58. Consider invoice factoring to turn accounts receivables into cash.
     Source: www.prnfunding.com/temporary-medical-staffing-testimonials

2.0 Company Summary

_____ (company name) will be a ____ (city) Health Care Staffing Agency. _____ (company name) is a start-up _____ (Corporation/Limited Liability Company) consisting of _____ (#) principle officers with combined industry experience of _____ (#) years.

The owner of the company will be investing $ ___ of ____ (his/her) own capital into the company and will also be seeking a loan of $ __ to cover start-up costs and future growth. _____ (company name) will be located in a _____ (purchased/rented) _____ (suite/complex) in the ____ on _____ (address) in _____ (city), __ (state). The owner, _____ , has ___ (#) years of experience in managing _____ (retail businesses?).

The company plans to use its existing contacts and customer base to generate short-term revenues. Its long-term profitability will rely on focusing on referrals, networking within community organizations and a comprehensive marketing program that includes public relations activities and a structured referral program.

Sales are expected to reach $_____ within the first year and to grow at a conservative rate of ____ (20?) percent during the next two to five years.

Facilities Renovations

The necessary renovations are itemized as follows: Estimate
    Partition of space into functional areas.   _____
    Build record storage areas.   _____
    Painting and other general cosmetic repairs   _____
    Install computer equipment   _____
    Other _____   _____
Total: _____

Hours of Operations

_____ (company name) will open for business on _____ (date) and will maintain the following office business hours:
    Monday through Thursday: _____   (7 AM to 11 PM?)
    Friday: _____
    Saturday: _____
    Sunday: _____

The company will invest in customer relationship management software (CRM) to track real-time sales data and collect customer information, including names, email addresses, key reminder dates and preferences. This information will be used with email, e-newsletter and direct mail campaigns to build personalized fulfillment programs, establish customer loyalty and drive revenue growth.

2.0.1   Traction (optional)

We will include this section because investors expect to see some traction, both before and after a funding event and investors tend to judge past results as a good indicator of future projections. It will also show that we can manage our operations and develop a business model capable of funding inventory purchases. Traction will be the best form of market research and present evidence of customer acceptance.

Period	_____
Product/Service Focus	_____
Our Sales to Date:	_____
Our Number of Users to Date:	_____
Number of Repeat Users	_____
Number of Pending Orders:	_____
Value of Pending Orders:	_____
Reorder Cycle:	_____
Key Reference Sites	_____
Mailing List Subscriptions	_____
Competitions/Awards Won	_____
Notable Product Reviews	_____
Actual Percent Gross Profit Margin	_____
Industry Average: GPM	_____
Actual B/(W) Industry Average	_____

Note: Percent Gross Profit Margin equals the sales receipts less the cost of goods sold divided by sales receipts multiplied by 100.

2.1   Company Ownership

_____ (company name) is a _____ (Sole-proprietorship /Corporation/Limited Liability Corporation (LLC)) and is registered to the principal owner, _____ (owner name). The company was formed in _____ (month) of ____ (year). It will be registered as a Subchapter S to avoid double taxation, with ownership allocated as follows: _____ (owner name) ____ % and _____ (owner name) ____ %.

The owner is a _____ (year) graduate of _____ (institution name), in _____ (city, ____ (state), with a _____ degree. He/she _____ has a second degree in _____ and certification as a _____. He/she also has ____ years of executive experience in the ____ (staffing?) industry as a _____, performing the following roles: _____.

His/her major accomplishments include: _____

Ownership Breakdown:

Shareholder Name	Responsibilities	Number and Class of Shares	Percent Ownership

The remainder of the issued and outstanding common shares are retained by the Company for __ (future distribution / allocation under the Company's employee stock option plan).

Shareholder Loans
The Company currently has outstanding shareholder loans in the aggregate sum of $_____. The following table sets out the details of the shareholder loans.

Shareholder Name	Loan Amount	Loan Date	Balance Outstanding

Directors
The Company's Board of Directors, which is made up of highly qualified business and industry professionals, will be a valuable asset to the Company and be instrumental to its development. The following persons will make up the Board of Directors of the Company:

Name of Person	Educational Background	Past Industry Experience	Other Companies Served

2.2 Company Licensing & Liability Protection

We will use the services of a local attorney or Health Care Staffing Agency consultant to help us with starting our agency, as these individuals have more experience with the process, and typically have more insight into the people who will be in a position to approve or deny our application for a business license. They will also help to work through all the various legal issues that will surface, including what kind of entity to use for our business, how to best protect against liability problems, what rules apply to advertising, and so forth. We will contact an insurance agent to find out how much insurance will cost.

Our business will consider the need to acquire the following types of insurances. This will require extensive comparison shopping, through several insurance brokers, listed with our state's insurance department:
1.   Workers' Compensation Insurance,

2.   Business Policy: Property & Liability Insurance
3.   Health insurance.
4.   Commercial Auto Insurance
5.   State Unemployment Insurance
6.   Business Interruption Insurance (Business Income Insurance)
7.   Disability Insurance
8.   Life Insurance
9.   Fidelity Bond Insurance
10.   Professional Liability Insurance (Malpractice Insurance for nurses/doctors)

Note: Some medical staffing firms decide to hire only independent contractors to limit
       their insurance costs, but this arrangement should be checked with your
       attorney or CPA, and their insurance coverage must be verified.

We will provide professional liability coverage to all our healthcare professionals. We
will carry business liability and property insurance and any other insurance we deem
necessary after receiving counsel from our lawyer and insurance agent.

Health insurance and workers' compensation will be provided for our full-time employees
as part of their benefit package. We feel that this is mandatory to ensure that they do not
leave the company for one that does offer these benefits.

Workers' Compensation covers employees in case of harm attributed to the workplace.
Most states require businesses to maintain workers' compensation insurance for its
employees. If we provide long-term placement services, the placed employee is
considered to be a long-term employee of our staffing company and will require workers'
compensation coverage under our staffing agency.

The Property and Liability Insurance protects the building from theft, fire, natural
disasters, and being sued by a third party.   Life and Disability Insurance may be
required if a bank loan is obtained.

Fidelity Insurance is insurance guaranteeing the fidelity of persons holding positions of
public or private trust.
Liability Insurance includes protection in the face of day-to day accidents, unforeseen
results of normal business activities, and allegations of abuse or molestation, food
poisoning, or exposure to infectious disease.
Property Insurance - Property Insurance should take care of the repairs less whatever
deductible you have chosen.
Loss of Income Insurance will replace our income during the time the business is shut-
down. Generally this coverage is written for a fixed amount of monthly income for a
fixed number of months.

To help save on insurance cost and claims, management will do the following:
1.   Stress employee safety in our employee handbook.
2.   Screen employees with interview questionnaires and will institute pre-

employment drug tests and comprehensive background checks.

3. Videotape our equipment and inventory for insurance purposes.
4. Create an operations manual that shares safe techniques.
5. Limit the responsibilities that we choose to accept in our contracts.
6. Consider the financial impact of assuming the exposure ourselves.
7. Establish loss prevention programs to reduce the hazards that cause losses.
8. Consider taking higher deductibles on anything but that which involves liability insurance because of third-party involvement.
9. Stop offering services that require expensive insurance coverage or require signed releases from clients using those services.
10. Improve employee training and initiate training sessions for safety.
11. Require Certificate of Insurance from all subcontractors.
12. Make staff responsible for a portion of any damages they cause.
13. We will investigate the setting-up of a partial self-insurance plan.
14. Convince underwriters that our past low claims are the result of our ongoing safety programs and there is reason to expect our claims will be lower than industry averages in the future.
15. At each renewal, we will develop a service agreement with our broker and get their commitment to our goals, such as a specific reduction in the number of incidents.
16. We will assemble a risk control team, with people from both sides of our business, and broker representatives will serve on the committee as well.
17. When an employee is involved in an accident, we will insist on getting to the root cause of the incident and do everything possible to prevent similar incidents from re-occurring.
18. At renewal, we will consult with our brokers to develop a cost-saving strategy and decide whether to bid out our coverage for competitive quotes or stick with our current carrier.
19. We will set-up a captive insurance program, as a risk management technique, where our business will form its own insurance company subsidiary to finance its retained losses in a formal structure.
20. Review named assets (autos and equipment), drivers and/or key employees identified on policies to make sure these assets and people are still with our company.
21. As a portion of our business changes, that is, closes, operations change, or outsourcing occurs, we will eliminate unnecessary coverage.
22. We will make sure our workforce is correctly classified by our workers' compensation insurer and liability insurer because our premiums are based on the type of workers used.
23. We will become active in Trade Organizations or Professional Associations, because as a benefit of membership, our business may receive substantial insurance discounts.
24. We will adopt health specific changes to our work place, such as adopting a no smoking policy at our company and allow yoga or weight loss classes to be held in our break room.
25. We will consider a partial reimbursement of health club membership as a benefit.

26.   We will find out what employee training will reduce rates and get our employees involved in these programs.

The required business insurance package will be provided by _____ (insurance carrier name) . The business will open with a ____ (#) million dollar liability insurance policy, with an annual premium cost of $ _____..

The business will need to acquire the following special licenses, accreditations, certifications and permits:
1.   A Sales Tax License is required through the State Department of Revenue.
2.   Use Tax Registration Certificate
3.   A County and/or City Occupational License.
4.   Standard Business License from State Licensing Agency
5.   Building Code Inspections by the County Building Department.
6.   Employment Agency License issued by the Department of Labor (some states)

The Joint Commission Medical Staffing Certification Program
The Joint Commission accredits and certifies more than 17,000 Medical organizations and programs in the U.S. Joint Commission accreditation and certification are recognized nationwide as symbols of quality that reflect a company's commitment to meeting certain performance standards.

We will strive to obtain and maintain the following industry certifications:
1.   Joint Commission Accreditation
2.   Women's Business Enterprise National Council Certification
3.   8(a) Business Development Certification
4.   Women Owned Small Business Certification
5.   Small Disadvantaged Business Certification
6.   Local Small Business Enterprise Certification
7.   Government Certified Contractor Certification
8.   Health Insurance Portability & Accounting Act Certification
9.   National Associates of LT Organization
10.   Council for Affordable Quality Healthcare Standards

Note: In most states, you are legally required to obtain a business license, and a dba certificate. A business license is usually a flat tax assessment and a percentage of your gross income. A dba stands for Doing Business As, and it is the registration of your trade name if you have one. You will be required to register your trade name within 30 days of starting your business. Instead of registering a dba, you can simply form an LLC or Corporation and it will have the same effect, namely register your business name.

Resources:
Workers Compensation Regulations
            http://www.dol.gov/owcp/dfec/regs/compliance/wc.htm#IL
New Hire Registration and Reporting
            www.homeworksolutions.com/new-hire-reporting-information/
State Tax Obligations

www.sba.gov/content/learn-about-your-state-and-local-tax-obligations

Note: Check with your local County Clerk and state offices or Chamber of Commerce to make sure you follow all legal protocols for setting up and running your business.

Notes: Most states do not require staffing agencies to have any special license other than a standard business license, but employees working for an agency can and should be bonded and properly licensed in their Medical specialty.

Some states require specialty staffing organizations to acquire specific licenses in order to place employees. To determine whether our state requires these licenses, we will seek assistance from our city's business development office or representative.

Summary of Medical Staffing Business Licenses
Business Licenses
A state business license is the main document required for tax purposes and conducting other basic business functions.
Occupations and Professions
State licenses are frequently required for certain occupations. Since each state is different, check with your states licensing authorities.
Tax Registration
If the state in which you operate has a state income tax, you'll have to register and obtain an employer identification number from your state Department of Revenue or Treasury Department.
Trade Name Registration
If your business will only be operated in your local community, registering your company name with the state may be sufficient. This will not protect your name from anyone else using it. It just creates a paper trail of who is doing business under a certain name. Check with your County Clerk's office to see if you need a *staffing business license.*

Employer Registrations
If you have any employees, you may be required to make unemployment insurance contributions for your staffing business. For more information, contact your state Department of Revenue or Department of Labor.

Resources:
Insurance Information Institute   www.iii.org/individuals/business/
National License Directory   www.sba.gov/licenses-and-permits
National Association of Surety Bond Producers   www.nasbp.org
Independent Insurance Agents & Brokers of America   www.iiaa.org
Century Surety Group   www.centurysurety.com
B & W Insurance Agencies   www.bwinsurance.com
Find Law   http://smallbusiness.findlaw.com/starting-business/starting-business-licenses-permits/starting-business-licenses-permits-guide.html

Business Licenses   www.iabusnet.org/business-licenses
Legal Zoom   www.legalzoom.com

2.3   Start-up To-Do Checklist

1. Describe your business concept and model, with special emphasis on planned multiple revenue streams and services to be offered.
2. Create Business Plan and Opening Menu of Products and Services.
3. Determine your start up costs of Health Care Staffing Agency business, and operating capital and capital budget needs.
4. Seek and evaluate alternative financing options, including SBA guaranteed loan, equipment leasing, social networking loan (www.prosper.com) and/or a family loan (www.virginmoney.com).
5. Do a name search: Check with County Clerk Office or Department of Revenue and Secretary of State to see if the proposed name of business is available.
6. Decide on a legal structure for business.
   Common legal structure options include Sole Proprietorship, Partnership, Corporation or Limited Liability Corporation (LLC).
7. Make sure you contact your State Department of Revenue, Secretary of State, and the Internal Revenue Service to secure EIN Number and file appropriate paperwork. Also consider filing for Sub-Chapter S status with the Federal government to avoid the double taxation of business profits.
8. Protect name and logo with trademarks, if plan is to go national.
9. Find a suitable location with proper zoning for a nurse staffing agency.
10. Research necessary permits and requirements your local government imposes on your type of business. (Refer to: www.business.gov & www.ttb.gov)
11. Call for initial inspections to determine what must be done to satisfy Fire Marshall, and Building Inspector requirements.
12. Adjust our budget based on build-out requirements.
13. Negotiate lease or property purchase contract.
14. Obtain a building permit.
15. Obtain Federal Employee Identification Number (FEIN).
16. Obtain State Sales Tax ID/Exempt Certificate.
17. Open a Business Checking Account.
18. Obtain Merchant Credit Card /PayPal Account.
19. Obtain City and County Business Licenses
20. Create a prioritized list for equipment, furniture and décor items.
21. Comparison shop and arrange for appropriate insurance coverage with product liability insurance, public liability insurance, commercial property insurance and worker's compensation insurance.
22. Locate and purchase all necessary equipment and furniture prior to final inspections.
23. Get contractor quotes for required alterations.
24 Manage the alterations process.

25. Obtain information and price quotes from possible supply distributors.
26. Set a tentative opening date.
27. Install 'Coming Soon' sign in front of building and begin word-of-mouth advertising campaign.
28. Document the preparation, project and payment process flows.
29. Create your accounting, purchasing, payroll, marketing, loss prevention, employee screening and other management systems.
30. Start the employee interview process based on established job descriptions and interview criteria.
31. Contact and interview the following service providers: uniform service, security service, trash service, utilities, telephone, credit card processing, bookkeeping, cleaning services, etc.
32. Schedule final inspections for premises.
33. Correct inspection problems and schedule another inspection.
34. Set a Grand Opening date after a month of regular operations to get the bugs out of the processes.
35. Make arrangements for website design.
36. Train staff.
37. Schedule a couple of practice lessons for friends and interested prospects.
38. Be accessible for direct customer feedback.
39. Distribute comment cards and surveys to solicit more constructive feedback.
40. Remain ready and willing to change your business concept and offerings to suit the needs of your actual customer base.

2.3.1 EMPLOYER RESPONSIBILITIES CHECKLIST

1. Apply for your SS-4 Federal Employer Identification Number (EIN) from the Internal Revenue Service. An EIN can be obtained via telephone, mail or online.
2. Register with the State's Department of Labor (DOL) as a new employer. State Employer Registration for Unemployment Insurance, Withholding, and Wage Reporting should be completed and sent to the address that appears on the form. This registration is required of all employers for the purpose of determining whether the applicants are subject to state unemployment insurance taxes.
3. Obtain Workers Compensation and Disability Insurance from an insurer. The insurance company will provide the required certificates that should be displayed.
4. Order Federal Tax Deposit Coupons – Form 8109 – if you didn't order these when you received your EIN. To order, call the IRS at 1-800-829-1040; you will need to give your EIN. You may want to order some blanks sent for immediate use until the pre-printed ones are complete. Also ask for the current Federal Withholding Tax Tables (Circular A) – this will explain how to withhold and remit payroll taxes, and file reports.
5. Order State Withholding Tax Payment Coupons. Also ask for the current Withholding Tax Tables.
6. Have new employees complete an I-9 Employment Eligibility Verification form. You should have all employees complete this form prior to beginning work. Do

not send it to Immigration and Naturalization Service – just keep it with other employee records in your files.

7. Have employees complete aW-4 Employees Withholding Allowance Certificate.

2.4.0 Company Location

_____ (company name) will be located in the _____ (complex name) in _____ (city), ___ (state). It is situated on a _____ (turnpike/street/avenue) just minutes from _____ (benchmark location), in the neighborhood of _____. It borders a large parking lot which is shared by all the businesses therein. Important considerations relative to office location are competition, accessibility, community growth trends, and area demographics.

The office location has the following advantages: (Select Choices)

1. It is easy to locate and accessible to a number of major roadways.
2. Parking.
3. Proximity to _____ and _____ income growth areas.
4. Reasonable rent.
5. Proximity to the growing residential community of _____.
6. Low crime rate with good police and fire protection.
7. Proximity to hospitals, clinics, adult daycare centers and private practices.

2.4.1 Company Facilities

_____ (company name) signed a _____ (#) year lease for _____ (#) square foot of office space. The cost is very reasonable at $____/sq. foot. We also have the option of expanding into an additional _____ sq. ft. of space. A leasehold improvement allowance of $___ /sq. ft. would be given. Consolidated area maintenance fees would be $___/month initially. _____ (company name) has obtained a _____ (three) month option on this space effective _____ (date), the submission date of this business plan, and has deposited refundable first and last lease payments, plus a $ _____ security deposit with the leasing agent.

The facilities will incorporate the following room parameters into the office layout:

		Percentage	Square Footage
1.	Supplies Storage	_____	_____
2.	Reception Area	_____	_____
3.	Conference/Training Room	_____	_____
4.	Admin Offices	_____	_____
5.	Utility/Computer Room	_____	_____
6.	Recruiter Cubicles	_____	_____
7.	Interview Rooms	_____	_____
8.	Restrooms	_____	_____
Totals:		_____	_____

2.5.0   Start-up Summary

The start-up costs for the Health Care Staffing Agency will be financed through a combination of an owner investment of $ _____ and a short-term bank loan of $ _____. The total start-up costs for this business are approximately $ _____ and can be broken down in the following major categories:

1.	Computer Equipment and Installation Expenses	$ _____
2.	Web Software Development	$ _____
3.	Office Furniture: Work Tables and Cabinets	$ _____
4.	Working Capital Requirements (12 months)	$ _____
	For day-to-day operations, including payroll, etc.	
5.	Renovate Office Space	$ _____
	Includes lighting update, flooring, etc.	
6.	Marketing/Advertising Expenses	$ _____
	Includes sales brochures, direct mail, opening expenses.	
7.	Utility/ (Rent?) Deposits	$ _____
8.	Licenses and Permits	$ _____
9.	Professional Services Expenses	$ _____
10.	Capital Expenditures	$ _____
11.	Contingent Cash Reserves	$ _____
12.	Other (Includes training, etc.)	$ _____
Total:		$ _____

Medical Staffing Start-up Estimates:

Real Estate/Rent Deposit:	$5000	Utility Deposits	$200
Furniture Fixtures/Equip:	$5000	Insurance:	$2000
Training:	$5000	Grand Opening	$2000
Office Equipment/Supplies:	$9000	Signage:	$1000
Leasehold Improvements:	$4000	Legal/Accounting Licenses	$1000

The company will require $_____ in initial cash reserves and additional $_____ in assets. The start-up costs are to be financed by the equity contributions of the owner in the amount of $ _____ , as well as by a ____ (#) year commercial loan in the amount of $ _____. The funds will be repaid through earnings.
These start-up expenses and funding requirements are summarized in the tables below.

2.5.1   Inventory

Inventory:	Supplier	Qty	Unit Cost	Total
Cleaning Supplies				
Office Supplies				
Computer Supplies				

Marketing Materials	_____
Stationery	_____
Business Cards	_____
Company Brochures	_____
Business Forms	_____
Invoices	_____
Employment Contracts	_____
Facility Contracts	_____
Background Investigate Form	_____
Employee Policy Manuals	_____
Misc. Supplies	_____
Totals:	_____

2.5.2   Supply Sourcing

Initially, _____ (company name) will purchase all of its equipment from _____ and supplies from _____, the _____ (second/third?) largest supplier in _____ (state), because of the discount given for bulk purchases. However, we will also maintain back-up relationships with two smaller suppliers, namely _____ and _____. These two suppliers have competitive prices on certain products.

Resource:
https://americanstaffing.net/industry-suppliers/

Background Checks
The Corra Group (wwwcorragroup.com) has increased its sources for international background checks to help assure quicker turnaround in the healthcare industry, as more hospitals and medical facilities seek foreign talent to fill healthcare related positions, faster turnaround times mean a more expedient hiring process.

Prophecy Healthcare got its start as the first online Pre-Employment Testing Company exclusive to the Healthcare Industry.

2.5.4   Equipment Leasing

Equipment Leasing will be the smarter solution allowing our business to upgrade our equipment needs at the end of the term rather than being overly invested in outdated equipment through traditional bank financing and equipment purchase. We also intend to explore the following benefits of leasing some of the required equipment:

1.	Frees Up Capital for other uses.	2.	Tax Benefits
3.	Improves Balance Sheet	4.	Easy to add-on or trade-up
5.	Improves Cash Flow	6.	Preserves Credit Lines

| 7. | Protects against obsolescence | 8. | Application Process Simpler |

Our leasing strategy will also be shaped by the following factors:
1. Estimated useful life of the equipment.
2. How long our business plans to use the equipment.
3. What our business intends to do with the equipment at the end of the lease.
4. The tax situation of our business.
5. The cash flow of our business.
6. Our company's specific needs for future growth.

List Any Leases:

Leasing Company	Equipment Description	Monthly Payment	Lease Period	Final Disposition

Resource:

LeaseQ   www.leaseq.com
An online market place that connects businesses, equipment dealers, and leasing companies to make selling and financing equipment fast and easy. The LeaseQ Platform is a free, cloud based SaaS solution with a suite of on-demand software and data solutions for the equipment leasing industry. Utilizes the Internet to provide business process optimization (BPO) and information services that streamline the purchase and financing of business equipment across a broad array of vertical industry segments.

Innovative Lease Services   http://www.ilslease.com/equipment-leasing/
This company was founded in 1986 and is headquartered in Carlsbad, California. It is accredited by the Better Business Bureau, a long standing member of the National Equipment Finance Association and the National Association of Equipment Leasing Brokers and is the official equipment financing partner of Biocom.

2.5.4   Funding Source Matrix

Funds Source	Amount	Interest Rate	Repayment Terms	Use

2.5.5   Distribution or Licensing Agreements   (if any)
Note: These are some of the key factors that investors will use to determine if we have a competitive advantage that is not easily copied.

Licensor	License Rights	License Term	Fee or Royalty

2.5.6   Trademarks, Patents and Copyrights (if any)

Our trademark will be virtually our branding for life. Our choice of a name for our business is very important. Not only will we brand our business and services forever, but what may be worthless today will become our most valuable asset in the years to come. A trademark search by our Lawyer will be a must, because to be told down the road that we must give up our name because we did not bother to conduct a trademark search would be a devastating blow to our business. It is also essential that the name that we choose suit the expanding product or service offerings that will be coming down the pike.
Note: These are some of the key factors that investors will use to determine if we have a competitive advantage that is not easily copied.

Resources: Patents/Trademarks www.uspto.gov / Copyright www.copyright.gov

2.5.7   Innovation Strategy   (optional)

_____ (company name) will create an innovation strategy that is aligned with not only our firm's core mission and values, but also with our future technology, supplier, and growth strategies. The objective of our innovation strategy will be to create a sustainable competitive advantage . Our education and training systems will be designed to equip our staff with the foundations to learn and develop the broad range of skills needed for innovation in all of its forms, and with the flexibility to upgrade skills and adapt to changing market conditions. To foster an innovative workplace, we will ensure that employment policies facilitate efficient organizational change and encourage the expression of creativity, engage in mutually beneficial strategic alliances and allocate adequate funds for research and development. Our radical innovation strategies include _____ to achieve first mover status. Our incremental innovation strategies will include modifying the following _____ (products/services/processes) to give our clients added value for their money.

2.5.9   Summary of Sources and Use of Funds

Sources:

Owner's Equity Investment	$ _____
Requested Bank Loans	$ _____
Total:	$ _____

Uses:

Capital Equipment	$ _____
Beginning Inventory	$ _____
Start-up Costs	$ _____

Working Capital	$	_____
Total:	$	_____

2.5.9 Funding To Date (optional)

To date, _____ 's (company name) founders have invested $_____ in _____
(company name), with which we have accomplished the following:
1. _____ (Designed/Built) the company's website
2. Developed content, in the form of ___ (#) articles, for the website.
3. Hired and trained our core staff of __(#) full-time people and ___ (#) part-time
    people.
4. Generated brand awareness by driving ___ (#) visitors to our website in a ___(#)
    month period.
5. Successfully _____ (Developed/Test Marketed) ___ (#) new staffing services,
    which compete on the basis of _____.
6. _____ (Purchased/Developed) and installed the software needed to _____
    (manage _____ operations?)
7. Purchased $ _____ worth of _____ (type of supplies)
8. Purchased $ _____ worth of _____ equipment to make _____.

2.6 Start-up Requirements

Start-up Expenses:		Estimates
Legal	_____	15000
Accountant	_____	300
Accounting Software Package	_____	300
State Licenses & Permits	_____	40000?
Store Set-up	_____	25000
Unforeseen Contingency	_____	3000
Market Research Survey	_____	300
Office Supplies	_____	300
Sales Brochures	_____	300
Direct Mailing	_____	500
Other Marketing Materials	_____	2000
Logo Design	_____	500
Advertising (2 months)	_____	2000
Consultants	_____	5000
Insurance	_____	
Rent (2 months security)	_____	3000
Rent Deposit	_____	1500
Utility Deposit	_____	1000
DSL Installation/Activation	_____	100

Telecommunications Installation	_____		3000
Telephone Deposit	_____		200
Expensed Equipment	_____		1000
Website Design/Hosting	_____		2000
Computer System	_____		12000
Used Office Equipment/Furniture	_____		2000
Organization Memberships	_____		300
Cleaning Supplies	_____		200
Staff Training	_____		5000
Other	_____		
Total Start-up Expenses	_____	**(A)**	

Start-up Assets:

Cash Balance Required	_____	(T)	15000
Start-up Equipment	_____	See schedule	
Start-up Inventory	_____	See schedule	
Other Current Assets	_____		
Long-term Assets	_____		
Total Assets	_____	**(B)**	
Total Requirements	_____	(A+B)	

Start-up Funding

Start-up Expenses to Fund	_____	(A)
Start-ups Assets to Fund	_____	(B)
Total Funding Required:	_____	**(A+B)**

Assets

Non-cash Assets from Start-up	_____	
Cash Requirements from Start-up	_____	(T)
Additional Cash Raised	_____	(S)
Cash Balance on Starting Date	_____	(T+S=U)
Total Assets:	_____	**(B)**

Liabilities and Capital

Short-term Liabilities:

Current Borrowing	_____	
Unpaid Expenses	_____	
Accounts Payable	_____	
Interest-free Short-term Loans	_____	
Other Short-term Loans	_____	
Total Short-term Liabilities	_____	**(Z)**

Long-term Liabilities:

Commercial Bank Loan	_____
Other Long-term Liabilities	_____

Total Long-term Liabilities _____ **(Y)**
Total Liabilities _____ **(Z+Y = C)**

Capital

Planned Investment
Owner _____
Family _____
Other _____
Additional Investment Requirement _____
Total Planned Investment _____ **(F)**
Loss at Start-up (Start-up Expenses) (-)_____ **(A)**
Total Capital (=)_____ **(F+A=D)**
Total Capital and Liabilities _____ **(C+D)**
Total Funding _____ **(C+F)**

2.6.1   Capital Equipment List

Equipment Cost	Model No.	New/ Used	Lifespan	Quantity	Unit Cost	Total Cost
Computer System						
Laptop						
Fax Machine						
Copy Machine						
Laser Printer						
Land line Phone System						
Scanner						
Cell Phones						
Digital Camera						
Answering Machine						
Office Furniture						
Accounting Software						
Database Management Software						
Microsoft Office Suite Software						
Tutorial Skills Training Software						
High Speed Internet Connection						
Shelving Units						
Lockers						
Telephone headsets						
Calculator						
Filing & Storage Cabinets						
Cabinetry						
Credit Card Verification Machine						
Paper Shredder						

Other _____

Total Capital Equipment _____

Note: Equipment costs are dependent on whether purchased new or used or leased. All items that are assets to be used for more than one year will be considered a long-term asset and will be depreciated using the straight-line method.

Estimated Formation Expenses

- Rental Deposit $ 600 – $ 4,000
- Software: $ 500 – $ 2000
- Signs $ 500 – $ 1,500
- Legal / Accounting $ 200-3000
- Advertising $ 500 – $ 2000
- Contingency Fund $1000 - $3000

- Equipment: $ 2,000 – $ 5,000
- Insurance:$ 100 – $ 4,000
- Leasehold improvements $ 0 – $ 3,000
- Owner Salary $ 3,000 – $ 5,000
- Telephone / Utilities $ 200 – $ 700
- Misc $ 200 – $500

2.7.0   SBA Loan Key Requirements

In order to be considered for an SBA loan, we must meet the basic requirements: 1. Must have been turned down for a loan by a bank or other lender to qualify for most SBA Business Loan Programs. 2. Required to submit a guaranty, both personal and business, to qualify for the loans. 3. Must operate for profit; be engaged in, or propose to do business in, the United States or its possessions; 4. Have reasonable owner equity to invest; 5. Use alternative financial resources first including personal assets.

All businesses must meet eligibility criteria to be considered for financing under the SBA's 7(a) Loan Program, including: size; type of business; operating in the U.S. or its possessions; use of available of funds from other sources; use of proceeds; and repayment. The repayment term of an SBA loan is between five and 25 years, depending on the lift of the assets being financed and the cash needs of the business. Working capital loans (accounts receivable and inventory) should be repaid in five to 10 years. The SBA also has short-term loan guarantee programs with shorter repayment terms.

A Business Owner Cannot Use an SBA Loan:

To purchase real estate where the participant has issued a forward commitment to the developer or where the real estate will be held primarily for investment purposes. To finance floor plan needs. To make payments to owners or to pay delinquent withholding taxes. To pay existing debt, unless it can be shown that the refinancing will benefit the small business and that the need to refinance is not indicative of poor management.

SBA Loan Programs:
Low Doc: www.sba.gov/financing/lendinvest/lowdoc.html
SBA Express www.sba,gov/financing/lendinvest/sbaexpress.html

Basic 7(a) Loan Guarantee Program

For businesses unable to obtain loans through standard loan programs. Funds can be used for general business purposes, including working capital, leasehold improvements and debt refinancing.
www.sba.gov/financing/sbaloan/7a.html

Certified Development Company 504 Loan Program

Used for fixed asset financing such as purchase of real estate or machinery.
www. Sba.gov/gopher/Local-Information/Certified-Development-Companies/

MicroLoan 7(m) Loan Program

Provides short-term loans up to $35,000.00 for working capital or purchase of fixtures.
www.sba.gov/financing/sbaloan/microloans.html

2.7.1 Other Financing Options

1. Grants:

   Healthcare grants, along with education grants, represent the largest percentage of grant giving in the United States. The federal government, state, county and city governments, as well as private and corporate foundations all award grants. The largest percentage of grants are awarded to non-profit organizations, health care agencies, colleges and universities, local government agencies, tribal institutions, and schools. For profit organizations are generally not eligible for grants unless they are conducting research or creating jobs.

   A. Contact your state licensing office.
   B. Foundation Grants to Individuals: www.fdncenter.org
   C. US Grants   www.grants.gov
   D. Foundation Center   www.foundationcemter.org
   E. The Grantsmanship Center   www.tgci.com
   F. Contact local Chamber of Commerce
   G. The Catalog of Federal Domestic Assistance is a major provider of business grant money.
   H. The Federal Register is a good source to keep current with the continually changing federal grants offered.
   I. FedBizOpps is a resource, as all federal agencies must use FedBizOpps to notify the public about contract opportunities worth over $25,000.
   J. Fundsnet Services   http://www.fundsnetservices.com/
   K. SBA Women Business Center
      www.sba.gov/content/womens-business-center-grant-opportunities

   Local Business Grants

   Check with local businesses for grant opportunities and eligibility requirements. For example, Bank of America sponsors community grants for businesses that endeavor to improve the community, protect the environment or preserve the

neighborhood.
Resource:
www.bankofamerica.com/foundation/index.cfm?template=fd_localgrants

Green Technology Grants
If you install green technology in the business as a way to reduce waste and make the business more energy efficient, you may be eligible for grant funding. Check your state's Economic Development Commission. This grant program was developed as part of the American Recovery and Reinvestment Act.
Resource: www.recovery.gov/Opportunities/Pages/Opportunities.aspx

2.	Friends and Family Lending	www.virginmoney.com
3.	National Business Incubator Association	www.nbia.org/
4.	Women's Business Associations	www.nawbo.org/
5.	Minority Business Development Agency	www.mbda.gov/
6.	Social Networking Loans	www.prosper.com
7.	Peer-to-Peer Programs	www.lendingclub.com
8.	Extended Credit Terms from Suppliers	30/60/90 days.
9.	Community Bank	
10.	Prepayments from Clients	
11.	Seller Financing: When purchasing an existing Health Care Staffing Agency.	
12.	Business Funding Directory	www.businessfinance.com
13.	FinanceNet	www.financenet.gov
14.	SBA Financing	www.sbaonline.sba.gov
15.	Private Investor	
16.	Use retirement funds to open a business without taxes or penalty. First, establish a C-corporation for the new business. Next, the C-corporation establishes a new retirement plan. Then, the owner's current retirement funds are rolled over into the C-corporation's new plan. And last, the new retirement plan invests in stock of the C-corporation. Warning: Check with your accountant or financial planner. Resource: http://www.benetrends.com/	
17.	Business Plan Competition Prizes www.nytimes.com/interactive/2009/11/11/business/smallbusiness/Competitions-table.html?ref=smallbusiness	
18.	Unsecured Business Cash Advance based on future credit card transactions.	
19.	Kick Starter	www.kickstarter.com
20.	Tech Stars	www.techstars.org
21.	Capital Source	www.capitalsource.com
	www.msl.com/index.cfm?event=page.sba504	
	Participates in the SBA's 504 loan program. This program is for the purchase of fixed assets such as commercial real estate and machinery and equipment of a capital nature, which are defined as assets that have a minimum useful life of ten years. Proceeds cannot be used for working capital.	
22.	Commercial Loan Applications	www.c-loans.com/onlineapp/
23.	Sharing assets and resources with other non-competing businesses.	
24.	Angel Investors	www.angelcapitaleducation.org

25. The Receivables Exchange   http://receivablesxchange.com/
26. Bootstrap Methods: Personal Savings/Credit Card/Second Mortgages
27. Community-based Crowd-funding   www.profounder.com
     www.peerbackers.com
A funding option designed to link small businesses and entrepreneurs with pools of prospective investors. Crowdfunding lenders are often repaid with goods or services.
28. On Deck Capital   www.ondeckcapital.com/
Created the Short Term Business Loan (up to $100,000.00) for small businesses to get quick access to capital that fits their cash flow, with convenient daily payments.
29. Royalty Lending   www.launch-capital.com/
With royalty lending, financing is granted in return for future revenue or company performance, and payback can prove exceedingly expensive if a company flourishes.
30. Stock :Loans   Southern Lending Solutions, Atlanta. GA.
     Custom Commercial Finance, Bartlesville, OK
A stock loan is based on the quality of stocks, Treasuries and other kinds of investments in a businessperson's personal portfolio. Possession of the company's stock is transferred to the lender's custodial bank during the loan period.
31. Lender Compatibility Searcher   www.BoeFly.com
32. Strategic Investors
Strategic investing is more for a large company that identifies promising technologies, and for whatever reason, that company may not want to build up the research and development department in-house to produce that product, so they buy a percentage of the company with the existing technology.
33. Bartering
34. Small Business Investment Companies   www.sba.gov/INV
35. Cash-Value Life Insurance
36. Employee Stock Option Plans   www.nceo.org
37. Venture Capitalists   www.nvca.org
38. Initial Public Offering (IPO)
39. Meet investors through online sites, including LinkedIn (group discussions), Facebook (BranchOut sorts Facebook connections by profession), and CapLinked (enables search for investment-related professionals by industry and role).
40. SBA Community Advantage Approved Lenders
     www.sba.gov/content/community-advantage-approved-lenders

41. Small Business Lending Specialists
https://www.wellsfargo.com/biz/loans_lines/compare_lines
http://www.bankofamerica.com/small_business/business_financing/
https://online.citibank.com/US/JRS/pands/detail.do?ID=CitiBizOverview
https://www.chase.com/ccp/index.jsp?pg_name=ccpmapp/smallbusiness/home/page/bb_business_bBanking_programs
42. Startup America Partnership   www.s.co/about
Based on a simple premise: young companies that grow create jobs. Once startups

apply and become a Startup America Firm, they can access and manage many types of resources through a personalized dashboard.

43. United States Economic Development Administration   www.eda.gov/

44. Small Business Loans   http://www.iabusnet.org/small-business-loans

45. Tax Increment Financing (TIF)
A public financing method that is used for subsidizing redevelopment, infrastructure, and other community-improvement projects. TIF is a method to use future gains in taxes to subsidize current improvements, which are projected to create the conditions for said gains. The completion of a public project often results in an increase in the value of surrounding real estate, which generates additional tax revenue. Tax Increment Financing dedicates tax increments within a certain defined district to finance the debt that is issued to pay for the project. TIF is often designed to channel funding toward improvements in distressed, underdeveloped, or underutilized parts of a jurisdiction where development might otherwise not occur. TIF creates funding for public or private projects by borrowing against the future increase in these property-tax revenues.

46. Gust   https://gust.com/entrepreneurs
Provides the global platform for the sourcing and management of early-stage investments. Gust enables skilled entrepreneurs to collaborate with the smartest investors by virtually supporting all aspects of the investment relationship, from initial pitch to successful exit.

49. Goldman Sachs 10,000 Small Businesses   http://sites.hccs.edu/10ksb/

50. Earnest Loans   www.meetearnest.com

51. Biz2Credit   www.biz2credit.com

52. Funding Circle   www.fundingcircle.com
A peer-to-peer lending service which allows savers to lend money directly to small and medium sized businesses

53. Lending Club   www.lendingclub.com

54. Equity-based Crowdfunding www.Indiegogo.com
www.StartEngine.com
www.SeedInvest.com

55. National Funding   www.nationalfunding.com
Their customers can to get working capital, merchant cash advances, credit card processing, and, equipment leasing.

56. Quick Bridge Funding   www.quickbridgefunding.com
Offers a flexible and timely financing program to help assist small and medium sized businesses achieve their goals.

57. Kabbage   www.kabbage.com
The industry leader in providing working capital online.

Resource: www.sba.gov/category/navigation-structure/starting-managing-business/starting-business/local-resources

http://usgovinfo.about.com/od/moneymatters/a/Finding-Business-Loans-Grants-Incentives-And-Financing.htm

3.0   Products and Services   (Select)

In this section, we will not only list all of our planned products and services, but also describe how our proposed products and services will be differentiated from those of our competitors and solve a real problem or fill an unmet need in the marketplace.

Services:
Our basic services will include the following:

- Administrative Staffing
- Clinical Trials Research Staffing
- HIM/Medical Coding Staffing
- National Staffing Solutions
- Permanent Physician Staffing
- Travel Allied Health Staffing
- Home Medical Services
- Allied Health Staffing
- Government Medical Staffing
- Locum Tenens Staffing
- Nurse Staffing
- Phys./Speech/Occ. Therapy Staffing
- Travel Nurse Staffing
- Education & Training Services

We will provide the following services:
Assessment of employer needs
Verification of minimum requirements
Presentation of caregiver profiles that correspond to employer needs
Caregiver reference screening
Consulting services related to the employment of a foreign national worker
Preparation of employment offer and employment contract

_____ (company name) will recruit and place the following Medical professionals:

- Outpatient Nursing Supervisor
- Staff Nurse - RN - Recovery Room
- Staff Nurse - RN - Oncology
- Staff Nurse - RN - Operating Room
- Staff Nurse - RN - Critical Care Unit
- Staff Nurse - RN
- Staff Nurse - RN - Intensive Care Unit
- Medical Assistant
- Dermatology Technologist
- Medical Technologist
- Mammography Technologist
- Sonography Technologist
- Certified Respiratory Therapy Technician
- Electroencephalograph Technician
- Ophthalmic Technician
- Pharmacy Technician I & II
- Polysomnographic Technician
- Renal Dialysis Technician
- Respiratory Therapist
- Medical Clerk
- Outpatient Physician Office Staff Nurse RN
- Staff Nurse - RN - Critical Care Unit
- Staff Nurse - RN - Allergy
- Staff Nurse - RN - Obstetrics
- Staff Nurse - RN - Emergency Department
- Licensed Practical Nurse
- Certified Nursing Associate
- Certified Medical Assistant
- Gastroenterology Technologist
- Radiologic Technologist
- Ultrasound Technologist
- Otolaryngology Technologist
- Cardiac Technician
- Optical Technician
- EKG Technician
- Phlebotomist
- Certified Occupational/Physical Therapist
- Physical Therapists
- Sr Office Clerk
- Medical Records Technician

3.0.1   Our Service Benefits

Our convenient and cost-effective services will provide our Medical organization clients with the following benefits:

1. Rapid temporary staffing to fulfill unforeseen demand.
2. Fills short-term vacancies
3. Assists with changing workloads due to restructuring or mergers.
4. The concept of "test driving" new employees to minimize risk and ensure a good match for permanent positions.
5. Save the cost of paying for an expensive ad on a national job board, as well as the costs associated with pre-screening assessments, such as skills tests, drug screenings and background checks.
6. Frees up the client's HR person to perform regular job responsibilities.
7. Highly time efficient when there is a need to find a candidate with unique skill sets for a specialized position.
8. Allows the client company to 'try before they buy'.
9. The client saves on the cost of the benefit package to full-time permanent employees.

3.1   Service Descriptions

In creating our service descriptions, we will provide answers to the following types of questions:

1. What does the service do or help the customer to accomplish?
2. Why will people decide to buy it?
3. What makes it unique or a superior value?
4. How expensive or difficult is it to make or copy by a competitor?
5. How much will the service be sold for?

Administrative Staffing Service

Our Administrative Staffing Service understands that reliable administrative support is a crucial part of any organization. In an industry that demands special attention because of its fast-paced and evolving nature, our state-of-the-art administrative staffing service ensures that the client will remain efficient, even in times of staff shortages. We will specialize in placing pre-screened and qualified personnel on contract, temp-to-perm, and direct hire assignments. Our pre-employment screening process will include competency tests and a thorough background check. Our innovative recruitment methods will allow us to match the right candidates to our clients' specifications. Some of the temporary positions we will staff include the following:

Receptionists/Front Desk Coordinators	Data Entry/ Telemarketing
File Clerks	Customer Service/ Call Center Reps

General Office Assistants
Jr./ Sr. Executive Assistants
Human Resource Assistants
Research Assistants
Patient Service Reps
Accounts Payable
Payroll Reps
Transporters

Administrative Assistants I, II, III
Office Managers
Marketing Assistants
Transcriptionists
Medical Front Office
Accounts Receivable
Legal Secretaries
Material Handlers

Allied Health Staffing

_____ (company name) will work with Medical facilities to provide cost-effective solutions for Allied Health staffing. Maintaining staffing levels in Medical facilities can be expensive and time-consuming as Medical organizations must ensure that they have the most qualified Allied Medical candidates in place without risking valuable time and money during the recruitment process. We will offer innovative solutions to successfully maintain the client's Allied Health staffing levels. Out team of staffing consultants will specialize in locating and placing Allied Medical professionals to meet the client's specific requirements. Our comprehensive screening and interviewing process will ensure the quality of each and every Allied Health professional that we place. From recruitment to placement, we will handle every aspect of the staffing process and provide a level of service that is unparalleled in the industry. _____ (company name) will perform a variety of Allied Health staffing including:

Dental Staffing
Medical Administration Staffing
Occupational Therapy Staffing
Physical Therapy Staffing
Radiology/Imaging Staffing
Scientific/Laboratory Staffing
Travel Allied Medical Staffing

Hospital Technician Staffing
Medical Social Workers Staffing
Pharmacy Staffing
Physician Assistants Staffing
Respiratory Therapy Staffing
Speech Therapy Staffing

Clinical Trials Research Staffing

_____ (company name) will be focused on providing the world's leading Medical organizations with clinical research professionals and expertise essential in treating devastating disease. We will serve the clinical research needs of all the clients with whom we service. Our flexible engagement model will allow us to provide a wide range of tactical and strategic solutions to the primary challenges that Medical research organizations face. We will provide drug safety monitoring and contract research services to the pharmaceutical, biotech and Medical device industries while providing its Medical professional candidates with temporary or permanent clinical staffing career opportunities. Our clinical trials services business segment consists of service offerings that include traditional staffing, as well as clinical trials management, drug safety monitoring and regulatory services to pharmaceutical and biotechnology clients.

_____ (company name) will provides a broad range of services, including: Consulting Engagements, Tailored Situations, Advisory Services, and Staff Augmentation.

Government Medical Staffing

_____ (company name) understands the level of expectation for providing premier contract healthcare staff in state and federal government Medical facilities. We will provide Medical professionals on a long-term, contracted staff and traveling basis, as well as qualified pre-screened per diem and part-time staff to meet the client's immediate staffing demands. Our strategic recruiting abilities and superior customer service are two of our core competencies that will distinguish us from other staffing agencies. We will serve the needs of our clients at every level of our service delivery system. ___ (company name) will provide focused contract management services that accommodate all procedures required under federal government agencies to meet the specific requirements of government contracts. Our offices operate under corporate-mandated policies and procedures in accordance with The Joint Commission. Some of the positions our service staffs include the following:

Anesthesiologists

Cardiologists

Certified Emergency Med. Technicians

Clinical Lab Scientists

Cytotechnologists

Dental Laboratory Technicians

Dermatologists

Emergency Medicine

Genetic Counselors

Hematologists

Internal Medicine

Licensed Practical Nurses (LPNs)

Medical Assistants

Medical Technologists

Neurologists

Nutritionists

Occupational Therapists

Ophthalmic Medical Technicians

Optometrists

Orthopedic Surgeons

Otolaryngologists

Pediatric Cardiologists

Perfusion Technologists

Pharmacy Aides

Physical Medicine

Physical Therapists

Physician Assistants

Podiatrists

Psychiatrists

Radiologic Technologists

Registered Nurses

Social Workers

Surgeons

Audiologists

Certified Dental Assistants

Certified Pharmacy Technicians

Counseling Seniors

Dental Hygienists

Dentists

Dietitians

General and Family Practice

Gerontologists

Histotechnologists

Kinesiotherapists

Licensed Vocational Nurses (LVNs)

Medical Technicians

Nuclear Medicine Positions

Nurse Assistants

OB/Gynecologists

Occupational Therapy Assistants

Ophthalmologists

Orthotists

Orthopedics

Pathologists

Pediatricians

Pharmacists

Phlebotomy Technicians

Rehabilitation Services

Physical Therapy Assistants

Physicians

Prosthetists

Psychologists

Radiologists

Respiratory Therapists

Speech Language Pathologists

Surgical Technologists

Urologists

Health Information Services

We will provide the necessary resources and sound financial stability required to deliver superior Medical coding and auditing services to our Medical facility clients. We will actively recruit and retain the following HIM and Medical coding professionals:

On-Site Coders   Remote Coders
Auditors   Complete Outsourcing
Interim Management   Charge Description Master

We will assist clients with any of the following projects:

Loose filing projects   Purge projects
Long and short-term scanning projects

We will provide the following on-site coding support:

Inpatient (Medicare, Non-Medicare, CMS DRG & APR-DRG)
Outpatient Surgery
Outpatient Services including Observation
Emergency Services (with or without E&M assignment)
Inpatient or Outpatient Rehabilitation setting
Nursing home and long-term care setting
Inpatient or Outpatient Psychiatric setting
Home Health Agencies
Public sector facilities (Dept of Defense, Dept of Veterans' Affairs, State & County facilities)

Remote Medical Coding Support

In addition to on-site coding support, ____ (company name) will provide remote coding support for facilities, including Coding on Demand. Our Coding on Demand program will provide our clients with dedicated scan technicians who will scan the Medical records provided and make them electronically available to a coder. Our program will allow us to scan and code any type of Medical record including inpatient discharges, observation services, emergency department services, outpatient/ancillary services and same day surgery. We will offer the following deliverables for remote coding support:

Remote access to encoder for entering all codes.
Work area for scan technician.
High-speed Internet access for scan technician.
Staff to collect, assemble and analyze Medical records for scanning.
Ensure approximately __ (#) Medical records are available for scanning each day.
Designate a point of contact to serve as liaison between the Medical facility health system and our staff.

Medical Coding Audit Service

Our Medical Coding Auditing services will include:

Retrospective or Concurrent audits
Focus on both Physician and facility
Inpatient facility – including CMS DRG and APR-DRG
Outpatient facility – including APC, OP Surgery, ER

Physician – E&M Services
Physician – All specialties
Physician – Inpatient or Outpatient professional services
State required audits including HSCRC APR-DRG Audits

Our comprehensive auditing program will be customized to meet the client's needs and expectations and will include the following:
A written report of our findings and recommendations including a summary report, audit spreadsheets (password-protected)
Trending and analysis of coding errors identified
Trending and analysis by coder/provider
Exit conference with pertinent leadership
A 1-2 hour training session for coding staff to discuss audit results
Certified and qualified auditor(s)
Expert management team

HIM Departmental Outsourcing
Our HIM Departmental Outsourcing services will include:
Interim Management (Directors, Assistant Directors, Coding Supervisors, Transcription Supervisors, Clerical Staff Supervisors)
Technical Staff (Coders, Transcriptionists, Tumor Registrars or Technicians)
Clerical Staff (Release of Information, File Room, Assembly and Analysis, Chart Processing, Scan Technicians)

Locum Tenens Staffing (Temporary Physician Staffing)
Locum tenens involves placing physicians, both general practitioners and specialists, on temporary assignments in a variety of Medical settings. The locum tenens market represents a wide range of physician specialties including, anesthesiology, radiology, surgical specialties, family practice and internal medicine. We will use some of the most innovative recruiting technology available in the industry and offer clients access to the most qualified and talented physicians from across the nation. Our Physician Consultants will take the time necessary to learn about the client's practice or facility, and understand the specific staffing challenges being faced. Then, using our experience we will work with the client to customize a service plan that is designed to meet the physician's staffing expectations and goals. Our comprehensive staffing service will also meet the requirements of The Joint Commission and NCQA.

Our Locum Tenens Staffing Service will enjoy the following advantages:
1.   Credentialing: our stringent screening process includes maintaining a current and comprehensive database on all of our physicians. Education and training with Medical schools, residency programs, and fellowships will be primary-source verified in addition to work history and professional references. Queries to the NPDB and FSMB, as well as each individual state licensing board, are completed for each physician.
2.   Physician Licensure: we will handle the paperwork process for physician licensing requirements across the nation. Our clients will not need to worry about

gathering information or tracking down third party sources.
3. Malpractice Coverage: we will provide comprehensive malpractice coverage; amount will vary based on the state in which the physician is contracted, but will meet or exceed the state requirements.
4. Industry Expertise: as a member of the National Association of Locum Tenens Organizations (NALTO), we will work to set the industry standard and ethical guidelines for physician staffing services.
5. 24-Hour Accessibility: our Physician Consultants will be on-call 24-hours a day, 7 days a week to provide personal and prompt assistance.

National Staffing Solutions

_____ (company name) will offer a national solution for complete nursing, Allied Health, and administrative staffing services for companies and organizations with an existing regional or national footprint. Our clients will be able to staff multiple facilities through one point-of-contact. Benefits to a Single Point-of-Contact include:

Cost savings	Credentialed contingency staff
Vendor neutrality	Streamlined, automated process
Compliance assurance	Accurate reporting
Contingency staff tracking	Auditing functions
Invoicing	

Nurse Staffing

____ (company name) will be dedicated to staffing qualified nurses to fill a variety of facility shifts, including per diem, temp-to-perm, and contract assignments. We will offer clients the opportunity to select some of the most sought after nurses from many of the leading facilities across the country. We will staff the following nursing professions:

Registered Nurses (RN)	Licensed Practical Nurses (LPN)
Licensed Vocational Nurses (LVN)	Certified Nursing Assistants (CNA)

Permanent Physician Staffing

We will set ourselves apart from industry competitors through a business model that puts clients first, offering the ideal combination of services to achieve proven results. With ____ (company name), the client will enjoy:

Guaranteed physician placement
A firm with national coverage
A personalized approach to finding the right fit.
Financial reprieve or partial fee 'roll' for positions filled by the client on their own
Flat monthly billing
Volume discounts

Physical/Speech/Occupational Therapy Staffing

We will provide therapy staffing agency services to help staff hospitals, clinics, and other Medical facilities with quality Medical professionals, filling the positions of physical therapists, occupational therapists, speech therapists, and more. In addition to our unique e-mail marketing service, we will post client positions on the Internet on multiple sites and tele-recruit staff for positions in selected markets. We will staff both travel and permanent placement therapy and Medical positions. We will staff the following positions:

Physical Therapist (PT) Staffing
Occupational Therapist (OT) Staffing
Speech-Language Pathologist (SLP) Staffing
Physical Therapy Assistant (PTA) Staffing
Certified Occupational Therapy Assistant (COTA) Staffing

Travel Therapy Staffing

We will staff travel Medical professionals with the following terms:

8-26 week assignments (eight-week minimum)
Fulltime work (40 hours per week)
We secure housing and travel services for each traveler contracted.
We can negotiate a reduced fee if housing is provided by the client.
Our Travel Clinicians are employees of _____ (company name) with Workers
    Compensation and Liability Insurance.
We do not use independent contractors. (1099 Staff)

Some of the travel Medical professionals _____ (company name) staffs includes the following:

Physical Therapists
Occupational Therapists
Speech-Language Pathologists
Imaging including Specialties

Physical Therapist Assistants
Occupational Therapist Assistants
Respiratory Therapists

Travel Allied Health Staffing

We will offer cost-effective staffing solutions to successfully maintain the client's allied health staffing levels. Our staffing consultants will specialize in locating and placing travel Allied Health professionals to meet the client's local facility's specific requests. Our comprehensive screening and interviewing process ensures the quality of each Allied Health professional that we place. We will staff a wide range of Allied Health specialties including:

Cardiology
Medical Professionals
Radiology

Laboratory
Pharmacy
Respiratory Therapy

Travel Nurse Staffing

We will work with our partners to ensure we are providing the perfect nursing or Medical candidates for their staffing situations. Our goal is to manage the staffing process so our clients can focus more time on the quality of care being provided to their community. Our clients will be able to:

Reduce costs associated with recruiting candidates
Access pool of nurses outside clients' geographic boundaries
Eliminate shortages of staff
Avoid costly overstaffing
Increase long-term staff satisfaction through fully-staffed floors

Maintain high quality patient care set by the client

We will provide the following disciplines:
Registered Nurses (RN)   Licensed Practical Nurses (LPN)
Licensed Vocational Nurses (LVN)   Operating Room and Surgical Technicians
Therapists

Education & Training Services
____ (company name) will provide continuing education programs to the Medical industry. We will hold one-day seminars, as well as national conferences, on topics relevant to nurses and other Medical professionals. We will provide lifelong-learning opportunities for Medical professionals.

Home Medical Services
We will offer many services offered in hospitals and care facilities in the comfort and familiarity of the client's own home. Health and safety strategies are best taught in the home itself, and recovery from stroke and similar conditions goes more smoothly in the home environment. We will send nurses, therapists, aides, and Medical social workers to the more comfortable, less costly environment of the client's own home.

3.1.1   Service Benefits

The Benefits of using our staffing agency include:
1.   Interviews are made by telephone, or in person if requested.
2.   Broad, experienced and rigorously screened candidate base
3.   Candidates are initially pre-screened and, if qualified, a face-to-face interview is scheduled with a placement counselor.
4.   References and all information is carefully reviewed and verified.
5.   Evaluate candidates' strengths compared with clients' specific criteria.
6.   Identify, select and match the best candidate(s) for our clients' requirements
7.   Scheduled one-on-one interviews between client and candidate.
8.   Negotiate salary, wage rates, and other terms and conditions of employment with family and employee.
9.   Follow-up, support, and guidance to assure both parties' contentment.
10. Maintain relationships with client and employee.
11. All candidates undergo mandatory current criminal background checks.
12. Trial and Guarantee period.
13. Licensed • Bonded • Insured
14. Greater workforce flexibility in scheduling the permanent employees.
15. Able to satisfy specialized recruitment needs.
16. Our Temp-2-hire program allows clients to try out potential employees before deciding to hire them.
17.   Can reduce labor costs since we are able to supply staff on demand 24 hours a day.

Source:
www.allteamstaffing.com/the-benefits-of-using-a-staffing-agency-to-fill-your-healthcare-
staff/

3.2 Alternative Revenue Streams

1. Classified Ads in our Newsletter
2. Vending Machine Sales
3. Product Rentals.
4. Website Banner Ads
4. Content Area Sponsorship Fees
5. Online Survey Report Fees
6. Consulting Services
7. Facilities Sub-leases

3.3 Production of Products and Services

We will use the following methods to locate the best suppliers for our business:
- Attend trade shows and seminars to spot upcoming trends, realize networking
     opportunities and compare prices.

Staffing Conferences   http://recruitics.com/blog/2016-staffing-conferences/
                              www.aureusmedical.com/jobseekers/conferences.aspx

Healthcare Industry Events   www.healthcaresource.com/resources/events.html
Trade Show Listings   www.maximstaffing.com/tradeshows.aspx

Staffing Trade Shows
www.staffinghub.org/industry-news/7-cant-miss-staffing-recruiting-trade-shows-2017/

- Subscribe to appropriate trade magazines, journals, newsletters and blogs.

Staffing Industry News   www.staffinghub.org/
Healthcare Traveler   http://healthcaretraveler.modernmedicine.com
Staffing Industry Analysts   www.staffingindustry.com/
New Medical   www.news-medical.net
The Staffing Stream   www.thestaffingstream.com
Nurse Zone   www.nursezone.com
Staffing Talk   www.staffingtalk.com
Staffing Success Magazine
           https://americanstaffing.net/asa-publications/staffing-success-magazine/

- Join our trade association to make valuable contacts, get listed in any online
     directories, and secure training and marketing materials.

American Nursing Association   www.nursingworld.com
American Staffing Association   www.americanstaffing.net
American Hospital Association   www.aha.org/content/13/13wpmwhitepaperfinal.pdf

3.4 Competitive Comparison

The company owner is a veteran Medical Recruiter and has a profound knowledge and contacts that few recruiters possess. Furthermore, there are only ___ (#) other Medical Staffing Agencies in the _____ area. _____ (company name) will differentiate itself from its local competitors by offering a broader range of staffing services, maintaining a database of client preferences and transaction history patterns, offering membership club benefits to qualifying repeat clients, using a monthly newsletter to stay-in-touch with Medical Professionals and offering an array of comprehensive services.

We will also place a heavy emphasis on the development of a staff training program to meet client skills demands, while also serving to control operational costs.

_____ (company name) does not have to pay for under-utilized staff. Our flexible employee scheduling procedures and use of commissioned recruiters ensure that the agency is not burdened with fixed overhead. We will also adopt a pay-for-performance compensation plan, and use referral incentives to generate new business.

We will reinvest major dollars every year in professional and educational materials. We will participate in online webinars to bring clients the finest selection of domestic staffing services, and industry trend information. Our prices will be competitive with other Medical Staffing Agencies that offer far less in the way of service benefits, satisfaction guarantees and innovative services.

3.5 Sales Literature

____ (company name) has developed sales literature that illustrates a professional organization with vision. ____ (company name) plans to constantly refine its marketing mix through a number of different literature packets. These include the following:
- direct mail with introduction letter and product price sheet.
- product information brochures
- press releases
- new product/service information literature
- email marketing campaigns
- website content
- corporate brochures

A copy of our informational brochure is attached in the appendix of this document. This brochure will be available to provide referral sources, leave at seminars, and use for direct mail purposes.

3.6 Fulfillment

The key fulfillment and delivery of services will be provided by our director/owner, and certified agency recruiters. The real core value is the recruiting industry expertise of the founder, and company training programs. The company will utilize job fairs, a state-of--the-art company website and a multi-media campaign to identify domestic Medical provider requirements and locate qualified nurses. A network of training centers, internal recruiting agents, immigration attorneys and college recruiters will extend the search for qualified ____ (Medical professionals/physicians/nurses?) to countries with developed Medical education systems and English teaching programs.

3.7 Technology

_____ (company name) will employ and maintain the latest technology to enhance its office management, personnel management, payment processing, client needs matching, Medical Professional profiling and database management programs and record keeping systems.

We will seek to purchase software that provides the following services:
1. Online Application Process - Registration, Application, Skills Checklists, Competency Exams, Email Verification
2. Healthcare Employee Credentialing and Tracking - From Employee Prospect to Active Employee
3. Auto Forms Generation - Printable Applications, Profiles, Service Contracts
4. Facility Customer Documentation and Tracking (Sales team can track customers from Prospect to Contract Signature)
5. Employee Scheduling (Per-Diem, Travel, and Perm-Placement Job Orders, Employee Availability and Cancellation tracking)
6. Invoicing and Reporting with QuickBooks IIF file export functionality
7. Email, contacts, and task tracking for Recruiters, Sales Reps, and Administrators

We will also utilize a human capital management software system that allows us to accomplish the following:
Enable employees to manage timecard information
Ensure patients get the best healthcare professional attending to their needs
Manage payroll via a single web portal in real time
Track, manage, analyze and maintain human resource data
Monitor and control labor costs
Quickly convert qualified applicants into billable employees
Provide on demand web based temp staffing solutions.

Technological tools like online applications, resume parsing, timekeeping and credential management software will be a huge aid in achieving greater productivity and cost efficiency.
Source: http://www.people20.com/files/2013/09/Healthcare-Aug10.pdf

Bullhorn   **www.bullhorn.com**
Provides cloud-based CRM solutions for companies in business services industries.

Sertifi   **www.sertifi.com.**
The company has worked closely with health care agencies to provide a viable electronic signature solution that could reduce paperwork and speed signature processes. Sertifi is the industry's most trusted e-sign provider and has processed millions of electronic signature documents.

API Healthcare   **www.apihealthcare.com/software-solutions**
Centricity™ Solutions for Workforce Management by API Healthcare:

Their total workforce management software solutions are designed specifically for the healthcare industry by the experts in healthcare. Solutions for Staffing Agencies include: Staff Scheduling, Paperless Recruiting, Payroll Invoicing, Competency Testing and Compliance Management.
Resources: http://www.apihealthcare.com/staffing-agencies

Nursing Agency Staffing and Billing Software
                        www.startanursestaffingagency.com/bundledsoftware.html

August Systems   www.august-systems.com/nurse_staffing_agency.php
        A scheduling solution with Invoicing, Payroll, and Telephony Software.

Halogen TalentSpace™   http://www.halogensoftware.com/products/healthcare
        A single, integrated system that helps nursing, human resources and learning
        professionals effectively align, develop, and manage employees, and create a
        culture that's focused on improving patient satisfaction.

BlueSky Medical Staffing Software   http://whatisbluesky.com/
A web-based staffing and medical recruitment software designed specifically for healthcare staffing agencies.
Source:
http://info.whatisbluesky.com/blog/bid/282884/Three-Tips-to-Automate-Healthcare-
        Staffing-Credentialing

Credentialing Systems
Prophecy Healthcare   **www.prophecyhealth.com**
Provides online clinical competency testing and checklists for the healthcare industry. They continue to lead the industry with their new behavioral and situational exams created specifically for the healthcare professional.
Resource:
https://www.hubspot.com/customers/prophecy-healthcare

Universal Background Screening   **www.univeralbackground.com**
A healthcare industry leader in real time web-based background check technology.
 Using Universal's secure and cutting edge technology, through integration, healthcare staffing agency's can reduce the risk and liability of the background check process.

You Sign Here   **www.yousignhere.com**
An electronic signature software that is fully integrated with BlueSky to where you can not only manage all of credentials but also manage all facility contracts and healthcare provider conformation letters.

Mobile Payments
Mobile Phone Credit Card Reader   https://squareup.com/
Square, Inc. is a financial services, merchant services aggregator and mobile payments company based in San Francisco, California. The company markets several software and hardware products and services, including Square Register and Square Order. Square Register allows individuals and merchants in the United States, Canada, and Japan to accept offline debit and credit cards on their iOS or Android smartphone or tablet computer. The app supports manually entering the card details or swiping the card through the Square Reader, a small plastic device which plugs into the audio jack of a supported smartphone or tablet and reads the magnetic stripe. On the iPad version of the Square Register app, the interface resembles a traditional cash register.

Google Wallet   https://www.google.com/wallet/
A mobile payment system developed by Google that allows its users to store debit cards, credit cards, loyalty cards, and gift cards among other things, as well as redeeming sales promotions on their mobile phone. Google Wallet can be used near field communication (NFC) to make secure payments fast and convenient by simply tapping the phone on any PayPass-enabled terminal at checkout.

Apple Pay   http://www.apple.com/apple-pay/
A mobile payment and digital wallet service by Apple Inc. that lets users make payments using the iPhone 6, iPhone 6 Plus, Apple Watch-compatible devices (iPhone 5and later models), iPad Air 2, and iPad Mini 3. Apple Pay does not require Apple-specific contactless payment terminals and will work with Visa's PayWave, MasterCard's PayPass, and American Express's ExpressPay terminals. The service has begun initially only for use in the US, with international roll-out planned for the future. Resource: www.wired.com/2018/01/shadow-apple-pay-google-wallet-expands-online-reach/

WePay   https://www.wepay.com/
An online payment service provider in the United States. WePay's payment API focuses exclusively on platform businesses such as crowdfunding sites, marketplaces andsmall business software. Through this API, WePay allows these platforms to access its payments capabilities and process credit cards for the platform's users.

Chirpify
Connects a user's PayPal account with their Twitter account in order to enable payments through tweeting.

Article: www.prnewswire.com/news-releases/tips-to-leverage-mobile-payments-in-your-marketing-strategy-300155855.html

3.8   Future Products and Services

_____ (company name) will continually expand our offering of services based on industry trends and changing client needs. We will not only solicit feedback via surveys and comments cards from clients on what they need in the future, but will also work to develop strong relationships with all of our clients and vendors. We also plan to open ____ (#) additional locations in the _____ area starting in _____ (year).

____ (company name) plans to leverage its success, by expanding its domestic and global reach, and by exploiting synergistic business opportunities that may arise. This will include providing a web-based HIPAA-compliant Certification program for placed professionals.

Future Agency Consulting Services will include:

Business Plan writing	Editing business plans
Resume writing or critique	Exploring business ideas and options
Branding	Marketing
Logo Design	Basic business start-up
How to start a home Medical company	Growing your business

We will provide personalized agency consulting services from founder _____. Our consulting sessions can be customized to address the specific areas of the client's business, which are presenting challenges such as marketing and recruiting strategies, pricing and policy development, employee management, growth strategies, and more. We will conduct one to three hour-long teleconferences. On-site visits can also be arranged as needed. Other clients will find it useful to visit our agency in ____ (city) to meet with our staff and observe our Medical Professional interviews, orientations and meetings.

Online Staffing Platforms

We plan to work with exiting online staffing platforms to satisfy the overall contingent labor strategy of our clients.
Examples:
1.   Nesco Resource/Field Nation
2.   The Willis Group/NextCrew
3.   MBO Partners/Work Market.
4.   Kelly Services/oDesk.

We also intend to research self-employment opportunities by nursing specialties.
Resource:
https://nnbanow.com/www-nnba-net/self-employment-choices-by-nursing-specialties/

eLinkXchange   **www.elinkxchange.com**
A healthcare industry job board that combines the essential elements of employability matching, compatibility matching, advertising, recruiting and hiring all into one convenient system. Both employers and job seekers can get exactly what they are looking

for, in the most efficient way possible, which saves time, money and unnecessary frustration. Their mission behind eLinkXchange was to create a dedicated healthcare industry job board. eLink Connection is the parent company of eLinkXchange, which has already made an unprecedented name for itself in the healthcare recruiting industry. The company has attributed their fast-growing success to the fact that their website is unique. They have developed an industry-dedicated healthcare job board for employers and job seekers. eLinkXchange allows employers to instantly search clinical resumes and get the best-matched candidates sent directly to their inbox. For job seekers, eLinkXchange provides a platform where one can instantly search thousands of open clinical positions and find the best job for them.

Source:

www.nbcrightnow.com/story/34737529/bringing-innovation-to-the-healthcare-
　　　　recruitment

.

Service Customization Process

In order to improve our competitiveness in the marketplace, we will seek to differentiate our agency by customizing our services, according to the following methodology:

1.　Find out what services our competitors are offering.

2.　Determine what customers want and are willing to pay for if not covered by their insurance.
　　a.　Look at the complaint log for requested services.
　　b.　Conduct a phone survey, asking if they would be willing to pay for a certain list of services, if offered, such as massage therapy.

3.　Develop a comprehensive training program to accompany the service to ensure that the staff has the knowledge and expertise to provide excellent care.

4.　Stay abreast of advances in the knowledge and care of many disease specialties, and be prepared to provide ongoing education and training throughout the year to keep the staff informed of the latest developments.

5.　Track the success of the program, including sales, cost of sales, conversion rate, value of new and lost cases, number of employees hired and trained, etc.

IT Professional Staffing Service

We plan to expand our range of staffing services to include other professionals needed by the healthcare industry, such as IT/software engineers.

Example:　　RecruitIQ Staffing　　www.RecruitIQstaffing.com

Headquartered in Dallas, Texas, RecruitIQ Staffing specializes in the sourcing, recruiting and placement of Nurses and IT professionals for the healthcare industry. Through a ready supply of qualified candidates and the delivery of cost-efficient, custom-tailored workforce solutions, RecruitIQ Staffing is the intelligent way for companies to address their workforce challenges.

Source:
http://finance.yahoo.com/news/buffalo-ny-job-fair-recruiters-124000690.html

4.0 Market Analysis Summary

Our Market Analysis will serve to accomplish the following goals:
1. Define the characteristics, and needs and wants of the target market.
2. Serve as a basis for developing sales, marketing and promotional strategies.
3. Influence the e-commerce website design.

_____ (company name) is a local firm that costs less than an HR consultant, provides for both project and long-term personnel needs, and has an easy, pay and billing rate system that covers employee payroll and worker's compensation insurance.

There are a variety of reasons why businesses may need ___'s (company name) services:
   Spikes in work load
   Business expands into an area that in-house expertise does not yet match
   Special events
   Pregnancy leave or sabbatical
   Business increases after layoffs
   Smaller practices does not yet have staff on-hand to complete extra projects.

According to economic forecasters, Medical staffing agencies and financial services are expected to have the largest industry growth over the next 25 years. The trend toward businesses cutting back on employees and their benefits due to high costs creates the demand for _____'s (company name) temporary placement services.

The company approaches businesses primarily through networking and cold calls. Our intention is to utilize a PR agency for more coverage as soon as possible. _____ (company name) is a member of the area Chamber of Commerce and actively participates in as many activities as possible, the proprietor is a member of the Women's Business Network, the Professional Women's Organization, and we are in the process of connecting with the Society for Human Resource Management.

Prior to start-up, _____ (company name) also surveyed several area Medical practices about their use of contingent workers. The company will use its website and other marketing materials that describe what Medical staffing services we provide and explain how simple it is to work with us.

_____ (company name) advertises in local papers and Medical journals when necessary, but also uses the _____ (state) Employment Department, both community college and university campuses, and the networking groups we are members of to search out the right employee.

Prior to the agency start-up, the company started recruiting by administering ____ (#) personnel surveys and advertising locally to create a staff of qualified Medical contingent workers.

Forces and trends in the market environment will affect _____ (company name), like all businesses. These include economic, competitive, legal/political, technology, and recordkeeping issues.

Economic Environment—It is believed that the Health Care Staffing Agency business is basically recession proof because of the aging population.

Legal/Political Environment—Town of _____ supports the opening of this needed business venture and has issued and approved building permits and business licenses to support use of the chosen property.

Technology and Recordkeeping Environment—Use of computerized databases and web-based software programs will capture and generate accounting and personnel detail. Computer programs will greatly simplify candidate profile management, candidate/client matching services and financial recordkeeping and tax preparation functions, with which all businesses must comply. We will outsource the accounting tax functions, but will maintain the daily financial records in-house.

_____ (company name) has a defined target market of Medical organizations that will be the basis of this business. Effective marketing combined with an optimal staffing service offering mix is critical to our success. The owner possesses solid information about the recruiting industry and knows a great deal about the common attributes of those that are expected to be loyal clients. This information will be leveraged to better understand who we will serve, their specific needs, and how to better communicate with them. The owner strongly believes that as more and more products become commodities that require highly competitive pricing, it will be increasingly important to focus on the development of innovative services, that can be structured and professionally managed.

4.1   Secondary Market Research

We will research demographic information for the following reasons:
1. To determine which segments of the population, such as Hispanics and the elderly, have been growing and may now be underserved.
2. To determine if there is a sufficient population base in the designated service area to realize the company's business objectives.
3. To consider what products and services to add in the future, given the changing demographic profile and needs of our service area.

We will pay special attention to the following general demographic trends:
1. Population growth has reached a plateau and market share will most likely be increased through innovation and excellent customer service.
2. Because incomes are not growing and unemployment is high, process efficiencies and sourcing advantages must be developed to keep prices competitive.
3. The rise of non-traditional households, such as single working mothers, means developing more innovative and personalized programs.
4. As the population shifts toward more young to middle aged adults, ages 30 to 44, and the elderly, aged 65 and older, there will be a greater need for child-rearing and geriatric mobile support services.
5. Because of the aging population and high unemployment, new ways of dealing

with the resulting stress levels will need to be developed.

We will collect the demographic statistics for the following zip code(s):

_____

We will use the following sources: www.census.gov, www.zipskinny.com, www.city-data.com, www.demographicsnow.com, www.brainyzip.com and www.claritas.com/claritas/demographics.jsp. This information will be used to decide upon which targeted programs to offer and to make business growth projections.
Resource: www.sbdcnet.org/index.php/demographics.html

Snapshots of consumer data by zip code are also available online:
http://factfinder.census.gov/home/saff/main.html?_lang=en
http://www.esri.com/data/esri_data/tapestry.html
http://www.claritas.com/MyBestSegments/Default.jsp?ID=20

1.	**Total Population**	_____
2.	**Number of Households**	_____
3.	**Population by Race:**	White ____% Black ___%
		Asian Pacific Islander ___% Other ____%
4.	**Population by Gender**	Male ____% Female ____%
5.	**Income Figures:**	Median Household Income $_____
		Household Income Under $50K ____%
		Household Income $50K-$100K ____%
		Household Income Over $100K ____%
6.	**Housing Figures**	Average Home Value - $_____
		Average Rent $_____
7.	**Homeownership**:	Homeowners % _____
		Renters % _____
8.	**Education Achievement**	High School Diploma % _____
		College Degree % _____
		Graduate Degree % _____
9.	**Stability/Newcomers**	Longer than 5 years % _____
10.	**Marital Status**	___% Married ___% Divorced ___% Single
		__% Never Married __% Widowed __% Separated
11.	**Occupations**	___ %Service ___% Sales ___% Management
		___ % Construction ___% Production
		___% Unemployed ___% Below Poverty Level
12.	**Number of Children**	_____
13.	**Children Age Distribution**	___%Under 5 years ___ %5-9 yrs ___%10-12 yrs
		___ % 13-17 yrs ___ %18-years
		___ % 20-29 ___ % 30-39 ___% 40-49 __% 50-59
		___% 60-69 ___% 70-79 ___% 80+ years
14.	**Prior Growth Rate**	_____ % from _____ (year)
15.	**Projected Population Growth Rate**	_____ %
16.	**Employment Trend**	_____
17.	**Business Failure Rate**	_____

18.   Number of Hospitals   _____

Secondary Market Research Conclusions:
This area will be demographically good for our business for the following reasons:

_____

_____

Resources:
www.allbusiness.com/marketing/segmentation-targeting/848-1.html
http://www.sbdcnet.org/industry-links/demographics-links
http://factfinder2.census.gov/faces/nav/jsf/pages/index.xhtml

4.1.1   Primary Market Research

We plan to develop a survey for primary research purposes and mail it to a list of local business magazine subscribers, purchased from the publishers by zip code. We will also post a copy of the survey on our website and encourage visitors to take the survey. We will use the following survey questions to develop an Ideal Customer Profile of our potential client base, so that we can better target our marketing communications. To improve the response rate, we will include an attention-grabbing _____ (discount coupon/ dollar?) as a thank you for taking the time to return the questionnaire.

1.   What is your business zip-code?
2.   What is your annual sales volume?
3.   How many employees do you have?
4.   What is your business specialty focus?
5.   What is your educational level?
6.   What is your profession?
7.   What are your favorite trade magazines?
8.   What is your favorite local newspaper?
9.   What is your favorite radio station?
10.   What organizations are you a member of?   _____
11.   Does our community have an adequate number of Medical staffing agencies?
12.   Does your practice currently patronize a local Health Care Staffing Agency?
13.   Are you satisfied with your current Health Care Staffing Agency?   Yes / No
14.   How many times on average per year do you use an Health Care Staffing Agency?
15.   What services do you typically purchase?   _____
16.   On average, how much do you spend on Health Care Staffing Agency services per year? __
17.   What is the name of your currently patronized Health Care Staffing Agency?
18.   What are their strengths as service providers?
19.   What are their weaknesses or shortcomings?
20.   What would it take for us to earn your Health Care Staffing Agency business?
21.   What is the best way for us to market our Health Care Staffing Agency?

22. Do you live in _____ community?
23. Do you work or study in _____ community?
24. What are your perceived future Medical professional recruiting needs?
25. Would you be interested in joining our Agency Club that would offer special Membership benefits?
26. Describe your experience with other Medical staffing agencies.
27. Please rank (1 to 14) the importance of the following factors when choosing an Health Care Staffing Agency:

___ Quality of Services	___ Service Selection
___ Reputation	___ Speed of Service
___ Flexibility	___ Screening Process
___ Convenient location	___ Competitive Pricing
___ Referral/References	___ Complaint Handling
___ Personnel Availability	___ Access to Hire Talent
___ Placement Guarantees	___ Understand Business Needs
___ Other _____	

28. What though processes are undertaken when considering hiring issues?
29. What information would you like to see in our agency newsletter?
30. Which online social groups have you joined? Choose the ones you access.

___ Facebook	___ MySpace
___ Twitter	___ LinkedIn
___ Ryze	___ Ning

31. What types of Health Care Staffing Agency services would most interest you?
32. What is your general need for an Health Care Staffing Agency?
Circle Months: J F M A M J J A S O N D (All)
Circle Days: S M T W T F S (All)
Indicate Hours: _____ or (24 hours)
33. What are your suggestions for realizing a better Health Care Staffing Agency experience?
34. Are you on our mailing list? Yes/No   If No, can we add you? Yes / No
35. Would you be interested in attending a free seminar on Medical employment trends?
36. Can you supply the name and contact info of person who might be interested in our Medical staffing services?

Please note any comments or concerns about medical staffing services in general.

We very much appreciate your participation in this survey. If you provide your name, address and email address, we will sign you up for our e-newsletter, inform you of our survey results, advise you of any new Health Care Staffing Agency opening in your community, and enter you into our monthly drawing for a free _____.
Name   Address
Email   Phone

4.1.2   Voice of the Customer

To develop a better understanding of the needs and wants of our Health Care Staffing Agency clients, we will institute the following ongoing listening practices:

1.   Focus Groups
    Small groups of clients (6 to 8) will be invited to meet with a facilitator to answer open-ended questions about priority of needs and wants, and our company, its products or other given issues. These focus groups will provide useful insight into the decisions and the decision making process of target consumers.
2.   Individual Interviews
    We will conduct face-to-face personal interviews to understand customer thought processes and preferences.
3.   Customer Panels
    A small number of clients will be invited to answer open-ended questions on a regular basis.
4.   Customer Tours
    We will invite clients to visit our facilities to discuss how our processes can better serve them.
5.   Visit Clients
    We will observe clients as they actually use our products to uncover the pains and problems they are experiencing during usage.
6.   Trade Show Meetings
    Our trade show booth will be used to hear the concerns of our clients.
7.   Toll-free Numbers
    We will attach our phone number to all products and sales literature to encourage the customer to call with problems or positive feedback.
8.   Customer Surveys
    We will use surveys to obtain opinions on closed-ended questions, testimonials, constructive feedback, and improvement suggestions.
9.   Mystery Shoppers
    We will use mystery shoppers to report on how our employees treat our   clients.
10.   Salesperson Debriefing
    We will ask our salespeople to report on their customer experiences to obtain insights into what the customer faces, what they want and why they failed to make a sale.
11.   Customer Contact Logs
    We will ask our sales personnel to record interesting customer revelations.
12.   Customer Serviceperson's Hotline
    We will use this dedicated phone line for service people to report problems.
13.   Discussions with competitors.
14.   Installation of suggestion boxes to encourage constructive feedback. The suggestion card will have several statements clients are asked to rate in terms of a given scale. There are also several open ended questions that allow the customer to freely offer constructive criticism or praise. We will work hard to implement reasonable suggestions in order to improve our service offerings as

well as show our commitment to the customer that their suggestions are valued.

4.2   Market Segmentation

Market segmentation is a technique that recognizes that the potential universe of users may be divided into definable sub-groups with different characteristics. Segmentation enables organizations to target messages to the needs and concerns of these subgroups. We will segment the market based on the needs and wants of select customer groups. We will develop a composite customer profile and a value proposition for each of these segments. The purpose for segmenting the market is to allow our marketing/sales program to focus on the subset of prospects that are "most likely" to purchase our medical staffing services. If done properly this will help to insure the highest return for our marketing/sales expenditures.

We will be serving several Medical segments: hospitals, nursing homes; private practices, home Medical centers, ambulatory care centers and laboratory services. Our nurses will work on permanent or temporary contract basis.

The total potential market in units is shown in the following table and chart.
>   There are approximately ___ (#) Medical-based businesses in ___ (city) that could potentially be our clients for our Event Child Care Services.
>   There are ____ (#) residents in ____ (city), according to the 200? U.S. Census, with __ (5) % projected growth over the next ten years.
>   There are ____ (#) seniors in the city of _____, requiring home Medical services.

Target Markets:

Hospitals	Outpatient Clinics.
Private Practices	Adult Day Care Centers
Nursing Homes	Government Agencies
Schools	Social Service Organizations
Home Healthcare Cos.	

Composite Customer Profile:

By assembling this composite customer profile we will know what needs and wants to focus on and how best to reach our target market. We will use the information gathered from our customer research survey to assemble the following composite customer profile:

Ideal Customer Profile

Who are they?
Location of business headquarters (city)   _____
Type of Business   _____
Number of employees   _____
Approximate annual revenues   _____
Years in business   _____
Company growth stage   _____

Publications subscribed to _____

Trade associations the company belongs to? _____

What is the total sq/ft. of the facility? _____

Where are they located (zip codes)? _____

Trend Preferences? Trendsetter/Trend follower/Other _____

How often do they buy? _____

What are most important purchase factors? Price/Brand Name/Quality/Terms/Service/ Convenience/Green/Other_____

What is their key buying motivator? _____

How do they buy it? Cash/Credit/Terms/Other_____

Where do they buy it from (locations)? _____

What problem do they want to solve? _____

What are the key frustrations/pains that these clients have when buying? _____

What info search methods do they use? _____

What is preferred problem solution? _____

Table: Market Analysis

Potential Clients	Growth	Number of Potential Clients 2017	2018	2019
Hospitals	10%			
Clinics	10%			
Private Practices	10%			
Adult Daycare Centers	10%			
Nursing Homes	10%			
Government Agencies	10%			
Other	10%			
Totals:	10%			

4.3   Target Market Segment Strategy

Our target marketing strategy will involve identifying a group of clients to which to direct our medical staffing services. Our strategy will be the result of intently listening to and understanding customer needs, representing clients' needs to those responsible for service delivery, and giving them what they want. In developing our targeted customer messages we will strive to understand things like: where they party and play, where they shop and go to school, how they spend their leisure time, what trade organizations they belong to, and where they volunteer their time. We will use research, surveys and observation to uncover this wealth of information to get our product details and brand name in front of our clients when they are most receptive to receiving our messaging.

Target Market Worksheet   (optional)

Product Benefits: Actual factor (cost effectiveness, design, performance, etc.) or perceived factor (image, popularity, reputation, etc.) that satisfies what a customer needs or wants. An advantage or value that the product will offer its buyer.

Products Features: One of the distinguishing characteristics of a product or service that helps boost its appeal to potential buyers. A characteristic of a product that describes its appearance, its components, and its capabilities. Typical features include size and color.

Product or Service	Product/ Service Benefits	Product/ Service Features	Potential Target Markets

We will focus on the following well-defined target market segments and emphasize our extensive candidate screening and matching practices, reliability, breadth of service selections, satisfaction guarantees and exceptional customer service. Target markets will include: hospitals, clinics, medical offices, hospices, nursing homes, home health care providers, schools, social service and nonprofit organizations and government-run health care programs. We will contact hospital directors, administrative directors, human resource managers, medical office managers, business owners and nonprofit organization leaders in our target markets to advertise our services and to determine their staffing needs in our area. l

Target Hospitals
We will target hospitals because they regularly use temporary Medical staffing to hire transcriptionists, certified nursing professionals, and other support staff. We will become members of the American Hospital Association, attend local chapter meetings to engage in networking activities, and consider placing ads in hospital directories. We will utilize the following Hospital Directories:

American Hospital Directory   www.ahd.com/freesearch.php3
Listings of hospital through the USA as well as statistical information.
US News & World Report   http://health.usnews.com/best-hospitals
Profiles of each of the more than 6,000 hospitals are presented here in snapshot form.

Medilexicon   www.medilexicon.com/hospitalsdirectory.php
Search through database of worldwide hospitals (currently 12,000 entries). Search by combination of country, alphabetical letter or keyword.

Hospital Link   www.hospitallink.com/
Use the HospitalLink.com® web site directory to locate more than 6,000 hospitals and 1,700 web sites by city, state, hospital name and/or zip code.

American Hospital Association   www.ahd.com/
Comprehensive reference book of U.S. hospitals includes service line offerings and detailed profile information such as facility ownership, C-suite contact names,

admissions, beds, outpatient visits, and more.

Target Nursing Homes
We will target nursing homes because they regularly use staffing agencies to temporarily fill scheduling gaps in the nursing staff.

Target Clinics and Private Practices
Clinics and private practices are always looking for temporary staff to fill vacation voids, take up the slack during staff shortages and cover unexpected peaks in admissions. We will join the trade associations of certain Medical practices and exhibit our staffing services at their trade show events. We will also place ads in their Medical journals.

Target Adult Day Care Centers
Adult day care centers are offering new jobs and caregiver roles for the assistance of disabled and elderly in their regular activities. These skilled Medical practitioners provide every possible assistance to those who need it. With new adult day care centers coming up every day, these centers are in great need of young professionals.

Target Federal or State Government Agencies
We will target Federal and State Agencies, such as CMS, NCHS, and State Medicaid Departments. We will respond to government bid requests and use independent sales reps to pursue these accounts.

Target Professional Organizations
We will target Professional Organizations such as AHIMA, CPC, AHA, and AMA and seek to establish mutual referral relationships.

Target Local Ethnic Groups
Ongoing demographic trends suggest that, in the coming decades, programs will be serving a population of people which is increasingly diverse in economic resources, racial and ethnic background, and family structure. Our plan is to reach out to professionals of various ethnic backgrounds, especially Hispanics, who comprise nearly 13 percent of the country's total population. In addition to embarking on an aggressive media campaign of advertising with ethnic newspapers and radio stations, we will set up programs to actively recruit bilingual employees and make our agency more accessible via signage printed in various languages based on the store's community. We will accurately translate our marketing materials into other languages. We will enlist the support of our bilingual employees to assist in reaching the ethnic people in our surrounding area through a referral program. We will join the nearest _____ (predominate ethnic group) Chamber of Commerce and partner with _____ (Hispanic/Chinese/Other?) Advocacy Agencies. We will also develop programs that reflect cultural influences and brand preferences.

Helpful Resources:
1.   U.S. census Bureau Statistics   www.census.gov
2.   U.S. Dept. of Labor/Bureau of Labor Statistics   www.bls.gov/data/home.htm

4.3.1   Market Needs

There are about 76 millions of baby boomers and only 44 millions of Generation X'ers. The baby boomers are creating a huge demand for nursing agency, nurse registry business, supplemental staffing agency for Medical professionals, and permanent placement Medical recruiters. With the 76 million of upcoming baby boomers, Medical staffing industry will continually grow in numbers.

Furthermore, a fading model of employment in the United States envisions a business enterprise with full-time employees who can expect to keep their jobs and perhaps advance so long as they perform satisfactorily and the business continues. Changing labor market conditions threaten the concept of full-time permanent employment. As reported by the *Conference Board* in September 1995, contingent workers account for at least 10 percent of the workforce at 21 percent of the companies surveyed, or almost double the 12 percent of respondents with that number in 1990.

Thus, client's have need for highly qualified, expertly trained Medical professionals. With access to thousands of Medical and administrative professionals across the country, we will be able to quickly fill Medical staffing requests with highly qualified personnel. Our plan is to serve our clients with personalized attention 24-hours a day, seven days a week.

With cost-effective staffing solutions that exceed industry standards, we will offer the complete Medical staffing package. Likewise, we will work with Medical professionals to find Medical jobs and employment opportunities that fit their personality and their needs.
____ (company name) will be able to attract high quality Medical professionals by offering a wide range of benefits, including health, dental, and life insurance, 401(k) savings plans, direct deposit, bonuses and incentives, and many more. Our Staffing Consultants will provide each candidate with personal attention, ensuring that they are carefully screened and qualified before matching them with the perfect position.

Demographic trends pointing to a greater need for Health Care Staffing Agency Services:
- The life expectancy in the U.S. continues to rise. Women live an average of 80 years, while men can expect to live to about 74 years of age.
- The number of Americans over 65 years of age will double to 70 million in the next thirty years.
- 75% of baby boomers are nearing retirement in the next decade.

Lifestyle trends pointing to a greater need for Health Care Staffing Agency services:
- About 80% of the elderly prefer to remain in their own homes, where comfort, independence and quality of life are enhanced.

- As many as 12.8 million Americans of all ages need assistance from others to carry out everyday activities.

4.4 Buying Patterns

A Buying Pattern is the typical manner in which /buyers consumers purchase goods or services or firms place their purchase orders in terms of amount, frequency, timing, etc. In determining buying patterns, we will need to understand the following:
- Why consumers make the purchases that they make?
- What factors influence consumer purchases?
- The changing factors in our society.

The Company provides recruiting and staffing services for permanent and contract positions, leaving options for both clients and candidates to decide the optimal formula for working together.

Supplemental Medical professionals are needed for a variety of reasons:
To fill in for an absent staff member.
To cover while physicians attend Continuing Medical Education (CME) courses.
To supplement regular staff during busy seasons.
To staff facilities while permanent doctors are recruited.
As an integral part of a master staffing plan.

In most cases, clients make the Medical staff hire decision on the basis of the following criteria:
1. Referrals and relationships with other clients.
2. Personality and expected relationship with the Placement Counselor.
3. Internet-based information gathering.
4. Personal interviews and judgments as to appearance, communication skills and expertise.

There is a recent trend of companies hiring temp workers and converting them to full-time employees. This allows them to spend less money up front on the worker and also allows them a trial period with the employee. While any employer can set up a trial or probationary period for a worker, the temp set up allows them to do this without investing much money into hiring or training of the worker. In essence it allows the firm to pay the temp agency to be their HR department, converting the temp worker into an employee of the firm after they have been impressed with the temp's work product, productivity, integrity and personality. This makes hiring significantly less risky and costly.

____ (company name) will gear its offerings, marketing, and pricing policies to establish a loyal client base. Our competitive pricing, satisfaction guarantee, accessibility, reliability, trustworthiness, superior customer service, strategic recruiting abilities, state-of-the-art technology based systems, and the offering of other Medical services will be welcomed in _____ (city) and contribute to our success.

4.5   Market Growth

We will assess the following general factors that affect market growth:

Current Assessment

1. Interest Rates _____
2. Government Regulations _____
3. Perceived Environment Impact _____
4. Consumer Confidence Level _____
5. Population Growth Rate _____
6. Unemployment Rate _____
7. Political Stability _____
8. Currency Exchange Rate _____
9. Innovation Rate _____
10. Home Sales _____
11. Gasoline Prices _____
12. Overall Economic Health _____

The staffing and recruiting industry grew twice as fast as the economy in 2015 and is on track to grow nearly two and a half times faster than the economy in 2016.

The U.S. temporary healthcare staffing market projected to grow 7% in 2017. The U.S. Administration on Aging projected that the number of Americans 65 years of age or older is expected to grow from 40.2 million in 2017 to 71.5 million in 2030. Among the trends noted in a March 2006 U.S. Census Bureau report, the number of Americans 65 years of age and older, currently the fastest growing segment of the U.S. population, will double in size within the next 25 years and by 2030, nearly 1 out of every 5 Americans will be 65 years or older. In a November 2007 report, the U.S. Bureau of Labor Statistics stated that more than 1.0 million additional nurses will be needed by 2020, making nursing the nation's top profession in terms of projected job growth. Additionally, there is pressure to restrict mandatory Medical worker overtime requirements by employers and to establish regulated nurse-patient ratios. Several states have enacted legislation establishing nurse to patient ratios and/or prohibiting mandatory overtime while other states have similar legislation pending. In conjunction with the aforementioned factors, the long-term prospects for the Medical staffing industry should improve as hospitals experience higher census levels, due in large part to an aging society, an increasing shortage of Medical workers and the potential of up to approximately 32 million U.S. residents gaining access to health insurance coverage following the passing of Medical reform by the U.S. government.

Economic downturns threaten temporary staffing companies, as clients prefer permanent staff to temporary professionals. Despite this, long-term growth in healthcare staffing is driven by the rising shortage of healthcare professionals, notably registered nurses, and growing demand fueled by the rapidly aging baby boomers.

American Demographics projects the number of U.S. households will grow by 15% to 115 million by the year 2017. These busy households will require a greater range of child care services.

We believe there is a market for our Medical staffing services in ____ (city) and that the market has potential for growth. _____ County's population in the year 2000 was ____ and is expected to grow at a rate of ____ (5)% over the next ten years. ____ (city) is dedicated to remaining a travel destination "hot spot" without losing its "small town" feel. Because of its unique appeal it is likely to attract many vacationers and settlers for years to come. Our business will grow as clients become familiar with our unrivaled Medical staffing services and hiring options.

The general industry analysis shows that _____ (city) is expected to experience _____ (double digit?) population, housing and commercial business growth. This suggests that as more families continue to move into the _____ area, there will be an increasing demand for quality Medical services, and this makes it a prime location for a Health Care Staffing Agency that is willing to think outside-of-the-box.

4.6.0 Service Business Analysis

Medical staffing companies operate with great economic immunity as there is currently a shortage of labor in the Medical industry. Additionally, people will continue to get sick and require Medical attention despite deleterious economic conditions, and the business will be able to remain profitable in any economic climate.

There are currently more than 125,000 vacancies for nurses. An estimate published in the Journal of the American Medical Association forecasts a shortage of more than 400,000 nurses by 2020. The number of foreign-educated nurses coming into the country more than tripled from 4,000 in 1998 to 15,000 in 2004. It's an increase born of necessity — and active recruitment. We know from speaking to competitors, as well as hospitals that this a great time to make an investment in a service that is highly visible and subject to acquisition.

The following long-term demand drivers seem to signify why there are increasing Medical staffing needs:
1.   An aging population.
2.   Accelerated early retirement of physicians.
3.   Changes in lifestyles of younger doctors wanting more leisure time.
4.   The rise of more complex treatments.
5.   Shifting physician demographics.
6.   Price increases due to high need.
7.   Overall population increases.
8.   Software based staffing systems are providing hospitals an effective means
        to fill open shifts.
Resource: www.staffcare.com/uploadedFiles/2014-survey-of-temp-physicians.pdf

The expected increase in the Medical staffing industry offers a positive outlook for recruitment firms. However, long-term indicators point to an imbalance in the years ahead due to increased demand for Medical services combined with shortages in the physician workforce. As these predictions are realized, the industry will compensate and adapt where necessary. By keeping abreast of these changes and planning accordingly, we can ease the growing pains and facilitate progressive outcomes for the years ahead.

The ongoing workforce shortage has most providers using external healthcare staffing agencies to source and recruit medical staff. It can be difficult for human resources to continually field telephone calls, emails, and instant messaging from various healthcare staffing agencies. Web-based Vendor Management Software (VMS) for the healthcare industry consolidates and centralizes external staffing agency communication. Through the software, staffing managers can communicate with hundreds of healthcare staffing agencies nationwide as well as analyze staffing metrics for continuous improvement initiatives.

4.7   Barriers to Entry

_____ (company name) will benefit from the following combination of barriers to entry, which cumulatively present a moderate degree of entry difficulty or obstacles in the path of other Medical staffing agencies wanting to enter our market.

1.	Business Experience.	2.	Community Networking
3.	Referral Program	4.	People Skills
5.	Marketing Skills	6.	Personnel Management
7.	Operations Management	8.	Cash Flow Management
9.	Website Design	10.	Capital Investment
11.	Computer Skills		

The owner and operator of a temporary help service does not have to be a nurse or have any special nursing education. Some states require that a registered nurse work for the company either as an employee or consultant. Business education is needed for nurses to understand the business aspects of being self-employed or a small business owner. Advanced nursing courses do not teach self-employment and small business ventures.

Staffing agencies need to be good judges of character. Sending workers out that do not have a good work ethic can result in damage to the practice bottom line. Organizational skills are needed to keep track of where workers are at any given time. We will listen to potential workers as we interview them. Choosing the right job for them depends on insights into their character, abilities, skills and personal needs.

4.7.1   Porter's Five Forces Analysis

We will use Porter's five forces analysis as a framework for the industry analysis and business strategy development. It will be used to derive the five forces which determine the competitive intensity and therefore attractiveness of our market. Attractiveness in this context refers to the overall industry profitability.

Competitors   The degree of rivalry is high in this segment, but less when compared to the overall category. There are _____ (#) major competitors in the _____ area and they include: _____

Threat of Substitutes

Substitutes are high for this industry. These include other medical staffing agencies, general employment agencies, etc.

Bargaining Power of Buyers

Buyer power is moderate in the business. Buyers are sensitive to quality and pricing as the segment attempts to capitalize on the pricing and quality advantage.

Bargaining Power of Suppliers

Supplier power is moderate in the industry. Inventory can be obtained from a number of distributors. A high level of operational efficiency for managing supplies can be achieved.

Threat of New Entrants

Relatively high in this segment. The business model can be easily copied.

Conclusions: _____ (company name) is in a competitive field and has to move fast to retain its competitive advantage. The key success factors are to develop operational efficiencies, innovative programs, cost-effective marketing and customer service excellence.

4.8   Competitive Analysis

Competitor analysis in marketing and strategic management is an assessment of the strengths and weaknesses of current and potential competitors. This analysis will provide both an offensive and defensive strategic context through which to identify our business opportunities and threats. We will carry out continual competitive analysis to ensure our market is not being eroded by developments in other firms. This analysis will be matched with the target segment needs to ensure that our products and services continue to provide better value than the competitors. The competitive analysis will show very clearly why our products and services are preferred in some market segments to other offerings and to be able to offer reasonable proof of that assertion.

We will conduct good market intelligence for the following reasons:
1.   To forecast competitors' strategies.
2.   To predict competitor likely reactions to our own strategies.
3.   To consider how competitors' behavior can be influenced in our own favor.

Overall competition in the area is _____ (weak/moderate/strong).

Competitive analysis conducted by the company owners has shown that there are __ (# or no other?) Medical staffing agencies currently offering the same combination of services in the __ (city) area. However, the existing competitors offer only a limited range of traditional services. In fact, of these, __ (# or none) of the competitors offered a range of services comparable with what _____ (company name) plans to offer to its clients.

Competitor	What We Can Do and They Can't	What They Can Do and We Can't

Self-assessment
Competitive Rating Assessment: 1 = Weak ....5 = Strong

	Our Company	Prime Competitor	Compare
Our Location	_____	_____	_____
Our Facilities	_____	_____	_____
Our Services and Amenities	_____	_____	_____
Our Management Skills	_____	_____	_____
Our Training Programs	_____	_____	_____
Our Research & Development	_____	_____	_____
Our Company Culture	_____	_____	_____
Our Business Model	_____	_____	_____
Overall Rating	_____	_____	_____

Rationale: _____

The following Medical staffing agencies are considered direct competitors in _____ (city):

Competitor	Address	Market Share	Primary Focus	Secondary Services	Strengths	Weaknesses

Indirect Competitors include the following (General Employment Agencies):

_____
_____

Alternative Competitive Matrix

Competitor Name:	Us			
Location:		_____	_____	_____
Location Distance (miles)		_____	_____	_____

Comparison Items:

Sales Revenue	_____
Service Focus	_____
Membership Programs	_____
Profitability	_____
Market Share	_____
Brand Name	_____
Specialty	_____

Other Services _____
Capitalization _____
Target Markets _____
Service Area _____
Operating Hours _____
Operating Policies _____
Payment Options _____
Other Financing _____
Pricing Strategy _____
Price Level L/M/H _____
Discounts _____
Yrs in Business _____
Reputation _____
Reliability _____
Quality _____
Marketing Strategy _____
Methods of Promotion _____
Alliances _____
Brochure/Catalog _____
Website _____
Sales Revenues _____
No. of Staff _____
Competitive Advantage _____
Credit Cards Accepted Y/N _____
Prescreening Methods _____
Guarantees _____
Comments _____

Competitor Profile Matrix

Critical Success Factors	Our Score	Competitor 1 Rating Score	Competitor 2 Rating Score	Competitor 3 Rating Score
Advertising				
Product Quality				
Price Competition				
Management				
Financial Position				
Customer Loyalty				
Brand Identity				
Market Share				
Total				

We will use the following sources of competition analysis information:
1. Competitor company websites.
2. Mystery shopper visits.
3. Annual Reports   (www.annual reports.com)

4. Thomas Net (www.thomasnet.com)
5. Trade Journals
6. Trade Associations
7. Sales representative interviews
8. Research & Development may come across new patents.
9. Market research can give feedback on the customer's perspective
10. Monitoring services will track a company or industry you select for news.
    Resources: www.portfolionews.com   www.Office.com
11. Hoover's   www.hoovers.com
12. www.zapdata.com   (Dun and Bradstreet) You can buy one-off lists here.
13. www.infousa.com   (The largest, and they resell to many other vendors)
14. www.onesource.com (By subscription, they pull information from many sources)
15. www.capitaliq.com   (Standard and Poors).
16. Obtain industry specific information from First Research
    (www.firstresearch.com) or IBISWorld, although both are by subscription only,
    although you may be able to buy just one report.
17. Get industry financial ratios and industry norms from RMA (www.rmahq.com) or
    by using ProfitCents.com software.
18. Company newsletters
19. Industry Consultants
20. Suppliers
21. Customer interviews regarding competitors.
22. Analyze competitors' ads for their target audience, market position, product
    features, benefits, prices, etc.
23. Attend speeches or presentations made by representatives of your competitors.
24. View competitor's trade show display from a potential customer's point of view.
25. Search computer databases (available at many public libraries).
26. Review competitor Yellow Book Ads.
27. www.bls.gov/cex/   (site provides information on consumer expenditures
    nationally, regionally, and by selected metropolitan areas).
28. www.sizeup.com
29. Business Statistics and Financial Ratios   www.bizstats.com

4.9 Market Revenue Projection

For each of our chosen target markets, we will estimate our market share in number of
clients, and based on consumer behavior, how often do they buy per year? What is the
average dollar amount of each purchase? We will then multiply these three numbers to
project sales volume for each target market.

Target Market	Number of Clients	No. of Purchases per Year	Average Dollar Amount per Purchase	Total Sales Volume
	A x	B	x C	= D

_____

_____

_____

Using the target market number identified in this section, and the local demographics, we have made the following assessments regarding market opportunity and revenue potential in our area:

Potential Revenue Opportunity =

	_____	Local No. of Medical Organizations
(x)	_____	Expected ___% Market Share
(=)	_____	Number of likely local clients
(x) $	_____	Average annual recruiting fee dollar amount
(=) $	_____	Annual Revenue Opportunity.

Or

	No. of Clients Per Week	(x)	Avg. Sale	(=)	Daily Income
Services	_____		_____		_____
Other	_____		_____		_____
Total:					_____
Annualized:				(x)	52
Annual Revenue Potential:					_____

Recap:

Month	Jan Feb Mar Apr May Jun Jul Aug Sep Oct Nov Dec	Total
Products		

Services

Gross Sales:	_____
(-) Returns	_____
Net Sales	_____

Revenue Assumptions:

1. The sources of information for our revenue projection are:
_____

2. If the total market demand for our product/service = 100%, our projected sales volume represents ____% of this total market.

3. The following factors might lower our revenue projections:
_____

83

5.0   Industry Analysis

SIC Code 7361   Employment Agencies   NAICS 52421001
Employment Contractors-Temporary Help + (7363-04)
As a whole, employment leasing services in the United States generate about $55 billion dollars with of revenue on a yearly basis. Approximately 1/3 of the industry is specifically geared toward the Medical segment of the market. With strong demand among hospitals and physicians for trained nurses, technicians, and physicians, the industry has grown to accommodate this need. The industry generates $44 billion dollars a year of payrolls, and employs almost 2 million people. The industry is expected to grow tremendously over the next two decades as more people (especially baby boomers) require Medical services. In the future, the Health Care Staffing Agency may be able to develop ancillary services such as direct in home nursing as a complementary service to the Medical employment services currently offered by the business. Several studies have indicated that there are more than 44 million Americans that active care for an elderly or developmentally disabled person.

Job growth drives demand for the personnel staffing industry. The profitability of individual companies depends on good marketing and availability of qualified employees. Large companies enjoy economies of scale in marketing and back-office operations. Small companies can compete successfully by specializing in an industry or a job function. The industry is labor-intensive: average annual revenue per worker is about $60,000

Currently, there are about 769 physician recruitment firms in the United States and over 1,767 in-house recruiters. Of the 769 firms, over 300 are members of the NAPR. The current size of the Medical staffing industry is $14 billion and is expected to increase 15-25 percent a year.

The staffing agencies can be broken down into four sectors:
1.   Retained: A recruitment firm that usually requires an up-front fee or monthly fee installments from a hospital/practice before the physician is placed.
2.   Contingency: A recruitment firm that is not paid by the hospital or practice until a physician is placed.
3.   Locum Tenens: A recruitment firm that provides short-term or temporary placement of physicians.
4.   In-house: A department run by the Medical facility itself that handles all recruitment for their own organization.

Using the statistics gathered, an average recruitment firm:
1.   Has three employees.
2.   Has been in business for less than 12 years.
3.   Makes over $400,000 in revenues.
4.   Completes searches in five months.
5.   Fills 81 percent of its searches.

While all four types of recruitment firms are listed as using the Internet, job boards and e-mail, there are some notable differences. For instance, retained firms utilize direct mail as an important part of recruitment while contingency firms more often rely on cold calls. Locum tenens companies are reported as using all three of these activities. In addition to using Internet/job boards and e-mail for recruitment, in-house departments also make use of advertisements in popular Medical journals as a means of attracting prospective candidates.

The NAPR cited websites and job boards as being the number one choice in advertising site of all four types of recruitment agencies. At a distant second, was the *New England Journal of Medicine*. However, locum tenens agencies are listed as favoring the American Academy of Family Practice as a second source for advertising.

Retained and contingency firms are reported to receive most of their placements from direct mail campaigns. However, retained firms also receive a great deal of leads that later place from Internet job boards, whereas contingency firms get their placements from telephone inquiries. According to the study, locum tenens agencies get a preponderance of placements from both telephone inquiries and referrals, while in-house departments tend to get theirs from advertising and referrals.

According to NAPR statistics, retained, contingency and locum tenens firms predict shortages in the fields of cardiology, gastroenterology and radiology. In contrast, in-house and contract management companies calculated that general surgery and ob-gyn would be in short supply for the year ahead.

The U. S. Bureau of Labor projects that Medical service jobs will show a significant increase resulting in 2.8 million new positions by 2017. Currently, there are approximately 727,000 practicing physicians in the United States. Out of this physician pool, an estimated eight percent or 58,160 physicians a year will be on the move. About a third, or 19,774, of these physicians will use recruitment firms to help them with their job searches.

5.1   Key Industry Statistics

The US Bureau of Labor Statistics projects that between 2010 & 2020 employment in the "Healthcare and Social Assistance" sector will generate the largest number of jobs (5.6 million) and have the fastest growth rate (3.0% annual) of all major industrial sectors. Source: http://www.staffingtalk.com/hottest-jobs-healthcare-staffing/

Statistics from the U. S. Bureau of Labor predict that physician jobs will increase from 727,000 to 887,300 in 2017, and by 2020, the job outlook for physicians will stand at 964,700.

More than $2 trillion was spent on temporary and contingent workers worldwide.

At the 'average' large company, 16 percent of the workforce is temporary, and this is up from 11 percent on 2005.

For U.S. staffing companies, an average 2.95 million contract and temporary staff were employed per business per day during the third quarter of 2012, which is 4.3 percent more than the third quarter of 2011.

Source: www.helpmates.com/2013/05/14/staffing-agencies-in-los-angeles-county-
internal-hiring-the-growth-of-the-staffing-industry/

Resource:
http://blog.realmatch.com/employers/healthcare-recruitment-trends-in-2016-infographic/

5.2   Industry Trends

We will determine the trends that are impacting our consumers and indicate ways in which our clients' needs are changing and any relevant social, technical or other changes that will impact our target market. Keeping up with trends and reports will help management to carve a niche for our business, stay ahead of the competition and deliver products that our clients need and want.

Shortage of nurses in the U.S. growing

Between 2000 and 2005, the shortage of qualified nurses in the U.S. increased from 110,800 to 218,800; in 2005, 10% of all demand went unmet as a result of this shortage. As nurses become more and more scarce relative to demand, hospitals and healthcare facilities turn to staffing agencies like AMN to meet their staffing needs. On the other hand, as competition increases for qualified nurses, companies have to offer higher compensation and more attractive benefits to stay competitive.

The aging U.S. population needs more medical care

According to estimates from the U.S. Census Bureau, the number of Americans age 65 or over is growing faster than the general population. As a wave of baby boomers hits 65, this growth is expected to outpace growth of people age 64 and younger by as much as four times by the year 2020. Older people require much more healthcare per capita than younger age groups, meaning that the U.S. healthcare industry is having to grow to accommodate the additional demand. As hospitals and healthcare facilities find themselves short of nurses, physicians, and other medical professionals, staffing firms like AMN benefit from the increased demand for trained medical staff.

More nurses are going back to work or increasing their hours to make up for shrinking retirement funds, a spouse's loss of income and other fallouts from the recession.

Physician recruiting is clearly seen as the most challenging area among clinical professionals because of the fiercely competitive environment.

The reduction in desired working hours and the onset of more retirements will lead to more staffing shortages, and these shortages, coupled with the increased patient load brought on by legislative reform, will require facilities to put a greater focus on recruitment and retention efforts and to consider staffing options.

When it comes to staffing plans, managers need to evaluate how they can use their funds for human capital most efficiently in the coming year.

Some steps to consider: hiring more nurse practitioners to handle some of the physician overload, consolidating supplemental staffing needs with vendor management, and bringing in temporary clinicians to cover absences, census fluctuations or major projects without committing to long-term overhead costs.

Many hospitals, Medical facilities, and Medical organizations across the country continue to struggle with quality assurance issues, low fill ratio, and other costly pitfalls in their efforts to locate dependable and cost-effective solutions to their supplemental staffing challenges.

Crowdsourced recruitment taps into communities of healthcare professionals, giving them opportunities to refer their friends and colleagues for positions employers need help filling.

There continues to be a significant number of mergers & acquisitions within this industry, but the size of the deals are diminishing.

Increasingly, physicians are avoiding the financial pressures of private practice and finding a work-life balance that can be found working for someone else, leaving self-employment to work for a hospital, clinic, staffing agency, government institution (VA), or among other doctors at a large group practice.
Source: www.forbes.com/sites/brucejapsen/2017/01/13/young-doctors-want-employment-not-marcus-welby-life/

It is becoming more commonplace for healthcare providers to adopt the team approach to healthcare delivery. The team approach naturally increases the demand for nurse practitioners, physician assistants and allied staff that can all work together to do those things previously handled by physicians. Nowhere is this more evident than the growing trend of providing primary care through pharmacy-based clinics. Staffing agencies can expect to hire more workers comprising a healthcare team rather than individuals filling a single position at a hospital.
Source: http://blog.healthjobsnationwide.com/healthcare-recruiting-trends-for-2014/

New patient focused positions include patient care coordinators, who advocate for patients; chronic disease management specialists, who help coach patients through the treatment process; and community health workers, who are trained by health and medical professionals to help promote healthy lifestyles.

Setting up physician consultations with as many as 12 patients with similar medical conditions, like cancer or diabetes help address the physician shortage without denying patients time with a doctor.

Using Telehealth Technologies, such as remote monitoring and "care at a distance", healthcare can help extend clinicians' knowledge and services to remote locations that have staffing shortages.

Besides retirement trends, many states in the US are passing laws mandating physicians to work fewer hours. which means that RNs are undertaking more duties traditionally performed by physicians and making RNs even more in demand.

Recruiters are looking beyond technical knowledge and skills to what is known as "soft skills", which involve listening skills, a good bedside manner, communication skills and even a customer service background.

Healthcare providers are using 'internships' as a means to directly attract new talent.

Hospitals continue to rely on healthcare staffing agencies to achieve efficient staffing levels because personnel currently represent 54% of total hospital expenses.

There is a growing demand for genetic counselors and physical therapists.

Sources:
http://info.staffingplus.com/bid/192282/Healthcare-Staffing-Trends-for-2014
www.thestaffingstream.com/2016/01/21/the-top-3-healthcare-staffing-trends-for-2016/
www.relode.com/blog/2017-healthcare-staffing-recruiting-trends
www.harriswilliams.com/sites/default/files/content/hwco._healthcare_staffing_
        update_-_11.18.15.pdf
https://hiring.monster.com/hr/hr-best-practices/recruiting-hiring-advice/strategic-
        workforce-planning/healthcare-recruiting-trends.aspx

5.3   Industry Key Terms

We will use the following term definitions to help our company to understand and speak the common language of our industry, and aid efficient communication.

Acuity-based Staffing
Delves deeper into optimal healthcare staffing strategies than nurse-to-patient ratios. It seeks to base staffing on patient need by ensuring an appropriate mix of skill sets and competencies. Contingent employees are often used to shore up staff and skill gaps.

Administrative or Clerical Staffing
Typically includes the following positions, among others: secretaries, general office clerks, receptionists, administrative assistants, word-processing and data entry operators, cashiers, and phone operators.

Allied Medical specialists
Includes: Radiology, Oncology, Respiratory Therapy, Physical/Occupational Therapy, Medical Laboratory, Medical Imaging, Administration and Pharmacy.
Benched
Temporary employees who are ready to work but not currently on assignment.
Candidate
A job seeker who has submitted his or her information to a staffing agency in the hopes of attaining a position that is best suited to their specific skill set. A candidate may be seeking a permanent or a temporary position and often will work with a recruiter to determine those positions for which they are best qualified.
Co-Employment
Used to describe the relationship among two or more organizations that exert some level of control over the same worker or groups of workers. Co-employers often share some degree of liability for shared employees.
Contingent
A work arrangement that differs from regular/permanent, direct wage, salary employment. Contingent workers most often include temporary employees provided by an outside staffing company and independent contractors/consultants. They do not include work done by consulting firms or by part-time regular employees, and are primarily defined by an explicitly defined tenure.
Contingent Workforce
A provisional group of workers who work for an organization on a non-permanent basis, also known as freelancers, independent professionals, temporary contract workers, independent contractors or consultants. VMS is a type of contingent workforce management. There are several other terms associated with VMS which are all relevant to the contingent workforce, or staffing industry.
Contingency Placement
The practice of charging a fee to either the applicant or the employer only after a successful referral of the applicant to the employer for employment.
Contractor
An individual hired to deliver a specific service as described in a contract. In some organizations, this term is used interchangeably with "temporary employee" to refer to individuals employed by a temporary staffing firm, typically at a professional level. An "independent contractor" is a self-employed individual performing services for a company under contract rather than as an employee, either on- or off-site.
Direct Hire (Permanent) Placement Staffing
Involves the placement of a candidate with a hiring firm on a full-time basis. In this method of staffing, the staffing firm often performs a comprehensive screening of all viable candidates and the hiring firm will then interview only the best pre-screened candidates. The staffing firm is typically compensated based on the yearly salary of the hired candidate.
Employee Leasing or PEO (Professional Employer Organization)
In an employee leasing or PEO arrangement, a business places all or most of its work force onto the payroll of a staffing firm and the staffing firm assumes responsibility for payroll, benefits, and other human resource functions. In this instance, the staffing firm essentially becomes the human resources department for its client.

Factoring

Converting the accounts receivable of a business into cash by selling outstanding invoices to a 'factor' for a discount. Accounts receivable factoring gives the business immediate cash to manage its operations more efficiently.

Health Care Staffing Agency

Typically finds employment or jobs for individuals who are seeking employment. Different from a staffing agency, an Health Care Staffing Agency may charge an individual an upfront fee to find them a job. The fee may be paid in advance or taken as a percentage of the salary of the obtained position.

Health Care Staffing Agency

Typically finds employment or jobs for individuals who are seeking employment. Different from a staffing agency, an Health Care Staffing Agency may charge an individual
an upfront fee to find them a job. The fee may be paid in advance or taken as a percentage of the salary of the obtained position.

Executive Search

Refers to the process of recruiting for exempt-level managers or professionals to be employed as traditional employees.

Independent Nurse Contractor

One who contracts with a Medical facility for nursing services. A contractual agreement is drawn up between you and the institution. Able to negotiate our compensation, hours worked and length of time your services will be needed. A self employed nurse that provides his/her services to Medical facilities, private individuals for a certain fee bypassing the agency.

Job Order

A request to a staffing firm or Health Care Staffing Agency to refer applicants for a specific position. A job order is the specific set of requirements set forth by an employer for an
actual position.

Job Board

A website that facilitates job hunting and range from large scale generalist sites to niche job boards for job categories such as engineering, legal, insurance, social
work, teaching, mobile app development as well as cross-sector categories such as green jobs, ethical jobs and seasonal jobs. Users can typically deposit their résumés and submit them to potential employers and recruiters for review, while employers and recruiters can post job ads and search for potential employees.

Resource: http://en.wikipedia.org/wiki/List_of_employment_websites

KPO (Knowledge Process Outsourcing)

A form of outsourcing in which knowledge-related and information related work is carried out by workers in a different company or by a subsidiary of the same organization, which may be in the same country or in an offshore location to save cost. Unlike the outsourcing of manufacturing, this typically involves high-value work carried out by highly skilled staff.

Long-Term Staffing (Contract Staffing)

Involves a staffing firm supplying employees to work on long-term, indefinite assignments. Employees are recruited, screened, and assigned by the staffing firm.

Managed Service Provider (MSP):
A company that takes on primary responsibility for managing an organization's contingent workforce program. An MSP may or may not be independent of a staffing supplier. MSPs often promote themselves as vendor neutral. Typical responsibilities of an MSP include overall program management, reporting and tracking, supplier selection and management, order distribution and often consolidated billing.

Managed Services Staffing
Long term and Contract Staffing involves a staffing firm supplying employees to work on long-term, indefinite assignments. Employees are recruited, screened, and assigned by the staffing firm.

Markup
The percentage added to the temporary employee's hourly pay rate to reach the bill rate.

Medical Staffing
Typically includes the following positions, among others: physicians, nurses, Medical technicians, therapists, home health aides, and custodial care workers. Some providers specialize in the office support positions within a Medical office including Medical assistants, lab technicians, Medical billing and Medical office receptionists.

Medical Staffing Agencies
Provide a pool of industry ready candidates for organizations at all levels and whenever the need arises.

Nursing Registry
An agency that provides nursing services to private individuals and Medical facilities on a contractual basis.

On-boarding
The process of bringing a contingent worker into a position with a goal of providing them all the necessary tools to be productive as soon as possible.

On-Premise
On-site coordination of a customer's temporary help services through an exclusive, long term general contractor relationship with a temporary help company. The designated vendor on premise may enter into subcontracting relationships with other temporary help suppliers, or such relationships may be specified by the customer.

Outplacement
A service to guide a terminated employee of a company to a satisfactory new position or career through the provision of counseling and support services, most often paid for by the terminating employer.

Payroll Services Staffing
The client recruits its own employees but asks a staffing firm to hire and assign them to perform services. Or workers currently employed by the customer are placed on the payroll of a staffing firm. Payroll services staffing is distinguished from PEO arrangements in that the workers generally are on temporary assignments and make up a small percentage of the customer's work force.

Per Diem Staffing
These assignments place medical professionals at hospitals and other healthcare facilities in response to clients' temporary staffing needs.

Placement

Occurs when a staffing firm brings together a job seeker and an employer for the purpose of establishing an ongoing employment relationship.

Private home care agency
An agency that provides nurses, nursing assistants, caregivers to private or corporate accounts to their place of residences. The home care agency collects payments from private individuals, insurances, or Medicare/Medicaid if certified by the government

Recruiter
The person within a staffing firm that is responsible for identifying and screening/ evaluating qualified candidates for an open position within a client business. The recruiter
generally works closely with the hiring firm to determine which candidates are best suited for any open positions.

Recruiting Firm
A firm that identifies and helps to procure employees for a company that is hiring. In contrast to a standard staffing firm, a recruiting firm does not typically place employees on temporary assignments within the company that is hiring and assume the administrative duties associated with the employees, such as payroll taxes, insurance, etc.

Recruitment Process Outsourcing (RPO)
Typically involves an organization taking on responsibility for all or most parts of an organization's recruiting process for direct hire employees.

Retained Search
Service provided by an executive search firm to locate a candidate for a specific position at a client company. Fee is payable whether or not a hire is made

Staffing Industry Analysts
A research and analysis firm covering the contingent workforce. Known for its independent and objective insights, the company's proprietary research, data, support tools, publications, and executive conferences provide a competitive edge to decision-makers who supply and buy temporary staffing. In addition to temporary staffing, Staffing Industry Analysts also covers these related staffing service sectors: third-party placement, outplacement, and staff leasing.

Statement of Work (SOW)
Contracts that describe the deliverables and activities promised for completion by a consultant or team of consultants.

Talent
Refers to individuals who possess the required skills to be potentially hired for a given position.

Supplemental Staffing Services
A business that provides temporary employment services for a short or long term contract to assist the needs of Medical facilities to fill in for vacations, long term disability, sick calls and employment strikes.

Temporary Full-Time Staffing
Involves the placement of a candidate in a full-time position within a hiring firm whose needs are only temporary.

Temporary Part-Time Staffing
Involves the placement of a candidate in a part-time position within a hiring firm whose

needs are only temporary.

Temporary Staffing

Involves the placement of human resources for non-permanent employment needs. The duration of the placement may have specific parameters or be undefined.

Temp-To-Hire Staffing

The placement of a candidate within a hiring firm for an often-predetermined evaluation period. During the evaluation, it is determined whether the candidate is suited for the position. The candidate is offered the position on a permanent basis at the end of the evaluation period. Temp-to-hire staffing is often preferred by companies that are hiring for a key position within the company.

Vendor

A person or organization that vends or sells contingent labor. Specifically a vendor can be an independent consultant, a consulting company, or staffing company (who can also be called a supplier – because they supply the labor or expertise rather than selling it directly).

VMS (Vendor Management System)

An internet-enabled, often Web-based application that acts as a mechanism for business to manage and procure staffing services (temporary help as well as, in some cases, permanent placement services) as well as outside contract or contingent labor. Typical features of a VMS include order distribution, consolidated billing and significant enhancements in reporting capability over many systems and processes.

5.4   Industry Leaders

We plan to study the best practices of industry leaders and adapt certain selected practices to our business model concept. Best practices are those methods or techniques resulting in increased customer satisfaction when incorporated into the operation.

The healthcare staffing market remains substantially fragmented, with the top ten participants commanding approximately 40% of the market. Additionally, a majority of the top firms provide multiple staffing services, enabling them to act as a one-stop-shop for hospitals and medical facilities seeking to efficiently manage their personnel needs.

Medical Staffing Network Holdings, Inc.   **www.msnnurse.com**

A national leader in Medical staffing with over 100 branch offices nationwide, Medical Staffing Network is a single source for healthcare staffing opportunities. And thanks to our merger with InteliStaf Medical, it now offers even more options and opportunities. Medical Staffing Network offers nurses, allied health, pharmacy, clinical research and anesthesia professionals a variety of flexible opportunities at thousands of top facilities nationwide. The company places temporary nurses and other Medical support staff with more than 7,000 Medical facilities such as hospitals and nursing homes. Options include per diem staffing (assignments lasting less than two weeks), travel staffing (temporary assignments that require relocation), and allied health assignments (staffing for specialized radiology or other clinical lab technicians). Investment firm Warburg Pincus owns 48% of the company.

AMN Healthcare   www.amnhealthcare.com/why-amn/our-clients.aspx
Operating under such brands as American Mobile Medical, Medical Express, NurseChoice, NursesRx, Preferred Medical Staffing, and O'Grady-Peyton International, the firm is one of the leading temporary Medical staffing companies in the world. The largest temporary healthcare staffing company in the U.S. by revenue, earning over $750 million in revenue. AMN provides temporary staffing of nurses, physicians (*locum tenens*), and medical assistants, as well as permanent physician placement services. It places nurses, technicians, and therapists for 13-week stints at hospitals, clinics, and schools nationwide. With professionals recruited from Australia, Canada, South Africa, the UK, and the US, AMN provides travel reimbursement and housing for its 6,800 nurse and Medical workers on assignment. The majority of temporary assignments for its 3,000 clients are at acute-care hospitals in the US.

Business Segments:
Nurse & Allied Healthcare Staffing (57% of revenue) - This segment provides hospitals and healthcare facilities with temporary professionals, typically for periods of four to 26 weeks. Nurses account for 84% of this segment's placements; since nurses account for around 25% of hospitals' operating expenses, they readily enlist staffing agencies to find temporary nurses. Therapists, medical assistants, and technical staff comprise the other 10% of the *Nurse & Allied Healthcare Staffing* segment's business.

Locum tenens staffing segment (38% of revenue) - Locum tenens staffing includes the temporary placement of physicians as independent contractors in healthcare settings. Assignment lengths range from a few days to one year, with the average assignment being a multi-week contract.

Physician permanent placement services segment (5% of revenue) - In this segment, AMN charges hospitals a fee to find permanent physicians, as well as variable fees tied to the physicians' work after their placement. The strong demand for physicians, coupled with the overlap of clients seeking physicians for temporary and permanent assignments, lets AMN cross-sell its *locum tenens* and permanent placement services.

C&A Industries Inc.
A national leader in staffing and recruiting. Through its affiliate firms, Aureus Medical Group (which places healthcare professionals in medical careers), Aureus Group, AurStaff and Celebrity Staff, C&A has provided Human Capital Management Solutions to a wide variety of industries for more than 40 years, including supplemental, contract-hire, and direct hire programs. C&A is headquartered in Omaha, Nebraska, with subsidiary offices located in Lincoln and Omaha, Nebraska; Kansas City, Missouri; and Des Moines, Iowa. Aureus Medical Group is a national leader in healthcare staffing specializing in the placement of Nursing, Advanced Practice, Cardiopulmonary, Diagnostic Imaging, Medical Laboratory, Neurodiagnostics, Radiation Oncology, and

Rehabilitation Therapy professionals, as well as Physicians, in hospitals and medical facilities nationwide. With more than 25 years of experience, Aureus Medical offers a full range of staffing options, including national contract (travel nursing, travel therapy, and in other areas of Allied Health), local contract, and direct hire. Aureus Medical is the largest division of Omaha-based C&A Industries, a leading provider of human capital management solutions for more than 40 years.

Resource:
http://blog.bluepipes.com/best-travel-nursing-companies-2014/

Medicus Healthcare Solutions
Has been providing supplemental and permanent placement of exceptional physicians and advanced practice providers at medical groups, practices, hospitals, and other facilities throughout the United States since 2004. Over the past 10 years, the company has pioneered Transition projects and has expanded its services to project and resource management services, including locum tenens vendor management and consulting services for building and optimizing medical service lines and revenue cycle processes. With nearly 300 employees—at company headquarters in Windham, New Hampshire, and offices in Denver, Colorado, and Houston, Texas—Medicus Healthcare Solutions is one of the fastest-growing companies in the healthcare staffing industry and has received local and national accolades for its efforts.

HealthCare Scouts, Inc.   **www.healthcarescouts.com**
Since 2005, HealthCare Scouts, Inc. has remained focused on a client-centered delivery model pairing standards in healthcare with the very best healthcare professionals that the active and passive marketplace has to offer. Focusing on candidates that are not just in the market but also on the market allows them the flexibility to extend multi-faceted solutions while remaining specialized experts in the healthcare staffing industry. Their national footprint and reputation builds upon their acute awareness and ability to hone in on evolving patterns in health care, staying current with developing trends, and remaining cognizant of their clients and candidates ever-changing needs. Internally, they have birthed a culture of quality over quantity. Externally, they put that culture into practice for those they represent.

Cross Country Healthcare, Inc.   **www.crosscountrystaffing.com/ccstaffing/**
One of the largest Medical staffing firms in the US. Under several brands, the company places traveling nurses and other Medical professionals through more than 5,000 contracts with acute care hospitals, pharmaceutical companies, nursing homes, schools, and other related facilities across the nation. The firm coordinates travel and housing arrangements for its nurses, whose assignments usually last about three months at a time. Cross Country also provides Medical education, training, and recruiting services for doctors and Medical executives. Subsidiaries and brands include Assignment America, Allied Health Group, NovaPro, Med-Staff, TravCorps, and Cejka Search.

A provider of healthcare staffing services. They also provide staffing of clinical research professionals and allied healthcare professionals, such as radiology technicians, rehabilitation therapists and respiratory therapists. Their staffing operations are complemented by other human capital management services, including search and recruitment, consulting, education and training and resource management services. The Company operates in three segments: Nurse and Allied Staffing, Physician Staffing and Other Human Capital Management Services. Its nurse and allied staffing segment is engaged in providing traditional staffing, including temporary and permanent placement of travel nurses and allied professionals, and branch-based local nurses and allied staffing through its Cross Country Staffing brand, MSN, AHG, Mediscan and DirectEd brands.

Franchises

Interim Healthcare   www.interimhealthcare.com
Founded in 1966, it is the nation's oldest national healthcare franchise organization providing the full continuum of home care, senior care, hospice and healthcare staffing services. Through a comprehensive network of more than 300 independently owned franchise offices, Interim HealthCare franchisees are the largest combined provider of community-based home care and healthcare staffing. It is unique in combining the commitment of local ownership with the support of a national organization that develops innovative programs and quality standards that improve the delivery of service through franchisees that employ more than 75,000 health care workers who serve 50,000 people each day. It provides a broad array of home care services including senior care focusing on personal care & support services such as bathing, grooming, transportation, companionship, Alzheimer's & Dementia care, and respite care. Also provides a variety of home nursing and pediatric nursing; IV therapy; chronic disease management, physical, occupational and speech therapy.

Total Investment: $115,500 - $188,500   Franchise Fee: $40,000
Ongoing Royalty Fee: 5%   Term of Franchise Agreement: 5 years, renewable
Financial Requirements
Net Worth: $250,000 - $750,000   Liquid Cash Available: $100,000 - $250,000
Training: Available at headquarters: up to 10 days. At franchisee's location: up to 10 days. Regional training : up to 5 days.
Ongoing Support: Newsletter, Meetings, Toll-free phone line, Grand opening, Internet, Security/safety procedures, Field operations/evaluations, Purchasing cooperatives,
Marketing Support: Co-op advertising, Ad slicks, National media, Regional advertising,

BrightStar Care
A healthcare staffing company that provides medical and non-medical care for all ages, in-home care for disabled adults and seniors, and supplemental staffing for corporate clients such as nursing homes and physicians' offices. Provides a customized care plan to match client needs with a qualified, pre-screened caregiver who is compatible with their needs. One of the few home healthcare providers that offer both medical and non-medical homecare, available to all clients 24/7.

Total Investment: $95,067 - $162,158   Franchise Fee: $47,500
Ongoing Royalty Fee: 5-7%   Term of Franchise Agreement: 10 years, renewable
Financial Requirements
Net Worth: $500,000   Liquid Cash Available: $75,000 - $100,000
Training: Available at headquarters: 8 days. At franchisee's location: 10 days.
Ongoing Support: Newsletter, Meetings, Toll-free phone line, Grand opening, Internet,
Security/safety procedures, Field operations/evaluations, Purchasing cooperatives,
Marketing Support: Co-op advertising, Ad slicks, National media, Regional advertising,

5.5   Industry News

Delta Medical Consulting released an updated version of its recruiting and retention
guidebook, "The Physician Recruiting Standard." This reference book includes the latest
trends in recruiting and retaining doctors and other health care providers.

6.0   Strategy and Implementation Summary

_____ (company name) intends to develop a referral network from doctors, surgeons, hospitals, and post operative clinics within the target market. Since the Company is marketing directly to Medical professionals and establishments, the costs associated with advertising are minimal. The Company will also use traditional forms of marketing that are targeted towards Medical professionals in the target market community. Management intends to market directly within locally based Medical journals for the Medical profession. In regards to larger clients, like hospitals and outpatient facilities, _____ (company name) will directly contact these businesses to establish ongoing business relationships. Registered nurse, technician, and physician outsourcing is the most profitable aspect of this business, and the Company will rapidly establish these relationships so that the business can immediately generate revenue from these sources. Finally, _____ (company name) will develop its own website that will feature information about the business, contact information, and preliminary pricing schedules for temporary and permanent Medical staffing solutions that the Company offers.

Our sales strategy is based on serving our niche markets better than the competition and leveraging our competitive advantages. These advantages include superior attention to understanding and satisfying customer needs and wants, creating a one-stop staffing solution, and value pricing.

The objectives of our marketing strategy will be to recruit new clients and job candidates, retain existing clients, get good clients to spend more and return more frequently to satisfy their staffing needs. Establishing a loyal customer base is very important because such core clients will not only generate the most lifetime sales, but also provide valuable referrals.

We will generate word-of-mouth buzz through direct-mail campaigns, exceeding customer expectations, developing a Web site, getting involved in community events with local businesses, and donating our services at charity functions in exchange for press release coverage. Our sales strategy will seek to convert potential and first-time clients into long-term relationships and referral agents. The combination of our competitive advantages, targeted marketing campaign and networking activities will enable _____ (company name) to continue increasing our market share.

6.1.0   Promotion Strategy

Given the importance of word-of-mouth/referrals among the area practices, we shall strive to efficiently service all our clients to gain their business regularly, which is the recipe for our long-term success. We shall focus on direct marketing, publicity, seminars, and advertising as proposed. Our promotion strategy will focus on generating referrals from existing clients and professionals, community involvement and direct mail campaigns.
Our promotional strategies will also make use of the following tools:

- **Advertising**
  - Yearly anniversary parties to celebrate the success of each year.
  - Yellow Pages ads in the book and online.
  - Flyers promoting special promotion events.
  - Doorknob hangers for private practices.

- **Local Marketing / Public Relations**
  - Client raffle for gift certificates or discount coupons
  - Participation in local civic groups.
  - Press release coverage of our sponsoring of events at the local community center for families and residents.
  - Article submissions to magazines describing Medical hiring trends.
  - Sales Brochure to convey our staffing program specialties.
  - Seminar presentations to local civic groups, explaining the importance of candidate pre-screening techniques.
  - Giveaway of free informational booklets with agency contact information.

- **Local Media**
  - Direct Mail - We will send quarterly postcards and annual direct mailings to private practices and clinics with a ___ (20?) mile radius of our agency. It will contain an explanation of the benefits of our candidate matching services.
  - Radio Campaign - We will make "live on the air" presentations of our trial home Medical service coupons to the disk jockeys, hoping to get the promotions broadcasted to the listening audience. We will also make our expertise available for talk radio programs.
  - Newspaper Campaign - Placing several ads in local community newspapers to launch our initial campaign. We will include a trial coupon.
  - Website – We will collect email addresses for a monthly newsletter.
  - Cable TV advertising on local community-based shows focused on news and child development.

6.1.1   Grand Opening

Our Grand Opening celebration will be a very important promotion opportunity to create word-of-mouth advertising results. We will advertise the date of our grand opening in local newspapers and on local radio. It is generally a good idea to provide the community with a reason to visit our agency, such as offering free wine and cheese.

We will do the following things to make the open house a successful event:
1. Enlist local business support to contribute a large number of door prizes.
2. Use a sign-in sheet to create an email/mailing list.
3. Sponsor a competition or trivia contest.
4. Schedule appearance by local celebrities.

5. Create a festive atmosphere with balloons, beverages and music.
6. Get the local radio station to broadcast live from the event and handout fun gifts.
7. Offer an application fee waiver.
8. Giveaway our logo imprinted T-shirts as a contest prize.
9. Allow potential clients to view your facility and ask questions.
10. Print promotional flyers and pay a few kids to distribute them locally.
11. Arrange for storytelling, and snacks for everyone.
12. Arrange for local politician to do the official opening ceremony so all the local newspapers came to take pictures and do a feature story.
13. Arrange that people can tour our facility on the open day in order to see our facilities, collect sales brochures and find out more about our staffing services.
14. Allocate staff members to perform specific duties, handout business cards and sales brochures and instruct them to deal with any questions or queries.
16. Organize a drawing with everyone writing their name and phone numbers on the back of business cards and give a voucher as a prize to start a marketing list.

Ex: _____ **(company name) Opens _____ (city) Branch**
_____ (company name), a provider of quality healthcare staffing solutions based in _____ (city), ____ (state) announced today that the company opened its newest office in _____ (city), _____ (state). _____ (Executive Name), who brings extensive healthcare staffing experience to the position, will manage the _____ (city) location.

_____ (company name) is an industry leader in placing healthcare professionals in contract, contract-to-hire, and direct hire opportunities for short- and long-term assignments. We staff facilities with qualified professionals in areas including nursing, clinical laboratory, rehab therapy, diagnostic imaging, respiratory, administration, dental, and pharmacy. Solely focused on the needs of healthcare facilities, we can match talent to opportunity within 24 to 48 hours.

6.1.2   Value Proposition

Our value proposition will summarize why a Medical organization should use our staffing services. We will enable quick access to our broad line of innovative services, out of our conveniently located agency offices in the _____ (city) area. Our value proposition will convince prospects that our staffing services will add more value and better solve their need for a convenient, one-stop Medical staffing service. We will add value to our clients by having the continual ability to provide new personnel with full credentials and guarantee an adherence to an on-going quality assurance process and standards.

We will use this value proposition statement to target clients who will benefit most from using our services. These are private practices looking to quickly deal employee terminations, absences and vacations. Our value proposition will be concise and appeal to the customer's strongest decision-making drivers, which are one-stop convenience, competitive pricing, remote online database access, satisfaction guarantee, thoroughness of the screening process, and quality of personal relationships.

Recap of Our Value Proposition:

Trust – We are known as a trusted business partner with strong customer and vendor endorsements. We have earned a reputation for quality, integrity, and delivery of successful event solutions.

Quality – We offer medical staffing experience and extensive professional backgrounds at competitive rates.

Experience – Our ability to bring people with years of healthcare management experience with deep technical knowledge is at the core of our success.

True Vendor Partnerships – Our true vendor partnerships enable us to offer the resources of much larger organizations with greater flexibility.

Customer Satisfaction and Commitment to Success – Through partnering with our clients and delivering quality solutions, we have been able to achieve an impressive degree of repeat and referral business. Since _____ (year), more than _____% of our business activity is generated by existing clients. Our philosophy is that "our clients' success is our success." Our success is measured in terms of our clients' success through the solutions we build for them.

6.1.3   Positioning Statement

Our positioning strategy will be the result of conducting in-depth consumer market research to find out what benefits consumers want and how our staffing services can meet those needs. Many service-oriented professions are leaning toward differentiating themselves on the basis of convenience. This is also what we intend to do. For instance, we plan to have extended, 24/7 "people" hours, 7 days of the week.

We also plan to develop specialized staffing services that will enable us to pursue a niche focus on specific interest based programs, such as nurse travel services, skills development services and HR consulting services. These objectives will position us at the _____ (mid-level/high-end) of the market and will allow the company to realize a healthy profit margin in relation to its low-end, discount rivals and achieve long-term growth.

Market Positioning Recap

Price: The strategy is to offer competitive prices that are lower that the market leader, yet set to indicate value and worth. .

Quality: The staffing quality will have to be very good as the finished service results will be showcased in highly visible situations.

Service: Highly individualized and customized service will be the key to success in this type of business. Personal attention to the clients will result in higher sales and word of mouth advertising.

6.1.4   Unique Selling Proposition (USP)

Our unique selling proposition will answer the question why a customer should choose to do business with our company versus any and every other option available to them in the marketplace. Our USP will be a description of a unique important benefit that our Health Care Staffing Agency offers to clients, so that price is no longer the key to our sales.

Our USP will include the following:
Who our target audience is: _____
What we will do for them: _____
What qualities, skills, talents, traits do we possess that others do not: _____
What are the benefits we provide that no one else offers: _____
Why that is different from what others are offering: _____
Why that solution matters to our target audience: _____

6.1.4   Distribution Strategy

Clients can contact the _____ (company name) by telephone, fax, internet and by dropping in. Our nearest competitors' are ___ (#) miles away in either direction.

Our clients will have the following access points:
1.   Order by Phone
        Clients can contact us 24 hours a day, 7days a week at _____.
        Our Customer Service Representatives will be available to assist clients Monday through Friday from ___ a.m. to ____ p.m. EST.
2.   Order by Fax
        Clients may fax their orders to _____ anytime.
        They must provide: Account number, Billing and shipping address, Purchase order number, if applicable, Name and telephone number, Product number/description, Unit of measure and quantity ordered and Applicable sales promotion source codes.
3.   Order Online
        Clients can order online at www._____.com.Once the account is activated, clients will be able to place orders, browse the catalog, check stock availability and pricing, check order status and view both order and transaction history.
4.   In-person
        All clients can be serviced in person at our facilities Monday through Friday from ___ a.m. to ____ p.m. EST.

We plan to pursue the following distribution channels: **(select)**

	Number	Reason Chosen	Sales Costs
1. Our own retail outlets _____			
2. Independent distributors _____			
3. Independent commissioned sales reps _____			

4. In-house sales reps _____
5. Direct mail using own catalog or flyers _____
6. In-house telemarketing _____
7. Contracted telemarketing call center _____
8. Cybermarketing via own website _____
9. TV and Cable Direct Marketing _____

6.1.6   Sales Rep Plan

The following parameters will help to define our sales rep plan:

1.	In-house or Independent	_____
2.	Salaried or Commissioned	_____
3.	Salary or Commission Rate	_____
4.	Salary Plus Commission Rate	_____
5.	Special Performance Incentives	_____
6.	Negotiating Parameters	Price Breaks/Added Services/
7.	Performance Evaluation Criteria	No. of New Clients/Sales Volume/
8.	Number of Reps	_____
9.	Sales Territory Determinants	Geography/Demographics/
10.	Sales Territories Covered	_____
11.	Training Program Overview	_____
12.	Training Program Cost	_____
13.	Sales Kit Contents	_____
14.	Primary Target Market	_____
15.	Secondary Target Market	_____

Rep Name	Compensation Plan	Assigned Territory

We will locate sales reps using the following techniques:
1. Place classified ads in trade magazines that serve medical practices.
2. Seek other agency owner recommendations.
3. Ask the managers of medical practices the names of reps showing products to them.
4. Attend trade shows where the reps are showing their product lines.

6.2.0   Competitive Advantages

A **competitive advantage** is the thing that differentiates a business from its competitors. It is what separates our business from everyone else. It answers the questions: "Why do clients buy from us versus a competitor?", and "What do we offer clients that is unique?". We will incorporate our key competitive advantages into all of our marketing materials. We will use the following competitive advantages to set us apart from our competitors. The distinctive competitive advantages which _____ (company name) brings to the marketplace are as follows: (Note: Select only those you can support)

Existing Medical staffing agencies are mainly generalists, with little experience in the Medical industry or in assessing the needs of the end users, who often rely on their own un-informed efforts to recruit qualified Medical professionals. _____ (company name), on the other hand, will have the specialized skills, technology and global contacts to dominate the existing competition.

Other competitive advantages include:
1. Around-the Clock Accessibility, with Staffing Consultants available 24-hours a day, 7 days a week to provide the most efficient service possible.
2. Maintenance of stringent screening processes to ensure that the professionals we send exceed our client's expectations in competency, skill level, professionalism and attitude.
3. Development of a thorough pre-employment screening process, which includes competency tests and a thorough background check.
4. We are able to recruit and maintain an abundance of qualified Medical professionals, enabling us to fill a variety of requests in a time efficient manner.
5. The facilities that we staff save thousands of dollars every year by eliminating recruitment fees from their budget. These fees include placing advertisements and valuable time spent reviewing resumes and interviewing candidates.
6. We have earned a glowing reputation of being a leader in temporary and direct hire (perm) rehab therapy staffing.
7. Our business revolves around motivated practitioners performing quality work. 8. We offer competitive salaries, insurance coverage, completion bonuses, and more to our allied staff.
8. Joint Commission Medical Staffing Services Certification.
9. With ___ (#) years of staffing experience, we know how to find the best Medical professionals for our client's needs and prepare them to make an immediate impact on assignment.
10. Our clients have access to the largest network of qualified Medical professionals in the country.
11. Our multi-brand approach to targeted online and print advertising, attendance at conferences and career fairs, along with our widely-known standing as a premier career option for nurses, physicians and allied Medical providers, allows us to attract top Medical professionals to fill almost any assignment need quickly.
12. Our Medical professionals meet or exceed the highest competency standards and must complete a rigorous assessment process, including:

An initial competency evaluation to verify education, certifications and work
  experience

A skills inventory review by our clinical experts

A thorough background and drug screening

A personal interview and client-specific evaluation

Ongoing competency testing

Continuing education courses, offered at no cost through our education
  partner.

13. By having owners of the company being the principle managers of the company
    we will reduce employee costs and will ensure the honesty and reliability of our
    staff.

14. Our involvement with the community and our presence and availability on a
    regular basis will give our clients the opportunity to give direct feedback.

15. We will enable our clients to have online access to our total inventory of job
    candidates.

16. We will train our staff to answer most clients questions, so that their time is
    valued.

17. We constantly are search of the latest technology to update our operations and
    reinforce the image in customer minds that we are among the most progressive
    recruiting professionals in the area.

18. We will utilize a software package that provides document management services
    and advanced management tools, such as basic and intermediate reporting
    functions, cost-benefit analysis, inventory management and audit functionality, in
    addition to electronic records storage and retrieval.

19. We will offer discounts and other incentives for referrals.

20. We have the technological and professional staffing capabilities to provide our
    clients with the highest possible level of personalized service.

21. We have an ethnically diverse and multilingual staff, which is critical for a
    service-oriented business.

22. We have formed alliances that enable us to provide one-stop shopping or an array
    of staffing services through a single access point.

23. We developed a specialized training program for the staff so they will be
    proficient at administering our agency service programs.

24. Our superior customer service, delivered through our trained staff, sets us apart
    and provides our competitive advantage

25. We regularly conduct focus groups to understand changing customer
    expectations.

26. We hire and train our employees to be responsive and empathetic to customer
    needs.

27. We do not service any other field except for the Medical Industry.

28. Our Proprietary Marketing Systems enable us to have more than twice as much
    traffic as any publicly traded Medical Recruitment Firm.

29. We provide customized solutions that meet the unique financial, clinical and
    operational goals of your facility.

30. For every professional we place, _____ (company name):

Arranges Medical malpractice insurance coverage.

Exceeds industry standards in qualifying independent allied health professionals through our Quality Assurance Department.

Uses an in-house licensing department that expedites licensure in all 50 states. Arranges all transportation and housing and handles necessary paperwork associated with privileging assistance, licensure and malpractice insurance.

31. Through cutting-edge business-to-business solutions, we support clients with access to the credentials of its healthcare professionals.

32. Our services also include staff utilization and fill rate reports, weekly financial reporting covering invoices and data trends, and real-time financial management of payments.

_____ (company name)has developed one of the largest and most comprehensive quality management programs in the staffing industry, the success of which is evident in our nursing division's corporate certification by the Joint Commission, endorsements of our physician and allied divisions by several state hospital associations, and by the large clinical services team who supports our Medical professionals and client facilities

In addition to great compensation, _____ (company name) will offer a superb benefits package to our personnel.

Referral Bonuses	Health Insurance
401(k) Retirement Plan	Housing Subsidies & Per Diem Allowances
Free Housing	Completion Bonuses
Transportation Reimbursement	Continuing Education Reimbursement
Hepatitis B Vaccination	Direct Deposit and Payroll Card
Paid Liability Insurance	Workers' Compensation Coverage

6.2.1   Branding Strategy

Our branding strategy involves what we do to shape what the customer immediately thinks our business offers and stands for. The purpose of our branding strategy is to reduce customer perceived purchase risk and improve our profit margins by allowing use to charge a premium for our Health Care Staffing Agency services.

We will invest $_____ every year in maintaining our brand name image, which will differentiate our health care staffing business from other companies. The amount of money spent on creating and maintaining a brand name will not convey any specific information about our products, but it will convey, indirectly, that we are in this market for the long haul, that we have a reputation to protect, and that we will interact repeatedly with our customers. In this sense, the amount of money spent on maintaining our brand name will signal to consumers that we will provide products and services of consistent quality.

We will use the following ways to build trust and establish our personal brand:

1. Build a consistently published blog and e-newsletter with informational content.
2. Create comprehensive social media profiles.
3. Contribute articles to related online publications.
4. Earn career certifications

Resources:
https://www.abetterlemonadestand.com/branding-guide/

Our key to marketing success will be to effectively manage the building of our brand platform in the marketplace, which will consist of the following elements:

Brand Vision - our envisioned future of the brand is to be the local source for medical staffing solutions to manage the complications of healthcare management.

Brand Attributes - Partners, problem solvers, responsive, comprehensive, reliable, flexible, recruiting experts, and easy to work with.

Brand Essence - the shared soul of the brand, the spark of which is present in every experience a customer has with our products, will be "Problem Solving" and "Responsive" This will be the core of our organization, driving the type of people we hire and the type of behavior we expect.

Brand Image - the outside world's overall perception of our organization will be that we are the 'medical staffing' pros who are alleviating the complications of selecting the right staffing level for the right period of time.

Brand Promise - our concise statement of what we do, why we do it, and why clients should do business with us will be, "To save money and improve the level of healthcare service with the help of our knowledgeable staff"

We will use the following methodologies to implement our branding strategy:
1. Develop processes, systems and quality assurance procedures to assure the consistent adherence to our quality standards and mission statement objectives.
2. Develop business processes to consistently deliver upon our value proposition.
3. Develop training programs to assure the consistent professionalism and responsiveness of our employees.
4. Develop marketing communications with consistent, reinforcing message content.
5. Incorporate testimonials into our marketing materials that support our promises.
6. Develop marketing communications with a consistent presentation style.
   (Logo design, company colors, slogan, labels, packaging, stationery, etc.)
7. Exceed our brand promises to achieve consistent customer loyalty.
8. Use surveys, focus groups and interviews to consistently monitor what our brand means to our clients.
9. Consistently match our brand values or performance benchmarks to our customer requirements.
10. Focus on the maintenance of a consistent number of key brand values that are tied to our company strengths.
11. Continuously research industry trends in our markets to stay relevant to customer needs and wants.
12. Attach a logo-imprinted product label and business card to all products,

marketing communications and invoices.

13. Develop a memorable and meaningful tagline that captures the essence of our brand.
14. Prepare a one page company overview and make it a key component of our sales presentation folder.
15. Hire and train employees to put the interests of clients first.
16. Develop a professional website that is updated with fresh content on a regular basis.
17. Use our blog to circulate content that establishes our niche expertise and opens a two-way dialogue with our clients.
18. Attractive and tasteful uniforms will also help our staff's morale. The branding will become complete with the addition of our corporate logo, or other trim or accessories which echo the style and theme of our establishment.
19. Create an effective slogan with the following attributes:
    a. Appeals to customers' emotions.
    b. Shows off how our service benefits customers by highlighting our customer service or care.
    c. Has 8 words or less and is memorable
    d. Can be grasped quickly by our audience.
    e. Reflects our business' personality and character.
    f. Shows sign of originality.
20. Create a Proof Book that contains before and after photos, testimonial letters, our mission statement , copies of industry certifications and our code of ethics.
21. Make effective use of trade show exhibitions and email newsletters to help brand our image.

The communications strategy we will use to build our brand platform will include the following items:

Website - featuring product line information, database searches, research, testimonials, cost benefit analysis, frequently asked questions, and policy information. This website will be used as a tool for both our sales team and our clients.

Presentations, brochures and mailers geared to the consumer, explaining the benefits of our product line as part of a comprehensive medical staffing plan.

Presentations and brochures geared to the corporate decision maker explaining the benefits of our programs in terms of positive outcomes, reduced cost from complications, and reduced risk of lawsuits or negative survey events.

A presentation and recruiting brochure geared to prospective sales people that emphasizes the benefits of joining our organization.

Training materials that help every employee deliver our brand message in a consistent manner.

6.2.2   Brand Positioning Statement

We will use the following brand positioning statement to summarize what our brand means to our targeted market:

To _____ (target market)
_____ (company name) is the brand of _____ (product/service
frame of reference) that enables the customer to _____ (primary
performance benefit) because ____ (company name) _____ (products/services)
_____ (are made with/offer/provide) the best _____ (key attributes)

6.3   Business SWOT Analysis

Definition: SWOT Analysis is a powerful technique for understanding our Strengths
and Weaknesses, and for looking at the Opportunities and Threats faced.

Strategy: We will use this SWOT Analysis to uncover exploitable opportunities and
carve a sustainable niche in our market. And by understanding the
weaknesses of our business, we can manage and eliminate threats that
would otherwise catch us by surprise. By using the SWOT framework, we
will be able to craft a strategy that distinguishes our business from our
competitors, so that we can compete successfully in the market.

Strengths   (select)
What Health Care Staffing Agency services are we best at providing?
What unique resources can we draw upon?
1.   Company led by a veteran recruiter and supported by a strong
management team   .
2.   The facility has been established as a computer center for ___ years.
3.   The nearest competition is __ miles and has a minimal inventory of
screened job candidates.
4.   Our agency offices have been extensively renovated, with many upgrades.
5.   Seasoned executive management professionals, sophisticated in business
knowledge, experienced in the Health Care Staffing Agency business.
7.   Strong networking relationships with many different organizations,
including _____.
8.   Excellent staff are experienced, highly trained and customer attentive.
9.   Wide diversity of Medical staffing service offerings.
10.   High customer loyalty.
11.   The proven ability to establish excellent personalized client service.
12.   Strong relationships with suppliers that offer flexibility and respond to
special customer requirements.
13.   Good referral relationships.
14.   Client loyalty developed through a solid reputation with repeat clients.
15.   Our agency has a focused target market of Registered Nurses.
16.   Sales staff with heath care education credentials.
17.   _____

Weaknesses

In what areas could we improve?

Where do we have fewer resources than others?

1.   Lack of developmental capital to complete Phase I start-up.
2.   New comer to the area.
3.   Lack of marketing experience.
4.   The struggle to build brand equity.
5.   A limited marketing budget to develop brand awareness.
6.   Finding dependable and people oriented staff.
7.   We need to develop the information systems that will improve our productivity and inventory management.
8.   Don't know the needs and wants of the local population.
9.   The owner must deal with the human resource learning curve.
10. Challenges caused by the seasonal nature of the business.
11. Inadequate monitoring of competitor strategies, reviews and responses.
12. Management expertise gaps.
13. _____

Opportunities

What opportunities are there for new and/or improved services?

What trends could we take advantage of?

1.   Seasonal changes in inventory.
2.   Could take market share away from existing competitors.
3.   Greater need for mobile home services by time starved dual income families.
4.   Growing market with a significant percentage of the target market still not aware that _____ (company name) exists.
5.   The ability to develop many long-term customer relationships.
6.   Expanding the range of product/service packaged offerings.
7.   Greater use of direct advertising to promote our services.
8.   Establish referral relationships with local businesses serving the same target market segment.
9.   Networking with non-profit organizations.
10. The aging population will need and expect a greater range of __ services.
11. Increased public awareness of the importance of 'green' matters.
12. Strategic alliances offering sources for referrals and joint marketing activities to extend our reach.
13. _____ (supplier name) is offering co-op advertising.
14. A competitor has overextended itself financially and is facing bankruptcy.
15. _____

Threats

What trends or competitor actions could hurt us?

What threats do our weaknesses expose us to?

1.   Another Health Care Staffing Agency could move into this area.
2.   Further declines in the economic forecast.
3.   Inflation affecting operations for gas, labor, and other operating costs.

4. Keeping trained efficient staff and key personnel from moving on or starting their own business venture.
5. Imitation competition from similar indirect service providers.
6. Price differentiation is a significant competition factor.
7. The government could enact legislation that could affect recruiting and licensing practices.
8. We need to do a better job of assessing the strengths and weaknesses of all of our competitors.
9. Sales of custom _____ by mass discounters..
10. _____

Recap:

We will use the following strengths to capitalize on recognized opportunities:
1. _____
2. _____

We will take the following actions to turn our weaknesses into strengths and prepare to defend against known threats.
1. _____
2. _____

6.4.0   Marketing Strategy

Overview:

We will make appointments with local Medical facilities to talk with the heads of human resource departments, office managers and recruiters. We will introduce our company and its staffing services through these meetings and hand out sales brochures highlighting the availability of our staff and the Medical specialties we cover. We will set up a phone line to handle the requests for staff on a 24-hour basis and purchase software that is specifically designed for Medical staffing agencies that can help track staff, record hours and payroll and client requests. We will create a website that job candidates can post their resumes to and clients can use to enter staffing requests and learn more about our company.

Our Marketing strategy will focus on the following:

1. Developing a reputation for a selection Medical staffing services, competitive prices, reliability and exceptional customer service.
2. Keeping the staff focused, satisfied and motivated in their roles, to help keep our productivity and customer service at the highest obtainable levels.
4. Maintaining the visibility of our agency offices through regular advertising to our target community.
5. Reaching out to potential hospitals, clinics, private practices and community organizations, with commissioned independent sales reps.

6. Doing activities that can stimulate additional business: seminars, publishing helpful articles about Medical Professional screening techniques, sharing interesting and educational training knowledge, publishing a newsletter, offering customer service through a website, and automatic reminder notices based on historical patterns.
7. Extending our market penetration beyond the physical boundaries of the office location through outside sales reps and a website.

In phase one of our marketing plan, we will gain exposure to our target markets through the use of discounts and grand opening promotional tactics. We will be taking a very aggressive marketing stance in the first year of business in hopes of gaining customer loyalty. In our subsequent years, we will focus less resources on advertising as a whole, but, we do plan to budget for advertising promotions on a continual and season specific basis.

We will start our business with our known personal referral contacts and then continue our campaign to develop recognition among other Medical professional groups and organizations. We will develop and maintain a database of our contacts in the field. We will work to maintain and exploit our existing relationships throughout the start-up process and then use our marketing tools to communicate with other potential referral sources.

The marketing strategy will create awareness, interest and appeal from our target market. Its ultimate purpose is to encourage repeat purchases and get clients to refer friends and professional contacts. To get referrals we will provide incentives and excellent service, and build relationships with clients by caring about what the client needs and wants to improve human resource utilization and productivity.

Our marketing strategy will revolve around two different types of media, flyers and a website. These two tools will be used to make clients aware of our broad range of staffing services. One focus of our marketing strategy will be to drive clients to our website for information about our service programs and candidate database search options.

A combination of local media and event marketing will be utilized. _____ (company name) will create an identity oriented marketing strategy with executions particularly in the local media. Our marketing strategy will utilize trade journal print ads, press releases, yellow page ads, flyers, and newsletter distribution. We will make effective use of direct response advertising, and include coupons for free consultations and HR audits in all print ads.

We will use comment cards, newsletter sign-up forms and surveys to collect customer email addresses and feed our client relationship management (CRM) software system. This system will automatically send out, on a predetermined schedule, follow-up materials, such as article reprints, seminar invitations, email messages, surveys and e-newsletters. We will offset some of our advertising costs by asking our alliance partners to place ads in our newsletter.

Current Situation

We will study the current marketing situation on a weekly basis to analyze trends and identify sources of business growth. As onsite owners, we will be on hand daily to insure exceptional customer service. Our services include domestic Medical field staffing services of the highest quality and a prompt response to feedback from clients. Our extensive and detailed financial statements, produced monthly, will enable us to stay competitive and exploit presented opportunities.

Marketing Budget

Our marketing budget will be a flexible $_____ per quarter. The marketing budget can be allocated in any way that best suits the time of year.
Marketing budget per quarter:

Newspaper Ads	$_____	Radio advertisement	$_____
Web Page	$_____	Customer raffle	$_____
Direct Mail	$_____	Sales Brochure	$_____
Home Shows	$_____	Seminars	$_____
Superpages	$_____	Google Adwords	$_____
Giveaways	$_____	Vehicle Signs	$_____
Business Cards	$_____	Flyers	$_____
Labels/Stickers	$_____	Videos/DVDs	$_____
Samples	$_____	Newsletter	$_____
Bench Signs	$_____	Email Campaigns	$_____
Sales Reps Comm.	$_____	Other	$_____

Total: $_____

Our objective in setting a marketing budget has been to keep it between _____ (5?) and _____ (7?) percent of our estimated annual gross sales.

Marketing Mix

New clients will primarily come from word-of-mouth and our referral program. The overall market approach involves creating brand awareness through targeted advertising, public relations, co-marketing efforts with select alliance partners, direct mail, email campaigns, seminars and a website.

Video Marketing

We will link to our website a series of YouTube.com based video clips that talk about our range of Medical staffing services, and demonstrate our expertise with certain Medical practices. We will create business marketing videos that are both entertaining and informational, and improve our search engine rankings. Studies have shown that videos are more than 50 times more likely to appear on the first page of search results as part of these blended results.

The video will include:

Client testimonials - We will let our best clients become our instant sales force because people will believe what others say about us more readily than what we say about ourselves.

Product Demonstrations - Train and pre-sell our potential clients on our most popular services by talking about and showing them. Often, our potential clients don't know the full range and depth of our services because we haven't taken the adequate time to show and tell them.

Include Business Website Address

Owner Interview: Explanation of agency mission statement and unique selling proposition.

Record Frequently Asked Questions Sessions - We will answer questions that we often get, and anticipate objections we might get and give great reasons to convince potential clients that we are the best Health Care Staffing Agency in the area.

Include a Call to Action - We have the experience and the know-how to supply your practice with Registered Nurses on a temporary basis. So call us, right now, and let's get started.

Seminar - Include a portion of a seminar on how to screen potential Medical Professionals.

Comment on industry trends and product news - We will appear more in-tune and knowledgeable in our market if we can talk about what's happening in our Medical industry and local marketplace.

Resources: www.businessvideomarketing.tv
                 www.hotpluto.com
                 www.hubspot.com/video-marketing-kit
                 www.youtube.com/user/mybusinessstory

Analytics Report
http://support.google.com/youtube/bin/static.py?hl=en&topic=1728599&guide=1
         714169&page=guide.cs

Note: Refer to Video Marketing Tips in rear marketing worksheets section.
Example:
www.youtube.com/watch?v=sVBrUOhhBvE

Top 12 places where we will share our marketing videos online:
YouTube   **www.youtube.com**
This very popular website allows you to log-in and leave comments and ratings on the videos. You can also save your favorite videos and allows you to tag posted videos. This makes it easier for your videos to come up in search engines.
Google Video   **http://video.google.com/**
A video hosting site. Google Video is not just focused on sharing videos online, but this is also a market place where you can buy the videos you find on this site using Google search engine.
Yahoo! Video   **http://video.yahoo.com/**
Uploading and sharing videos is possible with Yahoo Video!. You can find several types of videos on their site and you can also post comments and ratings for the videos.
Revver   **http://www.revver.com/**

This website lets you earn money through ads on your videos and you will have a 50/50 profit split with the website. Another great deal with Revver is that your fans who posted your videos on their site can also earn money.

Blip.tv   http://blip.tv/
Allows viewers to stream and download the videos posted on their website. You can also use Creative Commons licenses on your videos posted on the website. This allows you to decide if your videos should be attributed, restricted for commercial use and be used under specific terms.

Vimeo   http://www.vimeo.com/
This website is family safe and focuses on sharing private videos. The interface of the website is similar to some social networking sites that allow you to customize your profile page with photos from Flickr and embeddable player. This site allows users to socialize through their videos.

Metacafe   http://www.metacafe.com/
This video sharing site is community based. You can upload short-form videos and share it to the other users of the website. Metacafe has its own system called VideoRank that ranks videos according to the viewer reactions and features the most popular among the viewers.

ClipShack   http://www.clipshack.com/
Like most video sharing websites you can post comments on the videos and even tag some as your favorite. You can also share the videos on other websites through the html code from ClipShack and even sending it through your email.

Veoh   http://www.veoh.com/
You can rent or sell your videos and keep the 70% of the sales price. You can upload a range of different video formats on Veoh and there is no limit on the size and length of the file. However when your video is over 45 minutes it has to be downloaded before the viewer can watch it.

Jumpcut   http://download.cnet.com/JumpCut/3000-18515_4-10546353.html
Jumpcut allows its users to upload videos using their mobile phones. You will have to attach the video captured from your mobile phone to an email. It has its own movie making wizard that helps you familiarize with the interface of the site.

DailyMotion   www.dailymotion.com
As one of the leading sites for sharing videos, Dailymotion attracts over 114 million unique monthly visitors (source: comScore, May 2017) 1.2 billion videos views worldwide (source: internal). Offers the best content from users, independent content creators and premium partners. Using the most advanced technology for both users and content creators, provides high-quality and HD video in a fast, easy-to-use online service that also automatically filters infringing material as notified by content owners.
Offering 32 localized versions, their mission is to provide the best possible entertainment experience for users and the best marketing opportunities for advertisers, while respecting content protection.

CitySquares
A leader in video marketing and advertising solutions for local businesses working to expand their online exposure and generate new prospective clients. Building innovative video applications that deliver the best ways for local businesses to connect with clients. Their full-service video marketing platform makes it easy and affordable for any small or

medium sized business to utilize video to grow their online brand. Services include Video Creation and Online Distribution, YouTube In-Stream Advertising, Facebook Advertising and Lead Capturing, and CitySquares Local Business Directory, which is fast becoming the largest video business directory on the web.

Business Cards

Our business card will include our company logo, complete contact information, name and title, association logos, slogan or markets serviced, licenses and certifications. The center of our bi-fold card will contain a listing of the staffing services we offer. We will give out multiple business cards to friends, family members, business associates and to each customer, upon the completion of the service. We will also distribute business cards in the following ways:
1. Attached to invoices, surveys, flyers and door hangers.
2. Included in seminar handout packages.
3. We will leave a stack of business cards in a Lucite holder with the local Chamber of Commerce and any other businesses offering free counter placement.

We will use fold-over cards because they will enable us to list all of our services and complete contact instructions on the inside of the card. We will also give magnetic business cards to new clients for ease of posting.

We will place the following referral discount message on the back of our business cards:
- Our business is very dependent upon referrals. If you have associates who could benefit from our quality services, please write your name at the bottom of this card and give it to them. When your friend presents this card upon their first visit, he or she will be entitled to 10% off discount. And, on your next invoice, you will also get a 10% discount as a thank you for your referral.
Resource:
www.vistaprint.com

Direct Mail Package

To build name recognition and to announce the opening of our Health Care Staffing Agency, we will offer a mail package consisting of a tri-fold brochure containing a HR audit coupon to welcome our new clients. We plan to make a mailing to local subscribers of Medical Practice Journals. From those identified local clients, we shall ask them to complete a survey and describe their perception of the agency, and any staffing services they would like to see added. Those clients returning completed surveys would receive a premium (giveaway) gift.
Resource:
www.melissadata.com

Trade Shows

We will exhibit at as many local trade shows per year as possible. These include Professional Association Trade Shows, and business spot-lights with our local Chamber of Commerce, and more. The objective is to get our agency name and service out to as many people as possible. We will do our homework and ask other agencies where they exhibit their services. When exhibiting at a trade show, we will put our best foot forward and represent ourselves as professionals. We will be open, enthusiastic, informative and courteous. We will exhibit our staffing services with sales brochures, logo-imprinted giveaways, a photo book for people to browse through and a computer to run our video presentation through. We will use a 'free drawing' for a gift basket prize and a sign-in sheet to collect names and email addresses. We will also develop a questionnaire or survey that helps us to assemble an ideal customer profile and qualify the leads we receive. We will train our booth attendants to answer all type of questions and to handle objections. We will also seek to present educational seminars on hiring trends at the show to gain increased publicity, and name and expertise recognition. Most importantly, we will develop and implement a follow-up program to stay-in-touch with prospects.

Resources: www.tsnn.com   www.expocentral.com
              www.acshomeshow.com/   www.EventsInAmerica.com
              www.Biztradeshows.com

Our Proposed Trade Show Schedule

Event: Association of peri-Operative Registered Nurses (AORN) 58th Congress
Location: Philadelphia, Pennsylvania   Web site: www.aorn.org/

Event: MedAssets 2017 Healthcare Business Summit
Location: Las Vegas, Nevada   Web site: www.medassets.com

Event: American Association of Critical Care Nurses (AACN)
Location: Chicago, Illinois   Web site: www.aacn.org

Event: Clinical Laboratory Management Association ThinkLab'11 (CLMA)
Location: Baltimore, Maryland   Web site:www.clma.org

Event: American Academy of Nurse Practitioners Annual Conference (AANP)
Location: Las Vegas, Nevada   Web site:www.aanp.org

Event: Health Connect Partners Hospital O.R. and Surgery Conference
Location: Miami, Florida   Web site: www.hlthcp.com/

Event: Academy of Medical-Surgical Nurses (AMSN)
Location: Boston, Massachusetts   Web site: www.amsn.org

Event: Emergency Nurses Association (ENA)
Location: Tampa, Florida   Web site:www.ena.org

Event: Health Connect Partners Fall Pharmacy Conference
Location: Phoenix, Arizona   Web site: www.hlthcp.com/

Event: National Conference on Correctional Healthcare (NCCHC)
Location: Baltimore, Maryland   Web site: www.ncchc.org

Event: American Academy of Physician Assistants Annual PA Conference
Location: Las Vegas, Nevada   Website: www.aapa.org

Event: National Society for Histotechnology
Location: Cincinnati, OH   Website: www.nsh.org/content/registration

Event: Society of Diagnostic Medical Sonographers
Location: Atlanta, GA   Website:
www.sdms.org/meetings/default.asp

Bench Ads
These ads will provide us with an affordable way to improve our visibility.
Resource: www.BenchAds.net

Networking
Networking will be a key to success because referrals and alliances formed can help to
improve our community image and keep our agency growing. We will strive to build
long-term mutually beneficial relationships with our networking contacts and join the
following types of organizations:
1.   We will form a LeTip Chapter to exchange business leads.
2.   We will join the local BNI.com referral exchange group.
3.   We will join the Chamber of Commerce to further corporate relationships.
4.   We will join the Rotary Club, Lions Club, Kiwanis Club, Church Groups, etc.
5.   We will do volunteer work for American Heart Assoc. and Habitat for Humanity.
6.   We will become an affiliated member of the local board of Realtors and the
        Women's Council of Realtors.
7.   We will visit local chapters of Medical associations or groups, such as the
        American Nurses Association and the American Academy of Family Practice.

We will continue to network through Linkedin, Twitter, Facebook, and other social
networks, because it can be effective, and much less expensive than other options. We
will also join professional organizations, such as The American Staffing Association,
local staffing organizations, or attending trade shows / staffing conferences to bring
credibility to our organization, and provide excellent networking opportunities.
Source:
http://human-resources.promatcher.com/articles/10-Tips-for-Starting-a-Successful-
        Staffing-Agency-779

We will also stay up on our local networking events via the following organizations:
1.   www.meetup.com
2.   www.eventbite.com

3.   www.bizjournals.com
Source:
www.thestaffingstream.com/2013/05/30/7-tips-to-become-a-successful-recruiter/.

We will use our metropolitan _____ (city) Chamber of Commerce to target prospective business contacts. We will mail letters to each prospect describing our staffing services. We will follow-up with phone calls.

Newsletter

We will develop a one-page newsletter to be handed out to clients to take home with them as they visit the agency and our trade show booths. The monthly newsletter will be used to build our brand and update clients on special promotions. The newsletter will be produced in-house and for the cost of paper and computer time. We will include the following types of information:
1.   Our involvement with charitable events.
2.   New Staffing Service Introductions
3.   Featured employee/customer of the month.
4.   New Medical staffing industry technologies and trends.
5.   Customer endorsements/testimonials.
6.   Classified ads from local sponsors and suppliers.
7.   Announcements / Upcoming seminar events.

Resources:
Microsoft Publisher
www.getresponse.com
www.aweber.com

We will adhere to the following newsletter writing guidelines:
1.   We will provide content that is of real value to our subscribers.
2.   We will provide solutions to our subscriber's problems or questions.
3.   We will communicate regularly on a weekly basis.
4.   We will create HTML Messages that look professional and allow us to track how many people click on our links and/or open our emails.
5.   We will not pitch our business opportunity in our Ezine very often.
6.   We will focus our marketing dollars on building our Ezine subscriber list.
7.   We will focus on relationship building and not the conveying of a sales message.
8.   We will vary our message format with videos, articles, checklists, quotes, pictures and charts.
9.   We will recommend occasionally affiliate products in some of our messages to help cover our marketing costs.
10.   We will consistently follow the above steps to build a database of qualified prospects and customers.

Example:
http://yellowtelescope.com/newsletter-sign-up/

Resources:

www.constantcontact.com

www.vismedical.com/Newsletter/Volume1Issue1.html

www.mailchimp.com

http://lmssuccess.com/10-reasons-online-business-send-regular-newsletter-customers/

www.smallbusinessmiracles.com/how/newsletters/

www.fuelingnewbusiness.com/2010/06/01/combine-email-marketing-and-social-media-
for-ad-agency-new-business/

Vehicle Signs

We will place magnetic and vinyl signs on our vehicles and include our company name, phone number, company slogan and website address, if possible. We will create a cost-effective moving billboard with high-quality, high-resolution vehicle wraps. We will wrap a portion of the vehicle or van to deliver excellent marketing exposure.

Resource:

http://www.fastsigns.com/

Advertising Wearables

We will give all preferred club members an eye-catching T-shirt or sweatshirt with our company name and logo printed across the garment to wear about town. We will also give them away as a thank you for customer referral activities. We will ask all employees to wear our logo-imprinted shirts.

Stage Events

We will stage events to become known in our community. This is essential to attracting referrals. We will schedule regular events, such as seminar talks, job fairs, demonstrations, catered open house events and fundraisers. We will offer seminars through organizations to promote the benefits of our Medical staffing services. We will use event registration forms, our website and an event sign-in sheet to collect the names and email addresses of all attendees. This database will be used to feed our automatic customer relationship follow-up program and newsletter service.

Resource:

www.eventbrite.com

Educational Events

We will stage education courses and events because clinicians need continuing education credits to maintain their professional licenses. In addition, many are interested in furthering their knowledge in different specialty aspects of their work. Putting together an accredited continuing education course for nurses or occupational therapists, and then advertising it well, will be a great way to get recruits talking to our agency and wanting to benefit professionally from our instructional seminars. It will also serve to spread the word that our recruits think it is important to stay abreast of new technological and regulatory developments.

Host Healthcare Career Fair Events
The fairs will feature careers for which training can be completed in a few weeks to a few months: nursing assistant I, EKG technician, phlebotomy technician, healthcare billing and coding technician, cardiac/ECG monitor technician, medical insurance for pharmacy technician, drug collection specialist, and sleep disorders technician.

We will also stage workshop events that cover the vocabulary of the healthcare field, job descriptions and the daily activities of a healthcare professional. These programs will also enable each healthcare student to earn a Career Readiness Certificate and prepare a résumé.

Example:
RecruitIQ Staffing, a nursing and IT healthcare staffing company, is conducting a Job Fair, April 5th and 6th at the Northtown Center at Amherst, for their Travel Nursing Staffing Division located in Buffalo, New York.
Source:
http://finance.yahoo.com/news/buffalo-ny-job-fair-recruiters-124000690.html

Sales Brochures
The sales brochure will enable us to make a solid first impression when pursing business from commercial accounts and private practice clients. Our sales brochure will include the following contents and become a key part of our sales presentation folder and direct mail package:

- Contact Information
- Customer Testimonials
- Competitive Advantages
- Coupon
- Business Hours

- Business Description
- List of Services/Benefits
- Owner Resume/Bio
- Map of office location.
- Industry Trends

Sales Brochure Design
1. Speak in Terms of Our Prospects Wants and Interests.
2. Focus on all the Benefits, not Just Features.
3. Put the company logo and Unique Selling Proposition together to reinforce the fact that your company is different and better than the competition.
4. Include a special offer, such as a discount, a free report, a sample, or a free trial to increase the chances that the brochure will generate sales.

We will incorporate the following Brochure Design Guidelines:
1. Design the brochure to achieve a focused set of objectives (marketing of programs) with a target market segment (residential vs. commercial).
2. Tie the brochure design to our other marketing materials with colors, logo, fonts and formatting.
3. List capabilities and how they benefit clients.
4. Demonstrate what we do and how we do it differently.

5. Define the value proposition of our engineering installing services
6. Use a design template that reflects your market positioning strategy.
7. Identify your key message (unique selling proposition)
8. List our competitive advantages.
9. Express our understanding of client needs and wants.
10. Use easy to read (scan) headlines, subheadings, bullet points, pictures, etc.
11. Use a logo to create a visual branded identity.
12. The most common and accepted format for a brochure is a folded A3 (= 2 x A4), which gives 4 pages of information.
13. Use a quality of paper that reflects the image we want to project.
14. Consistently stick to the colors of our corporate style.
15. Consider that colors have associations, such as green colors are associated with the environment and enhance an environmental image.
16. Illustrations will be appropriate and of top quality and directly visualize the product assortment, product application and production facility.
17. The front page will contain the company name, logo, the main application of your product or service and positioning message or Unique Selling Proposition.
18. The back page will be used for testimonials or references, and contact details.

Sales Presentation Folder Contents

1.	Resumes	2.	Staff Photos
3.	Contract/Application	4.	Frequently Asked Questions
5.	Sales Brochure	6.	Business Cards
7.	Testimonials/References	8.	Program Descriptions
9.	Informative Articles	10.	Referral Program
11.	Company Overview	12.	Operating Policies
13.	Order Forms		

Coupons

We will use coupons with limited time expirations to get prospects to try our staffing service programs. We will also accept the coupons of our competitors to help establish new client relationships. We will run ads directing people to our Web site for a coupon certificate for a free HR consultation or hiring practices audit. This will help to draw in new clients and collect e-mail addresses for the distribution of a monthly newsletter.

Examples:
www.couponler.com/a-1-healthcare-staffing/free-staffing-services-try-it-before-you-buy-it
www.thenurseagency.com/Website%20Coupon%20Hosp%203%20for%20free.pdf

Cross-Promotions

We will develop and maintain partnerships with local businesses that cater to the needs of our clients, such as insurance companies, laboratories, equipment rental companies and adult daycare centers, and conduct cross-promotional marketing campaigns. These cross-promotions will require the exchanging of customer mailing lists and endorsements.

Premium Giveaways

We will distribute logo-imprinted promotional products at events, also known as giveaway premiums, to foster top-of-mind awareness (www.promoideas.org). These items include business cards with magnetic backs, mugs with contact phone number, drink recipe booklets and calendars that feature important celebration date reminders.

Local Newspaper Ads

We will use these ads to announce the opening of our agency and get our name established. We will adhere to the rule that frequency and consistency of message are essential. We will include a list of the positions we are looking to fill, and our top specialty staffing services and benefits. We will include a coupon to track the response in zoned editions of Community Newsletters and Newspapers. We will also submit public relations and informative articles to improve our visibility and establish our staffing expertise and trustworthiness. These publications include the following:

1.   Neighborhood Newsletters
2.   Local Chamber of Commerce Newsletter
3.   Realtor Magazines

Resource: Hometown News   www.hometownnews.com
               Pennysaver   www.pennysaverusa.com

Publication Type	Ad Size	Timing	Circulation	Section	Fee

Medical Journal Display Ads

We will consider placing display ads in medical journals read by professionals and possibly rent a list of their local subscribers for a planned direct mailing. The mailing will describe our temporary staffing service programs and benefits. We will use empirical data to prove how our temporary placement programs can actually save companies money, and help their staffs to be more productive.

Resource: The Business Journals http://www.bizjournals.com/
The premier media solutions platform for companies strategically targeting business decision makers. Delivers a total business audience of over 10 million people via their 42 websites, 62 publications and over 700 annual industry leading events. Their media products provide comprehensive coverage of business news from a local, regional and national perspective.

Medical Journals

- AHA News Now
- Contemporary Pediatrics
- Dental Economics
- Dentalproducts.net
- Dermatology Times

Contemporary Ob/Gyn
Cosmetic Surgery Times
Dental Office
Dental Products Report
Diagnostic Imaging

- dvm360 (veterinary medicine)
- HFM Magazine
- Health Facilities Management
- Healthcare Global
- Healthcare Traveler
- HomeCare
- Hearing Review
- Managed Care Magazine
- Materials Management in Health Care
- O&P Business News
- Outpatient Surgery Magazine
- Optometry Times
- Physicians Practice
- Psychiatric Times
- RT: Decision Makers in Resp. Care
- Veterinary Economics

Formulary
Health Data Management
Health Management Technology
Healthcare Informatics
Hearing Review
Hospitals & Health Networks
Imaging Economics
Managed Healthcare Executive
Medical Economics Magazine
Orthodontic Products
Ophthalmology Times
Physical Therapy Products
Plastic Surgery Practice
RDH (dental hygienists)
Urology Times
Veterinary Medicine

Source: http://libguides.rutgers.edu/content.php?pid=122317&sid=1051471
Resources: http://www.webwire.com/industrylist.asp
http://www.hiremedical.com/home/tradepub/tp_default.asp
http://en.wikipedia.org/wiki/List_of_trade_magazines

Publication Type	Ad Size	Timing	Circulation	Section	Fee

Article Submissions

We will pitch articles to medical and hospital trade journals, local newspapers, business magazines and internet articles directories to help establish our specialized expertise and improve our visibility. Hyperlinks will be placed within written articles and can be clicked on to take the customer to another webpage within our website or to a totally different website. These clickable links or hyperlinks will be keywords or relevant words that have meaning to our nurse staffing agency. We will create keyword-rich article titles that match the most commonly searched keywords for our topic. In fact, we will create a position whose primary function is to link our nurse staffing agency with opportunities to be published in local publications.

Publishing requires an understanding of the following publisher needs:
1.   Review of good work.
2.   Editor story needs.
3.   Article submission process rules
4.   Quality photo portfolio
5.   Exclusivity requirements.
6.   Target market interests

Our Article Submission Package will include the following:
1.   Well-written materials
2.   Good Drawings
3.   High-quality Photographs
4.   Well-organized outline.

Examples of General Publishing Opportunities:

1.	Document a new solution to old problem	2.	Publish a research study
3.	Addiction prevention advice	4.	Present a different viewpoint
5.	Introduce a local angle on a hot topic.	6.	Reveal a new trend.
7.	Share specialty niche expertise.	8.	Share health benefits

Examples of Specific Article Titles:
1. Everything You Ever Wanted to Know About the Medical Profession Screening Process
2. How to Evaluate and Compare Medical Staffing Agencies
3. Hospital Nurse Staffing and Quality of Care.
4. Trends in Nursing home Medical staffing
5. The Nursing Shortage: Fact or Fiction
6. A Study of Nursing-related Practice Problems
7. Nurses' Role in Improving Medical Quality.
8. The Advantages Of Working With A Health Care Staffing Agency
9. What You Need to Know When Choosing a Health Care Staffing Agency
10. Nurse Staffing Company–Business Due Diligence Tips
11. Locum Tenens: Lifestyle, Opportunities Attracting More Physicians
12. The ROI of Locum Tenens
13. The Increasing Demand for Temp Doctors
14. How to Become a Successful Recruiter
    Example:
    www.thestaffingstream.com/2013/05/30/7-tips-to-become-a-successful-recruiter/
15. How to Prepare for a Staffing Phone Interview
    www.medprostaffing.com/travel-healthcare-interview/
16. Tips for Working with a Recruiter
    Ex: https://masmedicalstaffing.com/blog/allied-health/medical-staffing-agencies-10-tips-for-working-with-a-recruiter/
17. How to Achieve Healthcare Staffing Optimization
    Ex: www.staystaffed.com/blog/index.php/leverage-workforce-data-to-optimize-healthcare-staffing/

Write Articles With a Closing Author Resource Box or Byline

1.	Author Name with credential titles.	2.	Explanation of area of expertise.
3.	Mention of a special offer.	4.	A specific call to action
5.	A Call to Action Motivator	6.	All possible contact information
7.	Helpful Links	8.	Link to Company Website.

Article Objectives:

Article Topic	Target Audience	Target Date

Article Tracking Form

Subject	Publication	Target Audience	Business Development	Resources Needed	Target Date

Possible Magazines to submit articles on healthcare staffing include:

1. The Wall Street Journal
2. The New York Times
3. HealthLeaders Media
4. Modern Healthcare
5. Medical Economics
6. New England Journal of Medicine
7. Columbia News Service
8. Managed Care Weekly
9. http://healthcaretraveler.modernmedicine.com/healthcaretraveler/

Resources: Writer's Market   www.writersmarket.com
            Directory of Trade Magazines   www.techexpo.com/tech_mag.html

Internet article directories include:

http://ezinearticles.com/
http://www.wahm-articles.com
http://www.articlecity.com
http://www.articledashboard.com
http://www.webarticles.com
http://www.article-buzz.com
www.articletogo.com
http://article-niche.com
www.internethomebusinessarticles.com
http://www.articlenexus.com
http://www.articlefinders.com
http://www.articlewarehouse.com
http://www.easyarticles.com
http://ideamarketers.com/
http://clearviewpublications.com/
http://www.goarticles.com/
http://www.webmasterslibrary.com/
http://www.connectionteam.com
http://www.MarketingArticleLibrary.com
http://www.dime-co.com
http://www.allwomencentral.com
http://www.reprintarticles.com
http://www.articlestreet.com
http://www.articlepeak.com
http://www.simplysearch4it.com
http://www.zongoo.com
http://www.mainstreetmom.com
http://www.valuablecontent.com
http://www.article99.com

http://www.mommyshelpercommunity.com
http://www.ladypens.com/
http://www.amazines.com
http://www.submityourarticle.com/articles
http://www.articlecube.com
http://www.free-articles-zone.com
http://www.content-articles.com
http://superpublisher.com
http://www.site-reference.com
www.articlebin.com
www.articlesfactory.com
www.buzzle.com
www.isnare.com
//groups.yahoo.com/group/article_announce
www.ebusiness-articles.com
www.authorconnection.com/
www.businesstoolchest.com
www.digital-women.com/submitarticle.htm
www.searchwarp.com
www.articleshaven.com
www.marketing-seek.com
www.articles411.com
www.articleshelf.com
www.articlesbase.com
www.articlealley.com
www.selfgrowth.com
www.LinkGeneral.com
www.articleavenue.com
www.virtual-professionals.com

Classified Ad Placement Opportunities

The following free classified ad sites, will enable our Health Care Staffing Agency to thoroughly describe the benefits of our using our services:

1.	**Craigslist.org**	2.	Ebay Classifieds
3.	Classifieds.myspace.com	4.	KIJIJI.com
5.	//Lycos.oodle.com	6.	Webclassifieds.us
7.	USFreeAds.com	8.	www.oodle.com
9.	Backpage.com	10.	stumblehere.com
11.	Classifiedads.com	12.	gumtree.com
13.	Inetgiant.com	14.	www.sell.com
15.	Freeadvertisingforum.com	16.	Classifiedsforfree.com
17.	www.olx.com	18.	www.isell.com
19.	Base.google.com	20.	www.epage.com
21.	Chooseyouritem.com	22.	www.adpost.com
23.	Adjingo.com	24.	Kugli.com
25.	global-free-classified-ads.com	26.	free4uclassifieds.com
27.	Salespider.com	28.	www.adsonmap.com
29.	www.usnetads.com	30.	Sawitonline.com
31.	www.freeclassifieds.com	32.	www.openclassifiedsads.com
33.	www.jwiz.com	34.	www.ClassifiedsGiant.com
35.	http://klondajk.us		

Examples:
http://www.medmatrix.org/_spages/employment_opportunities.asp
http://texmed.medbuzz.com/medical-classifieds.php

Sample Craigslist Classified Ad:
We will place the following types of classified ads through Craigslist to begin gathering a roster of potential employees.

WE ARE HIRING HOME HEALTH AIDES. FREE TRAINING AVAILABLE
Location: _____ (city).   No experience necessary and flexible hours. Please forward resumes to _____ (email address). Call _____ or visit our Website at _____
Or.
The _____ Health Care Staffing Agency can help you to locate prescreened and experienced Medical Professional and Home Care Specialists. If you are interested in our Health Care Staffing Agency services, please feel free to call us at _____ or email me at _____ for a no-obligation consultation to assess your staffing needs. Excellent references are available.   Thank you very much.

Health Care Staffing Agency
_____ **(company name)** was designed to deliver immediate results in searching for health care staff and does not impose the hassle of "upfront fees" that offer no guarantee that you will be happy with your new staff member. Our candidates range in experience and possess no less than two years experience in their field of expertise. Our Agency runs thorough license and reference checks, criminal background checks and drug screenings

on all of our candidates. We pre-select only qualified candidates and send you detailed profiles that you can review from the comfort of your home or office. We also offer a replacement guarantee should any unforeseen occurrence arise. All of our candidates are legal to work in the U.S. Call us now, and speak with one of our friendly client representatives that will assist you in beginning the process of finding a candidate that will make your search easier. Candidates we place include: Medical Professionals, Therapists, Lab Technicians, Physicians, Registered Nurses, etc. We are in the business of taking the burden of screening hundreds of resumes and delivering a relaxing hiring process to our clients. We will only send you candidate profiles that fit the exact job description you're looking to fill.

Contact us: _____ Email us: _____

Visit us online: _____

Two-Step Direct Response Classified Advertising
We will use 'two-step direct response advertising' to motivate readers to take a step or action that signals that we have their permission to begin marketing to them in step two. Our objective is to build a trusting relationship with our prospects by offering a free unbiased, educational report in exchange for permission to continue the marketing process. This method of advertising has the following benefits:

1. Shorter sales cycle.
2. Eliminates need for cold calling.
3. Establishes expert reputation.
4. Better qualifies prospects
5. Process is very trackable.
6. Able to run smaller ads.

Sample Two Step Lead Generating Classified Ad:
FREE Report Reveals "Top 10 Mistakes When Hiring a Medical Professional"
Or….. "Effective Medical Professional Screening Tips".
Call 24 hour recorded message and leave your name and address.
Your report will be sent out immediately.
Note: The respondent has shown they have an interest in our Health Care Staffing Agency services. We will also include a section in the report on our other Medical staffing services and our complete contact information, along with a time limited coupon and sales brochure.

Yellow Page Ads
Research indicates that the use of the traditional Yellow Page Book is declining, but that new residents or people who don't have many personal acquaintances will look to the Yellow Pages to establish a list of potential businesses to call upon. Even a small 2" x 2" boxed ad can create awareness and attract the desired target client, above and beyond the ability of a simple listing. We will use the following design concepts:

1. We will use a headline to sell people on what is unique about our agency service.
2. We will include a one year service guarantee to improve our credibility.
3. We will include a coupon offer and a tracking code to monitor the response rate and decide whether to increase or decrease our ad size in subsequent years.
4. We will choose an ad size equal to that of our competitors, and evaluate the response rate for future insertion commitments.
5. We will include our hours of operation, motto or slogan and logo.

6.   We will include our key competitive advantages.
7.   We will list under the same categories as our competitors.
8.   We will use some bold lettering to make our ad standout.
9.   We will utilize yellow books that also offer an online dimension.
Resource:
www.superpages.com
www.yellowpages.com

Examples:
www.yellowpages.com/laguna-niguel-ca/mip/oceans-medical-staffing-inc-479862247
 www.yellowpages.com/paterson-nj/mip/a-medical-staffing-agency-inc-228340
www.yellowpages.com/middletown-ny/medical-staffing-agency

Ad Information:

Book Title: _____	Coverage Area: _____
Yearly Fee: $_____	Ad Size: _____ page
Renewal date: _____	Contact: _____

Cable Television Advertising

Cable television will offer us more ability to target certain market niches or demographics with specialty programming. We will use our marketing research survey to determine which cable TV channels our clients are watching. It is expected that many watch Medical themed programs. Our plan is to choose the audience we want, and to hit them often enough to entice them to take action. We will also take advantage of the fact that we will be able to pick the specific upper income areas we want our commercial to air. Ad pricing will be dependent upon the number of households the network reaches, the ratings the particular show has earned, contract length and the supply and demand for a particular network.
Resources:

Spot Runner	www.spotrunner.com
Television Advertising	http://televisionadvertising.com/faq.htm

Ad Information:

Length of ad "spot": ___ seconds	Development costs: $____ (onetime fee)
Length of campaign: __ (#) mos.	Runs per month: Three times per day
Cost per month.: $_____	Total campaign cost: $_____.

Radio Advertising

Radio will give us the ability to target our audience, based on radio formats, such as news-talk, classic rock and the oldies. Radio will also be a good way to get repetition into our message, as listeners tend to be loyal to stations and parts of the day.
1.   We will use radio advertising to direct prospects to our Web site, advertise a limited time promotion or call for an informational brochure on staffing.
2.   We will try to barter our services for radio ad spots.
3.   We will use a limited-time offer to entice first-time clients to use our staffing services.
4.   We will explore the use of on-air community bulletin boards to play our public

announcements about community sponsored events.

5.   We will also make the radio station aware of our expertise in the Medical staffing field and our availability for interviews.
6.   Our choice of stations will be driven by the market research information we collect via our surveys.
7.   We will capitalize on the fact that many stations now stream their programming on the internet and reach additional local and even national audiences, and if online listeners like what they hear in our streaming radio spot, they can click over to our website.
8.   Our radio ads will use humor, sounds, compelling music or unusual voices to grab attention.
9.   Our spots will tell stories or present situations that our target audience can relate to, such as the growing demand for temporary Medical staffing,
10.   We will make our call to action, a website address or vanity phone number, easy to remember and tie it in with our company name or message.

Resources: Radio Advertising Bureau   www.RAB.com
              Radio Locator   www.radio-locator.com
              Radio Directory   www.radiodirectory.com

Ad Information:

Length of ad "spot": ___ seconds   Development costs: $____ (onetime fee)
Length of campaign: __ (#) mos.   Runs per month: Three times per day
Cost per month.: $_____   Total campaign cost: $_____.

Press Release Overview:

We will use market research surveys to determine the media outlets that our demographic clients read and then target them with press releases. We will draft a cover letter for our media kit that explains that we would like to have the newspaper print a story about the start-up of our new local business or a milestone that we have accomplished. And, because news releases may be delivered by feeds or on news services and various websites, we will create links from our news releases to content on our website. These links which will point to more information or a special offer, will drive our clients into the sales process. They will also increase search engine ranking on our site. We will follow-up each faxed package to the media outlet with a phone call to the lifestyle and employment section editors.

Media Kit

We will compile a media kit with the following items:
1.   A pitch letter introducing our company and relevant impact newsworthiness for their readership.
2.   A press release with helpful newsworthy story facts.
3.   Biographical fact sheet or sketches of key personnel.
4.   Listing of product and service features and benefits to customers.
5.   Photos and digital logo graphics
6.   Copies of media coverage already received.
7.   Frequently Asked Questions (FAQ)

8. Customer testimonials
9. Sales brochure
10. Media contact information
11. URL links to these online documents instead of email attachments.
12. Our blog URL address.

Press Releases

We will use well-written press releases to not only catch a reader's attention, but also to clearly and concisely communicate our business' mission, goals and capabilities.
The following represents a partial list of some of the reasons we will issue a free press release on a regular basis:
1. Announce Grand Opening Event and the availability of services.
2. Planned Open House Event
3   Addition of new product releases or service introduction.
4. Support for a Non-profit Cause or other local event, such as a Blood Drive.
5. Presentation of a free seminar or workshop on how to improve profitability with temporary Medical staffing practices.
6. Report Market Research Survey Results
7. Publication of an article or book on temporary Medical staffing trends.
8. Receiving a Medical Professional Staffing Association Award.
9. Additional training/certification/licensing received.

Example:

Valley Healthcare Staffing announced today that it has been named "Best Staffing Firms to Work For" by Staffing Industry Analysts in North America and the UK. The award was measured on 10 key engagement categories including teamwork, trust in senior leadership, manager effectiveness, compensation, feeling valued and benefits.
Source:
http://www.prweb.com/releases/2017/3/prweb14138694.htm

Example:

Medicus Healthcare Solutions, a leader and innovator in healthcare staffing, announced today that it has been recognized as a 2017 Best Staffing Firm to Work For in the large staffing firms category for North America. The award is given annually by Staffing Industry Analysts (SIA), the global advisor on staffing and workforce solutions, and recognizes employers for their top performance in engaging their employees and creating a workplace conducive to talent development, enjoyment, collaboration, and productivity.
Source:
http://finance.yahoo.com/news/medicus-healthcare-solutions-recognized-one-
        221100884.html

Example:

Maxim Healthcare Pays Special Tribute to Maxim Veteran Employees
Maxim Healthcare Services, an established provider of home healthcare, medical staffing and wellness services, has released a special video tribute commemorating Veterans Day.

The video features Maxim employees who have been a part of armed forces and served in its various branches. Maxim thanks them for their service and commitment and also thanks Maxim patients and clients.

We will use the following techniques to get our press releases into print:
1.   Find the right contact editor at a publication, that is, the editor who specializes in health, beauty and wellness issues.
2.   Understand the target publication's format, flavor and style and learn to think like its readers to better tailor our pitch.
3.   Ask up front if the journalist is on deadline.
4.   Request a copy of the editorial calendar--a listing of targeted articles or subjects broken down by month or issue date, to determine the issue best suited for the content of our news release or article.
5.   Make certain the press release appeals to a large audience by reading a couple of back issues of the publication we are targeting to familiarize ourselves with its various sections and departments.
6.   Customize the PR story to meet the magazine's particular style.
7.   Avoid creating releases that look like advertising or self-promotion.
8.   Make certain the release contains all the pertinent and accurate information the journalist will need to write the article and accurately answer the questions "who, what, when, why and where".
9.   Include a contact name and telephone number for the reporter to call for more information.

PR Distribution Checklist
We will send copies of our press releases to the following entities:
1.   Send it to clients to show accomplishments.
2.   Send to prospects to help prospects better know who you are and what you do.
3.   Send it to vendors to strengthen the relationship and to influence referrals.
4.   Send it to strategic partners to strengthen and enhance the commitment and support to our firm.
5.   Send it to employees to keep them in the loop.
6.   Send it to Employees' contacts to increase the firm's visibility exponentially.
7.   Send it to elected officials who often provide direction for their constituents.
8.   Send it to trade associations for maximum exposure.
9.   Put copies in the lobby and waiting areas.
10.   Put it on our Web site, to enable visitors to find out who we are and what our firm is doing, with the appropriate links to more detailed information.
11.   Register the Web page with search engines to increase search engine optimization.
12.   Put it in our press kit to provide members of the media background information about our firm.
13.   Include it in our newsletter to enable easy access to details about company activities.
14.   Include it in our brochure to provide information that compels the reader to contact our firm when in need of legal counsel.

15.   Hand it out at trade shows and job fairs to share news with attendees and establish credibility.

Media List

Journalist	Interests	Organization	Contact Info

Distribution: www.1888PressRelease.com   www.ecomwire.com
                  www.prweb.com   www.WiredPRnews.com
                  www.PR.com   www.eReleases.com
                  www.24-7PressRelease.com   www.NewsWireToday.com
                  www.PRnewswire.com   www.onlinePRnews.com
                  www.digitaljournal.com   www.PRLog.org
                  www.businesswire.com   www.marketwire.com
                  www.primezone.com   www.primewswire.com
                  www.xpresspress.com/   www.ereleases.com/index.html
                  www.Mediapost.com

Journalist Lists: www.mastheads.org   www.easymedialist.com
                      www.helpareporter.com

Media Directories
      Bacon's –   www.bacons.com/   AScribe –   www.ascribe.org/
      Newspapers – www.newspapers.com/   Gebbie Press – www.gebbieinc.com/

Support Services
      PR Web -   http://www.prweb.com
      Yahoo News –   http://news.yahoo.com/
      Google News –   http://news.google.com/

Direct Mail Campaign

A direct mail package consisting of a tri-fold brochure, letter of introduction, and reply card will be sent to a list of new businesses in _____ County. This list can be obtained from International Business Lists, Inc. (Chicago, IL) and is compiled from Secretary of State incorporation registrations, business license applications, announcements from newspaper clippings, and tax records. The letter will introduce _____ (company name), and describe our competitive advantages. The package will also include a promotional offer—the opportunity to try our Health Care Staffing Agency services at a limited-time special reduced rate. Approximately ten days after the mailing, a telephone follow-up will be conducted to make sure the brochure was received, whether the client has any questions, or would like to schedule an appointment.

Our direct mail program will feature the following key components:
1.   A call to action.
2.   Test marketing using a limited 100-piece mailing.
3.   A defined set of target markets.
4.   A follow up phone call.
5.   A personalized cover letter.

7.   A special trial offer with an expiration date.
Resource:
www.directmailquotes.com/rfq/quote1.cfm?affiliate=14

Postcards
1.   We will use a monthly, personalized, newsletter styled postcard, that includes Medical temporary staffing trends and hiring suggestions, to stay-in-touch with clients.
2.   Postcards will offer cheaper mailing rates, staying power and attention grabbing graphics, but require repetition, like most other advertising methods.
3.   We will develop an in-house list of potential clients for routine communications from open house events, seminar registrations, direct response ads, etc.
4.   We will use postcards to encourage users to visit our website, and take advantage of a special offer or engage in online Medical profile matching.
5.   We will grab attention and communicate a single-focus message in just a few words.
6.   The visual elements of our postcard (color, picture, symbol) will be strong to help get attention and be directly supportive of the message.
7.   We will facilitate a call to immediate action by prominently displaying our phone number and website address.
8.   We will include a clear deadline, expiration date, limited quantity, or consequence of inaction that is connected to the offer to communicate immediacy and increase response.
Resources:
www.Postcardmania.com
www.purepostcards.com/

Flyers
1.   We will seek permission to post flyers on the bulletin boards in local businesses, community centers, clinics, hospitals, job centers and colleges.
2.   We will also insert flyers into our direct mailings.
3.   We will use our flyers as part of a handout package at open house events and seminars.
4.   The flyers will feature an introductory coupon to track return on investment.
5.   The flyers will contain a listing of our service categories along with the benefits of temporary staffing services.
Resource:
www.stocklayouts.com/Templates/Flyer-Ads/Employment-Agency-Jobs-Fair-Flyer-Ad-
      Template-Design-GB0150701.aspx

Referral Program
We understand the importance of setting up a formal referral network through contacts with the following characteristics:
1.   We will give a premium reward based simply on people giving referral names on

the registration form or customer satisfaction survey.
2. Send an endorsed testimonial letter from a loyal customer to the referred prospect.
3. Include a separate referral form as a direct response device.
4. Provide a space on the response form for leaving positive comments that can be used to build a testimonial letter, that will be sent to each referral.
5. We will clearly state our incentive rewards, and terms and conditions.
6. We will distribute a newsletter to stay in touch with our clients and include articles about our referral program success stories.
7. We will encourage our staff at weekly meetings to seek referrals from their personal contacts.

Methods:
1. Always have ready a 30-second elevator speech that describes what you do and who you do it for.
2. Use a newsletter to keep our name in front of referrals sources.
3. Repeatedly demonstrate to referral sources that we are also thinking about their practice or business.
4. Regularly send referrals sources articles on unique yet important topics that might affect their businesses.
5. Use Microsoft Outlook to flag our contacts to remind us it is time to give them some form of personal attention.
6. Ask referral sources for referrals.
7. Get more work from a referral source by sending them work.
8. Immediately thank a referral source, even for the mere act of giving his name to a third party for consideration.
9. Remember referral sources with generous gift baskets and gift certificates.
10. Schedule regular lunches with former school classmates and new contacts.

We will offer an additional donation of $ _____ to any organization whose member use a referral coupon to become a client. The coupon will be paid for and printed in the organization's newsletter.

Referral Tracking Form

Referral Source Name	Presently Referring Yes/No	No. of Clients Referred	Anticipated Revenue	Actions to be Taken	Target Date

Sample Referral Program
We want to show our appreciation to established clients and business network partners for their kind referrals to our business. _____ (company name) wants to reward our valued and loyal clients who support our _____ Programs by implementing a new referral program. Ask any of our team members for referral cards to share with your family and friends to begin saving towards your next _____ (product/service) purchase. We will credit

your account $___ (?) for each new customer you refer to us as well as give them 10% off their first visit. When they come for their first visit, they should present the card upon arrival. We will automatically set you up a referral account.

Resources:
http://brightsmack.com/marketing-strategies/37-referral-ideas-to-grow-your-business/
http://www.nisacards.com/Business-Referral-Marketing-Cards.aspx
https://www.referralsaasquatch.com/resources/

Resources:
Referral Program Software Packages
      www.invitebox.com
      www.referralsaasquatch.com/

Statistics that support referral programs include:
92% of consumers trust peer recommendations, 40% trust advertising in search results, 36% trust online video ads, 36% trust sponsored ads on social networking sites and 33% trust online banner ads.

The average value of a referred customer is at least 16% higher than that of a non-referred customer with similar demographics and time of acquisition.

The Referral Details Are As Follows:
1. You will receive a $___ (?) credit for every customer that you refer for _____ (products/services). Credit will be applied to your referral account on their initial visit.
2. We will keep track of your accumulated reward dollars and at any time we can let you know the amount you have available for use in your reward account.
3. Each time you visit ____ (company name), you can use your referral dollars to pay up to 50% of your total charge that day
4. Referral dollars are not applicable towards the purchase of _____ products.
5. All referral rewards are for __products and cannot be used towards ___ services.

Referral Coupon Template
Company Name: _____
Address: _____
Phone: _____ Website: _____
Print and present this coupon with your first order and the existing customer who referred you will receive a credit for $_____ .

Current customer   **Referred customer**
Name: _____   Name: _____
Address: _____   Address: _____
Phone: _____   Phone: _____
Email: _____   Email: _____
Date referred:

Office use only
Credit memo number:_____
Credit issued date: _____   Credit applied by: _____

Invite-A-Friend

We will setup an aggressive invite-a-friend referral program. We will encourage new members or newsletter subscribers, during their initial registration process, to upload and send an invitation to multiple contacts in their email address books. We will encourage them by providing an added incentive, such as a free _____.

Customer Reward / Loyalty Program

As a means of building business by word-of-mouth, clients will be encouraged and rewarded as repeat clients with rebates or special 24/7 service privileges.

E-mail Marketing

We will use email marketing messages to keep current clients and prospective companies up to date on the candidates we have placed and the openings we have filled to show how our company is building its brand. We will use the following email marketing tips to build our mailing list database, improve communications, boost customer loyalty and attract new and repeat business.

1. Define our objectives as the most effective email strategies are those that offer value to our subscribers: either in the form of educational content or promotions. To drive sales, a promotional campaign is the best format. To create brand recognition and reinforce our expertise in our industry we will use educational newsletters.
2. A quality, permission-based email list will be a vital component of our email marketing campaign. We will ask clients and prospects for permission to add them to our list at every touch-point or use a sign-in sheet.
3. We will listen to our clients by using easy-to-use online surveys to ask specific questions about clients' preferences, interests and satisfaction.
4. We will send only relevant and targeted communications.
5. We will reinforce our brand to ensure recognition of our brand by using a recognizable name in the "from" line of our emails and including our company name, logo and a consistent design and color scheme in every email.

Every ___ (five?) to ____ (six?) weeks, we will send graphically-rich, permission-based, personalized, email marketing messages to our list of clients who registered on our website or in the office. The emails will alert clients in a ___ (50?)-mile radius to sales and promotions as well as other local events sponsored by the agency. This service will be provided by either ExactTarget.com or ConstantContact.com. The email will announce a special event and contain a short sales letter. The message will invite recipients to click on a link to the agency website to checkout more information about the event, then print out the page and bring it with them to the event. The software offered by these two companies will automatically personalize each email with the customer's name. The software also provides detailed click-through behavior reports that will enable us to evaluate the success of each message. The software will also allow the agency to dramatically scale back its direct mail efforts and associated costs. Our agency will send a promotional e-mail about a promotion that the customer indicated was important to them in their preferred membership application. Each identified market segment will get notified of new staffing services, specials and offers based on past buying patterns and what they've clicked on in our previous e-newsletters or indicated on their surveys. The objective is to tap the right customer's need at the right time, with a targeted subject line and targeted content. Our general e-newsletter may appeal to most clients, but targeted mailings that reach out to our various audience segments will build even deeper relationships, and drive higher sales.

Resources:

www.mailchimp.com

www.constantcontact.com/pricing/email-marketing.jsp

Voice Broadcasting

A web-based voice broadcast system will provide a powerful platform to generate thousands of calls to clients and clients or create customizable messages to be delivered to specific individuals. Voice broadcasting and voice mail broadcast will allow our company to instantly send interactive phone calls with ease while managing the entire process right from the Web. We will instantly send alerts, notifications, reminders, GOTV - messages, and interactive surveys with ease right from the Web. The free VoiceShot account will guide us through the process of recording and storing our messages, managing our call lists, scheduling delivery as well as viewing and downloading real-time call and caller key press results. The voice broadcasting interface will guide us through the entire process with a Campaign Checklist as well as tips from the Campaign Expert. Other advanced features include recipient targeting, call monitoring, scheduling, controlling the rate of call delivery and customized text to speech (TTS).

Resource:

http://www.voiceshot.com/public/outboundcalls.asp

Facebook.com

We will build our staffing agency's identity on Facebook with high-value and shareable content that is relevant to our potential candidates. Establishing a strong Facebook persona will help when our recruiters begin to reach out to candidates directly. We will use Facebook to move our businesses forward and stay connected to our clients in this fast-paced world. Content will be the key to staying in touch with our clients and keeping them informed. The content will be a rich mix of information, interactive questions, current trends and events, industry facts, education, promotions and specials, humor and fun.

Resource:

www.staffinghub.org/social-recruiting/how-your-staffing-company-should-be-using-facebook/

We will use the following step system to get clients from Facebook.com:
1. We will open a free Facebook account at Facebook.com.
2. We will begin by adding Facebook friends. The fastest way to do this is to allow Facebook to import our email addresses and send an invite out to all our   clients.
3. We will post a video to get our clients involved with our Facebook page. We will post a video called "How to Plan a Successful Temporary Medical Staffing Program." The video will be first uploaded to YouTube.com and then simply be linked to our Facebook page. Video will be a great way to get people active and involved with our Facebook page.
4. We will send an email to our clients base that encourages them to check out the new video and to post their feedback about it on our Facebook page. Then we will provide a link driving clients to our Facebook page.
5. We will respond quickly to feedback, engage in the dialogue and add links to our response that direct the author to a structured mini-survey.
6. We will optimize our Facebook profile with our business keyword to make it an invaluable marketing tool and become the "go-to" expert in our industry
7. On a weekly basis, we will send out a message to all Facebook fans with a special offer.
8. We will use Facebook as a tool for sharing success stories and relate the ways in which we have helped our clients.
9. We will use Facebook Connect to integrate our Facebook efforts with our regular website to share our Facebook Page activity. This will also give us statistics about our website visitors, and add social interaction to our site.
10. We will use a company called Payvment (www.payvment.com) that has a storefront application for Facebook, that requires a Facebook fan page set up for our dealership. We will install the application on our page, set up the look and feel of the storefront using the tools that Payvment provides, enter information about our dealership, and then start loading products.

Resources:
www.facebook.com/advertising/
http://www.socialmediaexaminer.com/how-to-set-up-a-facebook-page-for-business/
http://smallbizsurvival.com/2009/11/6-big-facebook-tips-for-small-business.html

Examples:
www.facebook.com/pages/RSI-Medical-Staffing/80326654224

Facebook Profiles represent individual users and are held under a person's name. Each profile should only be controlled by that person. Each user has a wall, information tab, likes, interests, photos, videos and each individual can create events.

Facebook Groups are pretty similar to Fan Pages but are usually created for a group of people with a similar interest and they are wanting to keep their discussions private. The members are not usually looking to find out more about a business - they want to discuss a certain topic. We will make sure that our recruiters join interest groups like "Science and Tech" along with professionally-oriented groups.

Facebook Fan Pages are the most viral of your three options. When someone becomes a fan of your page or comments on one of your posts, photos or videos, that is spread to all of their personal friends. This can be a great way to get your information out to lots of people...and quickly! In addition, one of the most valuable features of a business page is that you can send "updates" about new products and content to fans and your home building brand becomes more visible.

Facebook Live lets people, public figures and Pages share live video with their followers and friends on Facebook.
Source:
https://live.fb.com/about/
Resource:
http://smartphones.wonderhowto.com/news/facebook-is-going-all-live-video-streaming-your-phone-0170132/

Facebook Job Search
Facebook has added job search and position posting tools in the U.S. and Canada. Businesses can post openings, track applicants, and communicate directly with candidates on the new platform. Organizations can also pay for targeted ads to boost views of their open positions.

Small Business Promotions
This group allows members to post about their products and services and is a public group designated as a Buy and Sell Facebook group.
Source: https://www.facebook.com/groups/smallbusinesspronotions/

Best social media marketing practices:
1. Assign daily responsibility for Facebook to a single person on your staff with an affinity for dialoguing .
2. Set expectations for how often they should post new content and how quickly they should respond to comments – usually within a couple hours.
3. Follow and like your followers when they seem to have a genuine interest in your area of health and wellness expertise.
4. Post on the walls of not only your own Facebook site, but also on your most active, influential posters with the largest networks.
5. Periodically post a request for your followers to "like" your page.
6. Monitor Facebook posts to your wall and respond every two hours throughout your business day.

We will use Facebook in the following ways to market our Health Care Staffing Agency:
1. Promote our blog posts on our Facebook page
2. Post a video of our service people in action.
3. Make time-sensitive offers during slow periods

4. Create a special landing page for coupons or promotional giveaways
5. Create a Welcome tab to display a video message from our owner.
   Resource: Pagemodo.
6. Support a local charity by posting a link to their website.
7. Thank our clients while promoting their businesses at the same time.
8. Describe milestone accomplishments and thank clients for their role.
9. Give thanks to corporate accounts.
10. Ask clients to contribute stories about _____ occurrences.
11. Use the built-in Facebook polling application to solicit feedback.
12. Use the Facebook reviews page to feature positive comments from clients, and to respond to negative reviews.
13. Introduce clients to our staff with resume and video profiles.
14. Create a photo gallery of unusual ____ (requests/jobs?) to showcase our expertise.

We will also explore location-based platforms like the following:

- FourSquare
- Facebook Places
- GoWalla
- Google Latitude

As a Health Care Staffing Agency serving a local community, we will appreciate the potential for hyper-local platforms like these. Location-based applications are increasingly attracting young, urban influencers with disposable income, which is precisely the audience we are trying to attract. People connect to geo-location apps primarily to "get informed" about local happenings.

Foursquare.com

A web and mobile application that allows registered users to post their location at a venue ("check-in") and connect with friends. Check-in requires active user selection and points are awarded at check-in. Users can choose to have their check-ins posted on their accounts on Twitter, Facebook, or both. In version 1.3 of their iPhone application, foursquare enabled push-notification of friend updates, which they call "Pings". Users can also earn badges by checking in at locations with certain tags, for check-in frequency, or for other patterns such as time of check-in.]
Resource: https://foursquare.com/business/
Examples:
https://foursquare.com/v/medical-staffing-network/4eae8dccd3e32ee0decb260b

Instagram

Instagram.com is an online photo-sharing, video-sharing and social networking service that enables its users to take pictures and videos, apply digital filters to them, and share them on a variety of social networking services, such as
Facebook, Twitter, Tumblr and Flickr. A distinctive feature is that it confines photos to a square shape, similar to Kodak Instamatic and Polaroid images, in contrast to the 16:9 aspect ratio now typically used by mobile device cameras. Users are also able to record and share short videos lasting for up to 15 seconds.

Resources:
http://www.staffinghub.org/social-recruiting/recruiters-using-instagram/

We will use Instagram in the following ways to help amplify the story of our brand, get people to engage with our content when not at our store, and get people to visit our site:
1.   Let our customers and fans know about specific nurse staffing availability.
2.   Tie into trends, events or holidays to drive awareness.
3.   Let people know we are open and our responsiveness is spectacular.
4.   Run a monthly contest and pick the winning hashtagged photograph
       to activate our customer base and increase our exposure.
5.   Encourage the posting and collection of happy client photos.

Examples:
https://www.instagram.com/trinityhsg/
https://www.instagram.com/risestaffing/

Note: Commonly found in tweets, a hashtag is a word or connected phrase (no spaces) that begins with a hash symbol (#). They're so popular that other social media platforms including Facebook, Instagram and Google+ now support them. Using a hashtag turns a word or phrase into a clickable link that displays a feed (list) of other posts with that same hashtag. For example, if you click on #nurse staffing in a tweet, or enter #nurse staffing in the search box, you'll see a list of tweets all about nurse staffing.

Snapchat.com
This is a photo messaging app for iPhone and Android mobile devices. Users can take a picture or video and add text, drawings, and a variety of filters. They set a designated time limit, 1-10 seconds, and send to selected contacts from their list. Users can also set a "story" – a Snap that pins to their profile and is viewable for 24 hours after posting. Snapchat photos display for a maximum of 10 seconds (for 24 hours, in the case of a snap story) before becoming permanently inaccessible. The user may choose to save their snaps, but this will only save it to their local device. If the receiver uses the screenshot function on their phone, or chooses to replay a snap, the sender is notified. The point of Snapchat is to be fun and quirky, enticing and engaging your contacts with visual snippets of whatever you are doing. Teen and millennial users enjoy using Snapchat where they would traditionally send a text message. In many cases it's easier and more stimulating to send a quick clip of the property you are viewing, for example, than it would be to send a text description.

Snapchat is not useful as a lead generating tool, but it is exceptionally useful for client engagement and retention. When we meet with a client and exchange mobile contact information, we will ask if they use Snapchat and if we can add them to keep them updated on class schedules. The beauty of the Snap is that is draws the client or prospect into the environment and makes them want to see or learn more. We will use this limitation to our advantage and make our client feel compelled to request and attend more seminar and networking events. Snapchat is also a phenomenal tool to engage with existing clients. It will make job candidates feel connected to the recruiter and the job searching process, which is conducive to retaining these clients in the future. While the primary user demographic is in the millennial age range, the app is popular with many adults as well. Incorporating Snapchat into our client communication strategy will aid our ability to recruit candidates swiftly and form long term client relationships.

Resources:
http://www.staffinghub.org/social-recruiting/recruiters-using-snapchat/
https://blog.hootsuite.com/smart-ways-to-use-snapchat-for-business/
http://smallbiztrends.com/2014/10/how-businesses-can-use-snapchat.html
http://nymag.com/selectall/2016/04/the-snapchat-101-the-best-coolest-smartest-weirdest-
accounts.html

MySpace Advertising

MySpace.com offers a self-service, graphical "display" advertising platform that will enable our company to target our marketing message to our audience by demographic characteristics. With the new MySpace service, we will be able to upload our own ads or make them quickly with an online tool, and set a budget of $25 to $10,000 for the campaigns. We can choose to target a specific gender, age group and geographic area. We will then pay MySpace each time someone clicks on our ad. Ads can link to other MySpace pages, or external websites. MyAds will let us target our ads to specific groups of people using the public data on MySpace users' profiles, blogs and comments. MySpace will enable our company to target potential clients with similar interests to our existing customer base, as revealed via our marketing research surveys. Also the bulletin function on MySpace will allow us to update clients on company milestone achievements and coming events. We will also post a short video to our home page and encourage the sharing of the video with other MySpace users.
Examples:
http://www.myspace.com/advantagemedicalstaffing

LinkedIn.com

We will use Advanced LinkedIn accounts because they will automatically search and alert us to matching talent pools. We will get notified with smart search alerts when a candidate matches our search criteria, saving us time and effort. LinkedIn also ranks high in search engines and will provide a great platform for sending event updates to business associates. To optimize our LinkedIn profile, we will select one core keyword. We will use it frequently, without sacrificing consumer experience, to get our profile to skyrocket in the search engines. Linkedin provides options that will allow our detailed profile to be indexed by search engines, like Google. We will make use of these options so our staffing business will achieve greater visibility on the Web. We will publish our LinkedIn URL on all our marketing collateral, including business cards, email signature, newsletters, and web site. We will grow our network by joining industry and alumni groups related to our business. We will update our status examples of recent work, and link our status updates with our other social media accounts. We will start and manage a group or fan page for our staffing agency. We will share useful articles that will be of interest to clients, and request LinkedIn recommendations from clients willing to provide testimonials. We will post our presentations on our profile using a presentation application. We will ask our first-level contacts for introductions to their contacts and interact with LinkedIn on a regular basis to reach those who may not see us on other social media sites. We will link to articles posted elsewhere, with a summary of why it's valuable to add to our credibility and list our newsletter subscription information and archives. We will post discounts and package deals. We will buy a LinkedIn direct ad that our target market will see. We will find vendors and contractors through connections.

Examples:
http://www.linkedin.com/company/medical-staffing-services-inc

Resources:
http://www.staffinghub.org/social-recruiting/recruiters-using-advanced-linkedin/
https://www.linkedin.com/premium/products?family=talent

Podcasting
Our podcasts will provide both information and advertising. Our podcasts will allow us to pull in a lot of clients. Our monthly podcasts will be heard by ___ (#) eventual subscribers. Podcasts can now be downloaded for mobile devices, such as an iPod. Podcasts will give our company a new way to provide information and an additional way to advertise. Podcasting will give our business another connection point with clients. We will use this medium to communicate on important issues, what is going on with a planned event, and other things of interest to our agency clients. The programs will last about 10 minutes and can be downloaded for free on iTunes. The purpose is not to be a mass medium. It is directed at a niche market with an above-average educational background and very special child care interests. It will provide a very direct and a reasonably inexpensive way of reaching our targeted audience with relevant information about our Medical staffing services.

Resources:
www.apple.com/itunes/download/.
www.cbc.ca/podcasting/gettingstarted.html
www.healthediversity.com/index.php?action=podcasts-webcasts

Examples:
http://blog.bluepipes.com/category/travel-nursing/travel-healthcare-podcast/
http://blog.bluepipes.com/ttatn-030-how-agencies-and-recruiters-find-travel-nurses/

Blogging
Blogging will give our staffing agency and our medical staffing recruiters, the ability to show potential recruits that we are an expert in the medical staffing industry. This will help to establish our brand as an industry leader. We will share tips on what it means to

work in the healthcare industry such as, "How to deal with working the night shift," or "What are the best locations to travel to as a physical therapist."

Blogging will also allow our agency to keep our website up to date. As an example, when we sign a new healthcare facility as a client in an exotic location, we will blog about what life is like as a travel healthcare professional in that particular location.

We will use our blog to keep clients and prospects informed about events and services that relate to our Health Care Staffing Agency business, new releases, contests, and specials. Our blog will show readers that we are a good source of expert information that they can count on. With our blog, we can quickly update our clients anytime our company releases a new service, or the holding of a contest for referrals.

We will use our blog to communicate the following types of information:
1.   Share client testimonials and meaningful success stories.
2.   Recognize our employees of the quarter.
3.   Confirm our commitment to Healthcare Compliance
4.   Document our employee referral program.
5.   Share information on how to keep Travelers Mentally and Physically Fit.

Our visitors will be able to subscribe to our RSS feeds and be instantly updated without any spam filters interfering. We will also use the blog to solicit service usage recommendations and future program addition suggestions. Additionally, blogs are free and allow for constant ease of updating.

To get visitors to our blog to take the next action step and contact our firm we will do the following:
1.   Put a contact form on the upper-left hand corner of our blog, right below the header.
2.   Put our complete contact information in the header itself.
3.   Add a page to our blog and title it, "Become My Client.", giving the reader somewhere to go for the next sign-up steps.
4.   At the end of each blog post, we will clearly tell the reader what to do next; such as subscribe to our RSS feed, or to sign up for our newsletter mailing list.

Resources:
www.blogger.com
www.blogspot.com
www.wordpress.com

Examples:
www.candidatedirect.com/healthcare-staffing-blog/
https://www.medprostaffing.com/blog/

Twitter

We will use 'Twitter.com' as a way to produce new business from existing clients and generate prospective clients and recruit job candidates online. Twitter is a free social networking and micro-blogging service that allows its users to send and read other users' updates (otherwise known as tweets), which are text-based posts of up to 140 characters in length. Updates are displayed on the user's profile page and delivered to other users who have signed up to receive them. The sender can restrict delivery to those in his or her circle of friends, with delivery to everyone being the default. Users can receive updates via the Twitter website, SMS text messaging, RSS feeds, or email.

We will use Twitter's search feature to find candidates–and other job listings–by location, role, and niche. We will also search by hashtags, like #salesjob, applicable to the role we want to fill. Twitter will also give us the ability to have ongoing two-way conversations with our clients, which will allow us to get better at what we do and offer, while giving us the ability to express our own unique 'personality'. We will use our Twitter account to respond directly to questions, distribute news, solve problems, post updates, circulate information about fundraisers, hold trivia question contests for a chance to win a gift certificate and offer special discounts, known as 'Tweet Deals', on selected products and services. Our posts on Twitter will include our URL (address), our new offers, cooking recipe tips and new service offerings. On a long-term basis, using Twitter consistently and efficiently will help push our website up the rankings on Google. The intangible, that will only have a positive effect, are the hundreds of impressions that each tweet will get, not to mention the positive statements that will be posted about our service, staff, selection and product knowledge. Using TweetReach, we expect our special promotional offers to receive thousands of impressions. We will also add our website, company logo, personal photo and/or blog on our profile page.

We will provide the following instructions to register as a 'Follower' of _____ (company name) on Twitter:
1.   In your Twitter account, click on 'Find People' in the top right navigation bar, which will redirect to a new page.
2.   Click on 'Find on Twitter' which will open a search box that says 'Who are you looking for?'
3.   Type '_____ (company name) / _____ (owner name)' and click 'search'. This will bring up the results page.
4.   Click the blue '_____' name to read the bio or select the 'Follow' button.

Resources:
http://www.staffinghub.org/social-recruiting/recruiters-using-twitter/

Example:
http://twitter.com/clinicalone

Google Maps
We will first make certain that our business is listed in Google Maps. We will do a search for our business in Google Maps. If we don't see our business listed, then we will add our

business to Google Maps. Even if our business is listed in Google Maps, we will create a Local Business Center account and take control of our listing, by adding more relevant information. Consumers generally go to Google Maps for two reasons: Driving Directions and to Find a Business.

Resource: http://maps.google.com/

Bing Maps   www.bingplaces.com/
This will make it easy for customers to find our business.

Apple Maps
A web mapping service developed by Apple Inc. It is the default map system of iOS, macOS, and watchOS. It provides directions and estimated times of arrival for automobile, pedestrian, and public transportation navigation.

Resources:

http://www.stallcupgroup.com/2012/09/19/three-ways-to-make-your-pawn-business-more-profitable-and-sellable/

http://www.apple.com/ios/maps/

https://en.wikipedia.org/wiki/Apple_Maps

Google Places
Google Places helps people make more informed decisions about where to go for medical staffing services. Place Pages connect people to information from the best sources across the web, displaying photos, reviews and essential facts, as well as real-time updates and offers from business owners. We will make sure that our Google Places listing is up to date to increase our online visibility. Google Places is linked to our Google Maps listing, and will help to get on the first page of Google search page results when people search for a Health Care Staffing Agency in our area.

Resource:

www.google/com/places

Yelp.com
We will use Yelp.com to help people find our local business. Visitors to Yelp write local reviews, over 85% of them rating a business 3 stars or higher In addition to reviews, visitors can use Yelp to find events, special offers, lists and to talk with other Yelpers. As business owners, we will setup a free account to post offers, photos and message our clients. We will also buy ads on Yelp, which will be clearly labeled "Sponsored Results". We will also use the Weekly Yelp, which is available in 42 city editions to bring news about the latest business openings and other happenings.

Examples:

http://www.yelp.com/biz/medical-staffing-services-portland

Manta.com
Manta is the largest free source of information on small companies, with profiles of more than 64 million businesses and organizations. Business owners and sales professionals

use Manta's vast database and custom search capabilities to quickly find companies, easily connect with prospective clients and promote their own services. Manta.com, founded in 2005, is based in Columbus, Ohio.
Examples:
http://www.manta.com/c/mry8n29/universal-medical-staffing-agency

HotFrog.com

HotFrog is a fast growing free online business directory listing over 6.6 million US businesses. HotFrog now has local versions in 34 countries worldwide.
Anyone can list their business in HotFrog for free, along with contact details, and products and services. Listing in HotFrog directs sales leads and enquiries to your business. Businesses are encouraged to add any latest news and information about their products and services to their listing. HotFrog is indexed by Google and other search engines, meaning that clients can find your HotFrog listing when they use Google, Yahoo! or other search engines.
Resource:
http://www.hotfrog.com/AddYourBusiness.aspx

Local.com

Local.com owns and operates a leading local search site and network in the United States. Its mission is to be the leader at enabling local businesses and consumers to find each other and connect. To do so, the company uses patented and proprietary technologies to provide over 20 million consumers each month with relevant search results for local businesses, products and services on Local.com and more than 1,000 partner sites. Local.com powers more than 100,000 local websites. Tens of thousands of small business clients use Local.com products and services to reach consumers using a variety of subscription, performance and display advertising and website products.
Resource:
http://corporate.local.com/mk/get/advertising-opportunities

Autoresponder

An autoresponder is an online tool that will automatically manage our mailing list and send out emails to our clients at preset intervals. We will write a short article that is helpful to potential agency clients. We will load this article into our autoresponder. We will let people know of the availability of our article by posting to newsgroups, forums, social networking sites etc. We will list our autoresponder email address at the end of the posting so they can send a blank email to our autoresponder to receive our article and be added to our mailing list. We will then email them at the interval of our choosing with special offers. We will load the messages into our autoresponder and set a time interval for the messages to be mailed out.
Resource:
www.aweber.com

Pay-Per-Click Advertising

Google AdWords, Yahoo! Search Marketing, and Microsoft adCenter are the three largest network operators, and all three operate under a bid-based model. Cost per click (CPC) varies depending on the search engine and the level of competition for a particular keyword. Google AdWords are small text ads that appear next to the search results on Google. In addition, these ads appear on many partner web sites, including NYTimes.com (The New York Times), Business.com, Weather.com, About.com, and many more. Google's text advertisements are short, consisting of one title line and two content text lines. Image ads can be one of several different Interactive Advertising Bureau (IAB) standard sizes. Through Google AdWords, we plan to buy placements (ads) for specific search terms through this "Pay-Per-Click" advertising program. This PPC advertising campaign will allow our ad to appear when someone searches for a keyword related to our business, organization, or subject matter. More importantly, we will only pay when a potential customer clicks on our ad to visit our website. For instance, since we operate a Health Care Staffing Agency in _ (city), _(state), we will target people using search terms such as "Health Care Staffing Agency, Clinical Medical staffing, Medical Compliance, Medical IT, Medical staffing, Medical technology, Locum Staffing, Medical compliance, Medical internet, Nurse Staffing, Medical staffing, Medical technology in ____ (city), ____ (state)". With an effective PPC campaign our ads will only be displayed when a user searches for one of these keywords. In short, PPC advertising will be the most cost-effective and measurable form of advertising for our Health Care Staffing Agency.

Resources:

http://adwords.google.com/support/aw/?hl=en
www.wordtracker.com

Yahoo Local Listings

We will create our own local listing on Yahoo. To create our free listing, we will use our web browser and navigate to http://local.yahoo.com. We will first register for free with Yahoo, and create a member ID and password to list our business. Once we have accessed http://local.yahoo.com, we will scroll down to the bottom and click on "Add/Edit a Business" to get onto the Yahoo Search Marketing Local Listings page. In the lower right of the screen we will see "Local Basic Listings FREE". We will click on the Get Started button and log in again with our new Yahoo ID and password. The form for our local business listing will now be displayed. When filling it out, we will be sure to include our full web address (http://www.companyname.com). We will include a description of our Medical staffing services in the description section, but avoid hype or blatant advertising, to get the listing to pass Yahoo's editorial review. We will also be sure to select the appropriate business category and sub categories.

Examples:

https://search.yahoo.com/local/s?p=Temporary+Employment+Agencies&addr=
        Oxford,+MS&fr=local_lyc_lsyc_rd

Sales Reps/Account Executives

_____ (company name) will use independent commissioned sales reps to penetrate markets outside of _____ (city/state). Management will work to keep in constant communication with the sales reps to ensure that their placement service is professional and timely. Independent sales representatives will provide the best mode for distribution in order to maintain pricing controls and higher margins. Independent sales reps are not full-time employees, thus benefits are not necessary. Independent sales reps receive a flat commission based on gross sales. Our sales reps are set at a commission rate of __ (15?)% of gross sales. The average sales rep can service up to __ (#) accounts with the average location generating around $____ per year. We expect to have ___(#) independent sales reps covering ___ (#) states in place to sell the company's staffing services. In addition to field calls, sales reps will represent the staffing agency at all regional tradeshows, with the marketing director attending all national tradeshows.

Advertorials

An advertorial is an advertisement written in the form of an objective article, and presented in a printed publication—usually designed to look like a legitimate and independent news story. We will use quotes as testimonials to back up certain claims throughout our copy and break-up copy with subheadings to make the material more reader-friendly. We will include the "call to action" and contact information with a 24/7 voicemail number and a discount coupon. The advertorial will have a short intro about a client's experience with our medical staffing services and include quotes, facts, and statistics. We will present helpful information about HR planning, screening and recruiting.

Affiliate Marketing

We will create an affiliate marketing program to broaden our reach. We will first devise a commission structure, so affiliates have a reason to promote our business. We will give them ___ (10)% of whatever sales they generate. We will go after medical practice bloggers or webmasters who get a lot of web traffic for our keywords. These companies would then promote our Health Care Staffing Agency services, and they would earn commissions for the sales they generated. We will work with the following services to handle the technical aspects of our program.

ConnectCommerce	https://www.connectcommerce.com/
Commission Junction	https://members.cj.com
ShareASale	http://www.shareasale.com/
Share Results	
LinkShare	

Online Directory Listings

The following directory listings use proprietary technology to match clients with industry professionals in their geographical area. The local search capabilities for specific niche markets offer an invaluable tool for the customer. These directories help member businesses connect with purchase-ready buyers, convert leads to sales, and maximize the value of customer relationships. Their online and offline communities provide a quick and easy low or no-cost solution for clients to find a staffing agency quickly. We intend to sign-up with all no cost directories and evaluate the ones that charge a fee.

1.	Job Agencies Directory	www.jobagencies.com
2.	Directory of Recruiters	www.I-recruit.com
3.	Hospital Connection Network	www.hcnhealth.com
4.	Allied Health Jobs	//4alliedhealthjobs.com
5.	Recruitment Agencies	www.freeindex.com
6.	Hospital Jobs Online	www.hospitaljobsonline.com
7.	BOTW	www.botw.org/top/health/nursing/employment
8.	ABC Directory	http://search.abc-directory.com/medical+staffing?search=1
9.	American Staffing Association	http://asacentral.americanstaffing.net/asamemberdirectory/home

We will make certain that our listings contain the following information:

- Business Name
- Phone number
- Email address
- Contact Person: name, phone #, email
- Company logo
- Short Business description
- Specialties
- Twitter Business Page Link
- Address
- Days and Hours of operation
- Website URL
- Facility Photos
- Products/ Services offered
- Affiliations
- Facebook Business Page Link
- LinkedIn Business Page Link

Other General Directories Include:

Listings.local.yahoo.com
YellowPages.com
Bing.com/businessportal
Yelp.com
InfoUSA.com
Localeze.com
YellowBot.com
InsiderPages.com
CitySearch.com
Profiles.google.com/me
Jigsaw.com
Whitepages.com
Judysbook.com
Google.com
SuperPages.com
ExpressUpdate.com
MojoPages.com
BOTW

Switchboard Super Pages
MerchantCircle.com
Local.com
BrownBook.com
iBegin.com
Bestoftheweb.com
HotFrog.com
MatchPoint.com
YellowUSA.com
Manta.com
LinkedIn.com
PowerProfiles.com
Company.com
Yahoo.com
TrueLocal.com
Citysquares.com
DMOZ
Business.com

Get Listed
Universal Business Listing
http://getlisted.org/enhanced-business-listings.aspx
https://www.ubl.org/index.aspx
www.UniversalBusinessListing.org

Universal Business Listing (UBL) is a local search industry service dedicated to acting as a central collection and distribution point for business information online. UBL provides business owners and their marketing representatives with a one-stop location for broad distribution of complete, accurate, and detailed listing information.

Testimonial Marketing

We will either always ask for testimonials immediately after a completed project or contact our clients once a quarter for them. We will also have something prepared that we would like the client to say that is specific to a service we offer, or anything relevant to advertising claims that we have put together. For the convenience of the client we will assemble a testimonial letter that they can either modify or just sign off on. Additionally, testimonials can also be in the form of audio or video and put on our website or mailed to potential clients in the form of a DVD or Audio CD. A picture with a testimonial is also excellent. We will put testimonials directly on a magazine ad, slick sheet, brochure, or website, or assemble a complete page of testimonials for our sales presentation folder.

Examples:
http://www.alliantstaffing.com/testimonials/

We will collect customer testimonials in the following ways:
1. Our website – A page dedicated to testimonials (written and/or video).
2. Social media accounts – Facebook fan pages offer a review tab, which makes it easy to receive and display customer testimonials.
3. Google+ also offers a similar feature with Google+ Local.
4. Local search directories – Ask customers to post more reviews on Yelp and Yahoo Local.
5. Customer Satisfaction Survey Forms

We will pose the following questions to our customers to help them frame their testimonials:
1. What was the obstacle that would have prevented you from buying this product?
2. "What was your main concern about buying this product?"
3. What did you find as a result of buying this product?
4. What specific feature did you like most about this product?
5. What would be three other benefits about this product?
6. Would you recommend this product? If so, why?
7. Is there anything you'd like to add?

Resource:
https://smallbiztrends.com/2016/06/use-customer-testimonials.html

Reminder Service

We will use a four-tier reminder system in the following sequence: email, postcard, letter, phone call. We will stress the importance of staying in touch in our messages and keeping

their profile updated with their activities. We will also try to determine the reason for the non-response or inactivity and what can be done to reactivate the client. The reminder service will also work to the benefit of regular clients, that want to be reminded of an agreed upon special date or coming event.
Resource:
http://www.easyivr.com/reminder-service.htm

Business Logo

Our logo will graphically represent who we are and what we do, and it will serve to help brand our image. It will also convey a sense of uniqueness and professionalism. The logo will represent our company image and the message we are trying to convey. Our business logo will reflect the philosophy and objectives of staffing agency. Our logo will incorporate the following design guidelines:

1. It will relate to our industry, our name, a defining characteristic of our company or a competitive advantage we offer.
2. It will be a simple logo that can be recognized faster.
3. It will contain strong lines and letters which show up better than thin ones.
4. It will feature something unexpected or unique without being overdrawn.
5. It will work well in black and white (one-color printing).
6. It will be scalable and look pleasing in both small and large sizes.
7. It will be artistically balanced and make effective use of color, line density and shape.
8. It will be unique when compared to competitors.
9. It will use original, professionally rendered artwork.
10. It can be replicated across any media mix without losing quality.
11. It appeals to our target audience.
12. It will be easily recognizable from a distance if utilized in outdoor advertising.

Resources: www.freelogoservices.com/   www.hatchwise.com
              www.logosnap.com   www.99designs.com
              www.fiverr.com   www.freelancer.com

Logo Design Guide:
www.bestfreewebresources.com/logo-design-professional-guide
www.creativebloq.com/graphic-design/pro-guide-logo-design-21221

Examples:
www.google.com/search?q=healthcare+staffing+agency+logo&tbm=isch&tbo=u&source
       =univ&sa=X&ved=0ahUKEwjUlbj8yoHTAhUhjFQKHWcyCXUQsAQIGQ&bi
       w=1187&bih=514

Seminars

Seminars present the following marketing and bonding opportunities:
1. Signage and branding as a presenting sponsor.
2. Opportunity to provide logo imprinted handouts.

3. Media exposure through advertising and public relations.
4. The opportunity for one-on-one interaction with a targeted group of consumers to demonstrate an understanding of their needs and our matching expert solutions.
5. Use of sign-in sheet to collect names and email addresses for database build.
6. Present opportunity to sell products, such as workbooks.

Possible seminar funding sources:
1. Small registration fee to cover the cost of hand-outs and refreshments.
2. Get sponsorship funding from partner/networking organizations.
3. Sponsorship classified ads in the program guide or handouts.

We will establish our expertise and trustworthiness by offering free seminars on the following topics:
1. How to Locate and Evaluate Medical Staffing Agencies
2. How to Work with a Health Care Staffing Agency to Reduce Hiring Costs
3. The Growing Demand for Temporary Medical Staffing.

Seminar target groups include the following:

1.	Corporations	2.	Computer Companies
3.	Importers	4.	Property Managers
5.	High Tech Firms	6.	Real Estate Developers
7.	Construction Companies	8.	Manufacturers

Seminar marketing approaches include:
1. Posting to website and enabling online registrations.
2. Email blast to in-house database using www.constantcontact.com
3. Include seminar schedule in newsletter and flyer.
4. Classified ads using craigslist.org

Seminar Objectives:

Seminar Topic	Target Audience	Handout	Target Date

Webinars

A webinar is a presentation, lecture, workshop or seminar that is transmitted over the Web. A key feature of a Webinar is its interactive elements -- the ability to give, receive and discuss information. Webinars will be used as an effective vehicle for communicating a message, building awareness and buy-in about a particular topic, and offering an interactive educational experience.

Our Webinars will be educational in nature and allow our clinic to demonstrate the value of our Health Care Staffing Agency services and expertise, directly to prospects or existing clients without spending money to meet with them. Webinars allow prospects to listen to experts discuss uses, benefits and demand for certain products and services while gleaning insights about the unique benefits businesses provide. Webinars, like other forms of content marketing, should convey succinct messages and focus on one topic of interest. Webinars tend to run an hour, including Q&A time. Webinars are generally in the form of slide decks. While webinar marketing is a great tool for lead generation, the webinars, themselves, must be informative and cater to the learning needs of clients or prospects. Pairing webinars with blog posts and other website content, as well as placing calls to action at the end of the presentations, can direct prospects through conversion funnels.

Sample Webinar
Title: How to Evaluate the Benefits of Working with a Health Care Staffing Agency
As a result of the webinar participants will be able to:
                 Distinguish Good Job Candidates
Prerequisite: None
Target Audience: Hospital Administrators
Resources: www.gotomeeting.com/fec/webinar/secure_webinar_software
            www.webex.com/WebEx-Meetings-Purchase-FAQ.html?TrackID=
            1030070&hbxref=&goid=webex-meetings-FAQ

Cold Calling
Cold calling is the process of approaching prospective clients or clients, typically via telephone or actual visits, who were not expecting such an interaction.
1.   Requires visiting business premises and obtaining contact details of the person who is the responsible decision maker for hiring medical professionals.
2.   Involves outgoing telemarketing operations. A script will be developed with the objective of establishing a contact name and setting an appointment for a visit by our sales rep. Requires researching the prospects current pain points to offer remedies. We will send out a personalized letter that introduces our placement services and informs the prospect that we will be calling on a certain date.
3.   May involve walking in cold with a business suit and making introductions to both the gatekeeper and 'The Decision Maker' with the aid of small token gifts, such as a logo imprinted paperweight or pen set.

Autoresponder
An autoresponder is an online tool that will automatically manage our mailing list and send out emails to our clients at preset intervals. We will write a short article that is helpful to potential Health Care Staffing Agency clients. We will load this article into our autoresponder. We will let people know of the availability of our article by posting to newsgroups, forums, social networking sites etc. We will list our autoresponder email address at the end of the posting so they can send a blank email to our autoresponder to receive our article and be added to our mailing list. We will then email them at the interval of our choosing with special offers. We will load the messages into our autoresponder and set a time interval for the messages to be mailed out.
Resource: www.aweber.com

Database Marketing
Database marketing is a form of direct marketing using databases of clients or prospects to generate personalized communications in order to promote a product or service for

marketing purposes. The method of communication can be any addressable medium, as in direct marketing. With database marketing tools, we will be able to implement customer nurturing, which is a tactic that attempts to communicate with each customer or prospect at the right time, using the right information to meet that customer's need to progress through the process of identifying a problem, learning options available to resolve it, selecting the right solution, and making the purchasing decision. We will use our databases to learn more about clients, select target markets for specific campaigns, through customer segmentation, compare clients' value to the company, and provide more specialized offerings for clients based on their transaction histories, demographic profile and surveyed needs and wants. This database will gives us the capability to automate regular promotional mailings, to semi-automate the telephone outreach process, and to prioritize prospects as to interests, timing, and other notable delineators. The objective is to arrange for first meetings, which are meant to be informal introductions, and valuable fact-finding and needs-assessment events.

We will use sign-in sheets, coupons, surveys and newsletter subscriptions to collect the following information from our clients:

1.	Name	2.	Telephone Number
3.	Email Address	4.	Address
5.	Talent Needs	6.	Relevant Dates

We will utilize the following types of contact management software to generate leads and stay in touch with clients to produce repeat business and referrals:

1.	Act	www.act.com
2.	Front Range Solutions	www.frontrange.com
3.	The Turning Point	www.turningpoint.com
4.	Acxiom	www.acxiom.com/products_and_services/

We will utilize contact management software, such as ACT and Goldmine, to track the following:
1. Dates for follow-ups.
2. Documentation of prospect concerns, objections or comments.
3. Referral source.
4. Marketing Materials sent.
5. Log of contact dates and methods of contact.
6. Ultimate disposition.

Cause Marketing

Cause marketing or cause-related marketing refers to a type of marketing involving the cooperative efforts of a "for profit" business and a non-profit organization for mutual benefit. The possible benefits of cause marketing for business include positive public relations, improved customer relations, and additional marketing opportunities.
Cause marketing sponsorship by American businesses is rising at a dramatic rate, because clients, employees and stakeholders prefer to be associated with a company that is considered socially responsible. Our business objective will be to generate highly cost-effective public relations and media coverage for the launch of a marketing campaign

focused on _____ (type of cause), with the help of the _____ (non-profit organization name) organization.

Resources: www.causemarketingforum.com/
              www.cancer.org/AboutUs/HowWeHelpYou/acs-cause-marketing

Courtesy Advertising

We will engage in courtesy advertising, which refers to a company or corporation "buying" an advertisement in a nonprofit dinner program, event brochure, and the like. Our company will gain visibility this way while the nonprofit organization may treat the advertisement revenue as a donation. We will specifically advertise in the following non-profit programs, newsletters, bulletins and event brochures: _____

_____

Speaking Engagements

We will consider a "problem/solution" format where we describe a challenge and tell how our expertise achieved an exceptional solution. We will use speaking engagements as an opportunity to expose our areas of expertise to prospective clients. By speaking at conferences and forums put together by professional and industry trade groups, we will increase our firm's visibility, and consequently, its prospects for attracting new business. Public speaking will give us a special status, and make it easier for our speakers to meet prospects. Attendees expect speakers to reach out to the audience, which gives speakers respect and credibility. We will identify speaking opportunities that will let us reach our targeted audience. We will designate a person who is responsible for developing relationships with event and industry associations, submitting proposals and, most importantly, staying in touch with contacts. We will tailor our proposals to the event organizers' preferences.

Speaking Proposal Package:
1.   Speech Topic/Agenda/Synopsis
2.   Target Audience: Community and Civic Groups
3.   Speaker Biography
4.   List of previous speaking engagements
5.   Previous engagement evaluations

Possible Targets:

1.	Hospitals	2.	Nursing Homes
3.	Government Agencies	4.	Home Healthcare Services
5.	Adult Daycare Centers	6.	Assisted living residences
7.	Schools	8.	Physician practices
9.	Camps	10.	Ambulatory Centers
11.	Rehabilitation Centers	12.	Laboratory Services

Possible Speech Topics:
1.   The Benefits of Using a Health Care Staffing Agency
2.   Recruiting the Best Medical Professionals.

Speech Tracking Form

Group/Class	Subject/ Topic	Business Development Potential	Resources Needed	Target Date

We will use the following techniques to leverage the business development impact of our speaking engagements:

1. Send out press releases to local papers announcing the upcoming speech. We will get great free publicity by sending the topic and highlights of the talk to the newspaper.
2. Produce a flyer with our picture on it, and distribute it to our network.
3. Send publicity materials to our prospects inviting them to attend our presentation.
4. Whenever possible, get a list of attendees before the event. Contact them and introduce yourself before the talk to build rapport with your audience. Arrive early and don't leave immediately after your presentation.
5. Always give out handouts and a business card. Include marketing materials and something of value to the recipient, so that it will be retained and not just tossed away. You might include tips or secrets you share in your talk.
6. Give out an evaluation form to all participants. This form should request names and contact information. Offer a free consultation if it's appropriate. Follow up within 72 hours with any members of the audience who could become ideal clients.
7. Have a place on the form where participants can list other groups that might need speakers, along with the name of the program chairperson or other contact person.
8. Offer a door prize as incentive for handing in the evaluation. When you have collected all of the evaluations, you can select a winner of the prize.
9. Meet with audience members, answer their questions and listen to their concerns. Stay after your talk and mingle with the audience. Answer any questions that come up and offer follow-up conversations for additional support.
10. Request a free ad in the group's newsletter in exchange for your speech.
11. Send a thank-you note to the person who invited you to speak. Include copies of some of the evaluations to show how useful it was.

Speaking Engagement Package

1.	Video or DVD of prior presentation.	2.	Session Description
3.	Learning Objectives	4.	Takeaway Message
5.	Speaking experience	6.	Letters of recommendation
7.	General Biography	8.	Introduction Biography

Resource: www.toastmasters.com

Meet-up Groups

We will form a meet-up group to encourage people to participate in our recruiting programs.

Resource: http://www.meetup.com/create/

Examples:
http://recruiting.meetup.com/
http://healthcare-professionals.meetup.com/

BBB Accreditation

We will apply for BBB Accreditation to improve our perceived trustworthiness. BBB determines that a company meets BBB accreditation standards, which include a commitment to make a good faith effort to resolve any consumer complaints. BBB Accredited Businesses pay a fee for accreditation review/monitoring and for support of BBB services to the public. BBB accreditation does not mean that the business' products or services have been evaluated or endorsed by BBB, or that BBB has made a determination as to the business' product quality or competency in performing services. We will place the BBB Accreditation Logo in all of our ads.
Resource:
http://www.bbb.org/stlouis/accredited-business-directory/medical-staffing

Sponsor Events

The sponsoring of events, such as job fairs, will allow our company to engage in what is known as experiential marketing, which is the idea that the best way to deepen the emotional bond between a company and its clients is by creating a memorable and interactive experience. We will ask for the opportunity to prominently display our company signage and the set-up of a booth from which to handout sales literature. We will also seek to capitalize on networking, speech giving and workshop presenting opportunities.

Sponsorships

We will sponsor a local team, such as our child's little league team, the local soccer club or a bowling group. We will then place our company name on the shirts in exchange for providing the equipment and uniforms.

Patch.com

A community-specific news and information platform dedicated to providing comprehensive and trusted local coverage for individual towns and communities. Patch makes it easy to: Keep up with news and events, Look at photos and videos from around town, Learn about local businesses, Participate in discussions and Submit announcements, photos, and reviews.
Ex: http://greenfield.patch.com/listings/hcs-medical-staffing

MerchantCircle.com

The largest online network of local business owners, combining social networking features with customizable web listings that allow local merchants to attract new clients. A growing company dedicated to connecting neighbors and merchants online to help build real relationships between local business owners and their clients. To date, well over 1,600,000 local businesses have joined MerchantCircle to get their business more exposure on the Internet, simply and inexpensively.

Mobile iPhone Apps

We will use new distribution tools like the iPhone App Store to give us unprecedented direct access to consumers, without the need to necessarily buy actual mobile *ads* to reach people. Thanks to Apple's iPhone and the App Store, we will be able to make cool mobile apps that may generate as much goodwill and purchase intent as a banner ad. We will research Mobile Application Development, which is the process by which application software is developed for small low-power handheld devices, such as personal digital assistants, enterprise digital assistants or mobile phones. These applications are either pre-installed on phones during manufacture, or downloaded by clients from various mobile software distribution platforms. iPhone apps make good marketing tools. The bottom line is iPhones and smartphones sales are continually growing, and people are going to their phones for information. Apps will definitely be a lead generation tool because it gives potential clients easy access to our contact and business information and the ability to call for more information while they are still "hot". Our apps will contain: directory of staffers, publications on relevant issues, office location, videos, etc.

We will especially focus on the development of apps that can accomplish the following:
1. **Mobile Reservations:** Customers can use this app to access mobile reservations linked directly to your in-house calendar. They can browse open slots and book appointments easily, while on the go.
2. **Appointment Reminders:** You can send current customers reminders of regular or special appointments through your mobile app to increase your yearly revenue per customer.
3. **Style Libraries**
Offer a style library in your app to help customers to pick out a _____ style. Using a simple photo gallery, you can collect photos of various styles, and have customers browse and select specific _____.
4. **Customer Photos**
Your app can also have a feature that lets customers take photos and email them to you. This is great for creating a database of customer photos for testimonial purposes, advertising, or just easy reference.
5. **Special Offers**
Push notifications allow you to drive activity on special promotions, deals, events, and offers. If you ever need to generate revenue during a down time, push notifications allow you to generate interest easily and proactively.
6. **Loyalty Programs**
A mobile app allows you to offer a mobile loyalty program (buy ten ___, get one free, etc.). You won't need to print up cards or track anything manually – it's all done simply through users' mobile devices.
7. **Referrals**
A mobile app can make referrals easy. With a single click, a user can post to a social media account on Facebook or Twitter about their experience with your

business. This allows you to earn new business organically through the networks of existing customers.

8. **Product Sales**

We can sell _____ products through our mobile app. Customers can browse products, submit orders, and make payments easily, helping you open up a new revenue stream.

Resources: http://www.apple.com/iphone/apps-for-iphone/
                               http://iphoneapplicationlist.com/apps/business/
Software Development: http://www.mutualmobile.com/
                               http://www.avenuesocial.com/mob-app.php#
                               http://www.biznessapps.com/
Resource: http://www.appolicious.com/pages/services
Example: http://www.opportunitydrive.com/features

Transit Ads

According to the Metropolitan Transportation Authority, MTA subways, buses and railroads provide billions of trips each year to residents. Marketing our nurse staffing agency in subway cars and on the walls of subway stations will be a great way to advertise our business to a large, captive audience.

Restroom billboard advertising (Bathroom Advertising)

We will target a captive audience by placing restroom billboard advertising in select high-traffic venues with targeted demographics. A simple, framed ad on the inside of a bathroom stall door or above a urinal gets at least a minute of viewing, according to several studies. The stall door ads are a good choice for venues with shorter waiting times, such as small businesses, while large wall posters are well-suited to airports or movie theatres where people are more likely to be standing in line near the entrance or exit. Many new restroom based ad agencies that's specialize in restroom advertisement have also come about, such as; Zoom Media, BillBoardZ , Flush Media , Jonny Advertising, Insite Advertising, Inc, Wall AG USA, ADpower, NextMedia, and Alive Promo (American Restroom Association, 9/24/2009).
Resources:
http://www.indooradvertising.org/
http://www.stallmall.com/
http://www.zoommedia.com/

Tumblr.com

Tumblr will allow us to effortlessly share anything. We will be able to post text, photos, quotes, links, music, and videos, from our browser, phone, desktop, email, or wherever we happen to be. We will be able to customize everything, from colors, to our theme's HTML.

thumbtack.com

A directory for finding and booking trustworthy local services, which is free to

consumers. Thumbtack lets customers describe a job — anything from painting a house to fixing a leak — with lots of specifics, including location, timing and budget. It sends those leads to service providers, who pay from $3 to $20 for the customer's contact information so they can follow up with a quote. Each project can receive up to five quotes. The site facilitates more than 5 million projects a year, averaging about $500 each. Home improvement, Thumbtack's biggest category, is a lucrative and highly fragmented market worth well over $500 million annually in the United States. It lists 200,000 professionals in 1,500 categories.
Resource:
www.thumbtack.com/postservice

Citysearch.com
Citysearch.com is a local guide for living bigger, better and smarter in the selected city. Covering more than 75,000 locations nationwide, Citysearch.com combines in-the-know editorial recommendations, candid user comments and expert advice from local businesses. Citysearch.com keeps users connected to the most popular and undiscovered places wherever they are.

Publish e-Book
Ebooks are electronic books which can be downloaded from any website or FTP site on the Internet. Ebooks are made using special software and can include a wide variety of media such as HTML, graphics, Flash animation and video. We will publish an e-book to establish our healthcare staffing expertise, and reach people who are searching for ebooks on how to make better use our products and/or services. Included in our ebook will be links back to our website, product or affiliate program. Because users will have permanent access to it, they will use our ebook again and again, constantly seeing a link or banner which directs them to our site. The real power behind ebook marketing will be the viral aspect of it and the free traffic it helps to build for our website. ebook directories include:

> www.e-booksdirectory.com/
> www.ebookfreeway.com/p-ebook-directory-list.html
> www.quantumseolabs.com/blog/seolinkbuilding/top-5-free-ebook-directories-subscribers/

Resource: www.free-ebooks.net/

e-books are available from the following sites:

Amazon.com	Createspace.com
Lulu.com	Kobobooks.com
BarnesandNoble.com	Scribd.com
AuthorHouse.com	

Business Card Exchanges
We will join our Chamber of Commerce or local retail merchants association and volunteer to host a mixer or business card exchange. We will take the opportunity to invite social and business groups to our store to enjoy wine tastings, and market to local

businesses that will be looking for medical staffing solutions. We will also build our email database by collecting the business cards of all attendees.

Hubpages.com

HubPages has easy-to-use publishing tools, a vibrant author community and underlying revenue-maximizing infrastructure. Hubbers (HubPages authors) earn money by publishing their Hubs (content-rich Internet pages) on topics they know and love, and earn recognition among fellow Hubbers through the community-wide HubScore ranking system. The HubPages ecosystem provides a search-friendly infrastructure which drives traffic to Hubs from search engines such as Google and Yahoo, and enables Hubbers to earn revenue from industry-standard advertising vehicles such as Google AdSense and the eBay and Amazon Affiliates program. All of this is provided free to Hubbers in an open online community.

Resource: http://hubpages.crabbysbeach.com/blogs/
             http://hubpages.com/learningcenter/contents
Ex: http://elearn4life.hubpages.com/hub/What-Is-Staffing-How-Medical-Staffing-
        And-Other-Staffing-Companies-Afford-To-Stay-In-Business

Trivok.com

A totally free online directory that aims to provide information on businesses in USA and help its users find the best company.

Example:
www.trivok.com/company/inamax-medical-staffing-inc_1743917.html

Pinterest.com

The goal of this website is to connect everyone in the world through the 'things' they find interesting. They think that a favorite book or article topic can reveal a common link between two people. With millions of new pins added every week, Pinterest is connecting people all over the world based on shared tastes and interests. What's special about Pinterest is that the boards are all visual, which is a very important marketing plus. When users enter a URL, they select a picture from the site to pin to their board. People spend hours pinning their own content, and then finding content on other people's boards to "re-pin" to their own boards. We will use Pinterest for remote personal appointments. When we have a customer with specific needs, we will create a board just for them with resources we handle that would meet their needs, along with links to other tips and content. We will invite our customer to check out the board on Pinterest, and let them know we created it just for them.

Pinterest usage recommendation include:
1.   Conduct market research by showing photos of potential products or test launches, asking the customer base for feedback.
2.   Personalize the brand by showcasing style and what makes the brand different, highlighting new and exciting things through the use of imagery.
3.   Add links from Pinterest photos to the company webstore, putting price banners on each photo and providing a link where users can buy the products directly.
Example:

http://pinterest.com/advancedmedical/occupational-therapy-jobs/

Resources:
www.copyblogger.com/pinterest-marketing/
www.shopify.com/infographics/pinterest
www.pinterest.com/entmagazine/retail-business/
www.pinterest.com/brettcarneiro/ecommerce/
www.pinterest.com/denniswortham/infographics-retail-online-shopping/
www.cio.com/article/3018852/e-commerce/how-to-use-pinterest-to-grow-your-business.html

Topix.com
Topix is the world's largest community news website. Users can read, talk about and edit the news on over 360,000 of our news pages. Topix is also a place for users to post their own news stories, as well as comment about stories they have seen on the Topix site. Each story and every Topix page comes with the ability to add your voice to the conversation.
Example:
http://www.topix.com/med/physical-medicine-rehabilitation

Survey Marketing
We will conduct a survey in our target area to illicit opinions to our proposed business model. This will provide valuable feedback, lead to prospective clients and serve to introduce our Health Care Staffing Agency business, before we begin actual operations.

Google Calendar   www.google.com/calendar
We will use Google Calendar to organize our mobile Health Care Staffing Agency schedule and share events with friends.

'Green' Marketing
We will target environmentally friendly clients to introduce new clients to our business and help spread the word about going "green". We will use the following 'green' marketing strategies to form an emotional bond with our clients:
1.   We will use clearly labeled 'Recycled Paper' and Sustainable Packaging, such as receipts and storage containers.
2.   We will use "green", non-toxic cleaning supplies.
3.   We will install a 'green' lighting and heating systems to be more eco-friendly.
4.   We will use web-based Electronic Mail and Social Media instead of using paper advertisements.
5.   We will find local suppliers to minimize the carbon footprint that it takes for deliveries.
6.   We will use products that are made with organic ingredients and supplies.
7.   We will document our 'Green' Programs in our sales brochure and website.
8.   We will be a Certified Energy Star Partner.

9. We will install new LED warehouse lighting, exit signs, and emergency signs.
10. We will install motion detectors in low-traff7ic areas both inside and outside of warehouses.
11. We will implement new electricity regulators on HVAC units and compressors to lower energy consumption.
12. We will mount highly supervised and highly respected recycling campaigns.
13. We will start a program for waste product to be converted into sustainable energy sources.
14. We will start new company-wide document shredding programs.
15. We will use of water-based paints during the finishing process to reduce V.O.C.'s to virtually zero.
16. Use of solar panels for non-critical sections and facilities in the complex.
17. Use of only hybrid or electric vehicles.

Sticker Marketing

Low-cost sticker, label and decal marketing will provide a cost-effective way to convey information, build identity and promote our company in unique and influential ways. Stickers can be affixed to almost any surface, so they can go and stay affixed where other marketing materials can't; opening a world of avenues through which we can reach our target audience. Our stickers will be simple in design, and convey an impression quickly and clearly, with valuable information or coupon, printed optionally as part of its backcopy. Our stickers will handed out at trade shows and special events, mailed as a postcard, packaged with product and/or included as part of a mailing package. We will insert the stickers inside our product or hand them out along with other marketing tools such as flyers or brochures. Research has found that the strongest stickers are usually less than 16 square inches, are printed on white vinyl, and are often die cut. Utilizing a strong design, in a versatile size, and with an eye-catching shape, that is, relevant to our business, will add to the perceived value of our promotional stickers.

We will adhere to the following sticker design tips:
1. We will strengthen our brand by placing our logo on the stickers and using company colors and font styles.
2. We will include our phone number, address, and/or website along with our logo to provide clients with a call to action.
3. We will write compelling copy that solicits an emotional reaction.
4. We will use die-cut stickers using unusual and business relevant shapes to help draw attention to our business.
5. We will consider that size matters and that will be determined by where they will be applied and the degree of desired visibility to be realized.
6. We will be aware of using color on our stickers as color can help create contrast in our design, which enables the directing of prospect eyes to images or actionable items on the stickers.
7. We will encourage clients to post our stickers near their phones, on yellow page book covers, on party invitations, on notepads, on book covers, on gift boxes and packaging, etc.

8.   We will place our stickers on all the products we sell and marketing materials we distribute.

ZoomInfo.com
Their vision is to be the sole provider of constantly verified information about companies and their employees, making our data indispensible — available anytime, anywhere and anyplace the customer needs it. Creates just-verified, detailed profiles of 65 million businesspeople and six million businesses. Makes data available through powerful tools for lead generation, prospecting and recruiting.

CitySlick.net
CitySlick.net's unique approach to *online local advertising* helps distribute search traffic for local businesses. We will get more local clients through the internet via CitySlick's local citation network.

Zipslocal.com
Provides one of the most comprehensive ZIP Code-based local search services, allowing visitors to access information through our online business directories that cover all ZIP Codes in the United States. Interactive local yellow pages show listings and display relevant advertising through the medium of the Internet, making it easy for everyone to find local business information

Hold Biggest Fan Contest
Do you love _____ (company name)? Do you have a great story about how the team at ____ (company Name) helped you "get there" to achieve your goals? Well, then ____ (company name) wants to hear from you! _____ (company name) has launched the "Biggest Fan Contest" on its Facebook Page at the beginning of ____ (month), inviting current and former clients to share why they are _____'s (company name) "Biggest Fan." Participants are eligible to win a number of prizes including: _____.
To enter, visit www.facebook.com/_____ (company name), "like" the page, and click the "Biggest Fan Contest" tab on the right hand side. Participants are then asked to write a short blurb or upload a photo sharing why they love _____ (company name). If you have a story to tell or photo to share, enter today. Contest ends _____ (date). See contest tab for full details.

zip.pro
Zip.pro helps users discover local businesses, eateries, cafes, events et al. This is accomplished by giving them a 360 degree overview of the businesses in their area through client testimonials, guide maps, pictures, editorial reviews etc. all powered by a highly intuitive user-interface built specifically for achieving the end objective - Discovery

Data.com/connect/index.jsp
A dynamic community with connections to millions of B2B decision makers. It's the fastest way to reach the right people, and never waste time hunting down the wrong

person again.
Resource:
http://community.jigsaw.com/t5/How-to-Use-Jigsaw/bd-p/jigsawresourcecenter

Mobile Marketing

We will work with clients to create a mobile version of their websites to deliver a better and more appropriate experience to mobile based users. This will purely be an opt in campaign, and will let us create an ongoing conversation with our clients.
Our mobile site will provide quick, convenient access to key information, such as newly designed job search for travel nurses, an easy physician job application format, educational and testimonial videos for travelers, healthcare industry staffing news and announcements, and important information about our firm's staffing and recruiting programs.

We will use the following to leverage our mobile marketing program:
1. We will offer clients the opportunity to join a mobile loyalty club and receive special rewards and offers for mobile club members only.
2. We will encourage clients to sign up for the mobile program at the reception counter, on the website and on social media platforms.
3. We will develop compelling up-sell and cross-sell mobile coupon offers, such as a discount when purchasing a service, or up-selling through offering service packages.
4. We will use mobile loyalty programs to stay top of mind with existing clients and drive repeat sales.
5. Our mobile messages will include mobile coupons as well as announcements about new recruits or new available staffing services.
6. We will use mobile messaging on special occasions to drive traffic during the slower season.

Resources:
Mobile Marketing Association   www.mmaglobal.com
BxP Marketing visit   www.bxpmarketing.com.

Note: Google has partnered with Mountain View, Calif.-based startup DudaMobile to launch GoMo, a service that targets small business owners who want to create mobile-friendly websites. The service provides an easy-to-use website for small business owners who want to turn their websites into stripped-down versions for smartphones. The service is free for the first year, and costs $108 annually thereafter.

Trumpia.com
The only All-In-One Multi-Channel Marketing and Messaging platform that gives marketers and their clients the greatest level of choice by incorporating SMS and MMS text, email, voice broadcast, IM and social media. Trumpia's multi-channel technology integrates every popular messaging channel and the most comprehensive set of mobile text marketing features in the industry today. Trumpia allows marketers to orchestrate a coordinated cross-channel marketing strategy via a single, web-based system to dramatically increase response rates, brand awareness and return on investment. With

Trumpia's White Label Reseller program, savvy marketers are creating their own branded website using Trumpia's opt-in, permission based marketing software platform. Resellers can set-up their own pricing, profit margins and monthly plans.

Resource:
www.staffingrobot.com/2011/06/mobile-website-medical-staffing.html

Google+
We will pay specific attention to Google+, which is already playing a more important role in Google's organic ranking algorithm. We will create a business page on Google+ to achieve improved local search visibility. Google+ will also be the best way to get access to Google Authorship, which will play a huge role in SEO.
Resources:
https://plus.google.com/pages/create
http://www.google.com/+/brands/
https://www.google.com/appserve/fb/forms/plusweekly/
https://plus.google.com/+GoogleBusiness/posts
http://marketingland.com/beyond-social-benefits-google-business-73460

Examples:
https://plus.google.com/101490729229949899209/posts

Inbound Marketing
Inbound marketing is about pulling people in by sharing relevant healthcare staffing information, creating useful content, and generally being helpful. It involves writing everything from buyer's guides to blogs and newsletters that deliver useful content. The objective will be to nurture customers through the buying process with unbiased educational materials that turn consumers into informed buyers.
Resource:
www.Hubspot.com

Google My Business Profile   www.google.com/business/befound.html
We will have a complete and active Google My Business profile to give our healthcare staffing company a tremendous advantage over the competition, and help potential customers easily find our company and provide relevant information about our business.

Reddit.com
An online community where users vote on stories. The hottest stories rise to the top, while the cooler stories sink. Comments can be posted on every story, including stories about startup healthcare staffing companies.
Examples:
www.reddit.com/r/reddit.com/related/envlr/online_healthcare_staffing_company/

6.4.1   Strategic Alliances

We will form strategic alliances to accomplish the following objectives:
1.   To share marketing expenses.
2.   To realize bulk buying power on wholesale purchases.
3.   To engage in barter arrangements.
4.   To collaborate with industry experts.
5.   To set-up mutual referral relationships.

_____ (company name) will provides clinical staffing to a wide range of facilities and Medical practices including ambulatory surgery centers, government facilities, correctional facilities, rehabilitation facilities, school systems, long-term care facilities, home health agencies and Medical clinics. We plan to develop the largest network of physicians, nurses and allied Medical providers to meet the clinical staffing needs of almost any facility.

We will develop strategic alliances with the following service providers by conducting introductory 'cold calls' to their offices and making them aware of our capabilities by distributing our corporate brochures and business cards:

1.	Adult Daycare Centers	2.	Health Clubs
3.	Hospitals	4.	Nursing Homes
5.	Assisted living residences	6.	Schools
7.	Physician practices	8.	Camps
9.	Ambulatory Centers	10.	Rehabilitation Centers
11.	Home Medical Centers	12.	Laboratory Services
13.	Pharmacies	14.	Retirement homes
15.	Skilled Nursing Facilities	16.	Health Departments
17.	Insurance Companies	18.	Medical Equipment Companies
19.	Government Agencies	20.	Radiology Centers
21.	Urgent Care Centers	22.	Educational institutions
23.	Home Healthcare Agencies	24.	Nursing Clinics
25.	Outpatient Clinics	26.	Acute Care Centers
27.	Long term Treatment Care Centers		

We will assemble and present a sales presentation package that includes sales brochures, business cards, and a DVD presentation of basic temp hiring tips, and client testimonials. We will include coupons that offer a discount or other type of introductory deal. We will ask to set-up a take-one display for our sales brochures at the business registration counter.

We will promptly give the referring business any one or combination of the following agreed upon reward options:
1.   Referral fees   2.   Free services
3.   Mutual referral exchanges

We will monitor referral sources to evaluate the mutual benefits of the alliance and make certain to clearly define and document our referral incentives prior to initiating our referral exchange program.

6.4.2   Monitoring Marketing Results

To monitor how well _____ (company name) is doing, we will measure how well the advertising campaign is working by taking customer surveys. What we would like to know is how they heard of us and how they like and dislike about our staffing services. In order to get responses to the surveys, we will be give discounts as thank you rewards.

Response Tracking Methods
Coupons: ad-specific coupons that easily enable tracking
Landing Pages: unique web landing pages for each advertisement
800 Numbers: unique 1-800-# per advertisement
Email Service Provider: Instantly track email views, opens, and clicks
Address inclusion of dept # or suite #.

Our financial statements will offer excellent data to track all phases of sales. These are available for review on a daily basis. _____ (company name) will benchmark our objectives for sales promotion and advertising in order to evaluate our return on invested marketing dollars, and determine where to concentrate our limited advertising dollars to realize the best return. We will also strive to stay within our marketing budget.

Key Marketing Metrics
We will use the following two marketing metrics to evaluate the cost-effectiveness of our marketing campaign:
1.   The cost to acquire a new customer: The average dollar amount invested to get one new client. Example: If we invest $3,000 on marketing in a single month and end the month with 10 new clients, our cost of acquisition is $300 per new customer.
2.   The lifetime value of the average active customer. The average dollar value of an average customer over the life of their business with you. To calculate this metric for a given period of time, we will take the total amount of revenue our business generated during the time period and divide it by the total number of clients we had from the beginning of the time period.
3.   We will track the following set of statistics on a weekly basis to keep informed of the progress of our practice:
      A.   Number of total referrals.
      B.   Percentage increase of total referrals (over baseline).
      C.   Number of new referral sources.
      D.   Number of new clients/month.
      E.   Number of Leads

Key Marketing Metrics Table
We've listed some key metrics in the following table. We will need to keep a close eye on these, to see if we meet our own forecasted expectations. If our numbers are off in too

many categories, we may, after proper analysis, have to make substantial changes to our marketing efforts.

Key Marketing Metrics	2017	2018	2019
Revenue			
Leads			
Leads Converted			
Avg. Transaction per Customer			
Avg. Dollars per Customer			
Number of Referrals			
Number of PR Appearances			
Number of Testimonials			
Number of New Club Members			
Number of Returns			
Number of BBB Complaints			
Number of Completed Surveys			
Number of Blog readers			
Number of Twitter followers			
Number of Facebook Fans			

Metric Definitions

1. Leads: Individuals who step into the store to consider a purchase.
2. Leads Converted: Percent of individuals who actually make a purchase.
3. Average Transactions Per Customer: Number of purchases per customer per month. Expected to rise significantly as clients return for more and more items per month
4. Average $ Per Customer: Average dollar amount of each transaction. Expected to rise along with average transactions.
5. Referrals: Includes customer and business referrals
6. PR Appearances: Online or print mentions of the business that are not paid advertising. Expected to be high upon opening, then drop off and rise again until achieving a steady level.
7. Testimonials: Will be sought from the best and most loyal clients. Our objective is ___ (#) per month) and they will be added to the website. Some will be sought as video testimonials.
8. New Loyalty Club Members: This number will rise significantly as more clients see the value in repeated visits and the benefits of club membership.
9. Number of Returns/BBB Complaints: Our goal is zero.
10. Number of Completed Surveys: We will provide incentives for clients to complete customer satisfaction surveys.

6.4.3   Word-of-Mouth Marketing

We plan to make use of the following techniques to promote word-of-mouth

advertising:
1.   Repetitive Image Advertising
2.   Provide exceptional customer service.
3.   Make effective use of loss leaders.
2.   Schedule in-store activities, such as demonstrations or special events.
3.   Make trial easy with a coupon or introductory discount.
4.   Initiate web and magazine article submissions
5.   Utilize a sampling program
6.   Add a forward email feature to our website.
7.   Share relevant and believable testimonial letters
8.   Publish staff bios.
9.   Make product/service upgrade announcements
10.   Hold contests or sweepstakes
12.   Have involvement with community events.
13.   Pay suggestion box rewards
14.   Distribute a monthly newsletter
15.   Share easy-to-understand information (via an article or seminar).
16.   Make personalized marketing communications.
17.   Structure our referral program.
18.   Sharing of Community Commonalities
19.   Invitations to join our community of shared interests.
20.   Publish Uncensored Customer Reviews
21.   Enable Information Exchange Forums
22.   Provide meaningful comparisons with competitors.
23.   Clearly state our user benefits.
24.   Make and honor ironclad guarantees
25.   Provide superior post-sale support
26.   Provide support in the pre-sale decision making process.
27.   Host Free Informational Seminars or Workshops
28.   Get involved with local business organizations.
29.   Issue Press Release coverage of charitable involvements.
30.   Hold traveling company demonstrations/exhibitions/competitions.

6.4.4   Customer Satisfaction Survey

We will design a customer satisfaction survey to measure the "satisfaction quotient" of our Health Care Staffing Agency clients. By providing a detailed snapshot of our current customer base, we will be able to generate more repeat and referral business and enhance the profitability of our company.

Our Customer Satisfaction Survey will including the following basics:
1.   How do our clients rate our medical staffing business?
2.   How do our clients rate our competition?
3.   How well do our clients rate the value of our products or services?
4.   What new customer needs and trends are emerging?

5. How loyal are our clients?
6. What can be done to improve customer loyalty and repeat business?
7. How strongly do our clients recommend our business?
8. What is the best way to market our business?
9. What new value-added services would best differentiate our business from that of our competitors?
10. How can we encourage more referral business?
11. How can our pricing strategy be improved?

Our customer satisfaction survey will help to answer these questions and more. From the need for continual new products and services to improved customer service, our satisfaction surveys will allow our business to quickly identify problematic and underperforming areas, while enhancing our overall customer satisfaction.

Examples:
http://www.firstcallmedical.net/healthcare-staffing-client-satisfaction-survey
http://www.staffoflifenursing.com/nurse-staffing-client-satisfaction-survey

Resources:
https://www.survata.com/
https://www.google.com/insights/consumersurveys/use_cases
https://www.surveymonkey.com/mp/customer-satisfaction-survey-questions/
http://www.smetoolkit.org/smetoolkit/en/content/en/6708/Customer-Satisfaction-Survey-Template-
http://smallbusiness.chron.com/common-questions-customer-service-survey-1121.html

6.4.5   Marketing Training Program

Our Marketing Training Program will include both an initial orientation and training, as well as ongoing continuing education classes. Initial orientation will be run by the owner until an HR manager is hired. For one week, half of each day will be spent in training, and the other half shadowing the operation's manager.

Training will include:
Learning the entire selection of Health Care Staffing Agency services.
Understanding our Mission Statement, Value Proposition, Position Statement and Unique Selling Proposition.
Appreciating our competitive advantages.
Understanding our core message and branding approach.
Learning our store's policies; returns processing, complaint handling, etc.
Learning our customer services standards of practice.
Learning our customer and business referral programs.
Learning our Membership Club procedures, rules and benefits.
Becoming familiar with our company website, and online ordering options.
Service procedures specific to the employee's role.

Ongoing workshops will be based on customer feedback and problem areas identified by mystery buyers, which will better train employees to educate clients. These ongoing workshops will be held _____ (once?) a month for _____ (three?) hours.

6.5   Sales Strategy

The development of our sales strategy will start by developing a better understanding of our customer needs. To accomplish this task we will pursue the following research methods:
1.   Join the associations that our target clients belong to.
2.   Contact the membership director and establish a relationship to understand their member's needs, challenges and concerns.
3.   Identify non-competitive suppliers who sell to our customer to learn their challenges and look for partnering solutions.
4.   Work directly with our customer and ask them what their needs are and if our business may offer a possible solution.

The Management of our agency will focus on weekly sales revenue goals, and explaining any variances. Best value services will be identified to assist clients with smart purchase selections. The situation will be monitored to insure that the company invests adequately in its own operations.

In order to improve our sales strategy, we will do the following:
1.   Thoroughly explain the depth and nuances of our recruiting process.
2.   Be honest and helpful if we can't fill the role by suggesting another more specialized agency.
3.   Reduce turnover in our recruiting positions by supporting recruiter development appropriately.
4.   Facilitate the client meeting with everyone who will be working with their team to fill external needs, including the our managers, account reps, and recruiters.
5.   Continually seek to find new ways to add real value to the talent acquisition process of our clients.
6.   Use regular customer satisfaction surveys to solicit client inputs.

Sales feedback will be elicited to stimulate ideas, approaches, relate success stories, instruct in new techniques, share news, and implement improvements. Major corporate accounts will be solicited through networking, neighborhood solicitations via sales agents, and opportunistic encounters at any time by management.

_____ (company name) will keep its placement prices competitive with other Medical staffing agencies in a ___ (#) mile radius of our office. Clients that purchase more than $___ (10000) worth of combined services will be given ___ (5)% coupon on future purchases.

Our focus will be on making the staffing services we offer of the highest possible quality and improving the quality of our customer service. Only when those services are well-established, will we consider expanding our range of services offered. We will become a one-stop shop for staffing services, and specialized program offerings. We will also be very active in the community, building a solid reputation with professionals and community leaders.

We will continue to get job leads from job boards, Vendor Management Systems (VMS) and Managed Service Provider (MSP) programs. Retrieving, organizing and imputing data from these multiple systems and distributing them to other job boards, social sites and our internal Applicant Tracking System (ATS) will be challenging. We will acquire the systems and tools that automate as much of this process as possible.

Definitions:

A **MSP**, or Managed Service Provider, manages vendors and measure their effectiveness in recruiting according to the client's standards and requirements. MSPs generally do not recruit directly, but try to find the best suppliers of vendors according to the client's requirements. This, in essence, makes the MSP more neutral than a VOP in finding talent because they themselves do not provide the labor.

A **VOP**, or Vendor On Premise, is a vendor that sets up shop on the client's premises. They are concerned with filling the labor needs and requirements of the client.[3] The VOP does this either by sourcing labor directly from themselves, or from other suppliers, whom may be their competitors. Also, the VOP manages and coordinates this labor for the client.

VMS is a tool, specifically a software program, that distributes job requirements to staffing companies, recruiters, consulting companies, and other vendors (i.e. Independent consultants). It facilitates the interview and hire process, as well as labor time collection approval and payment.

A **CMS**, or Contractor Management System, is a tool which interfaces with the Access Control Systems of large refineries, plants, and manufacturing facilities and the ERP system in order to capture the real-time hours/data between contractors and client. This type of system will typically involve a collaborative effort between the contractor and facility owner to simplify the timekeeping process and improve project cost visibility.

An **ATS** or Applicant Tracking System is a software application that enables the electronic handling of recruitment needs. An ATS can be implemented on an enterprise or small business level, depending on the needs of the company. An ATS is very similar to customer relationship management systems, but are designed for recruitment tracking purposes. In many cases they filter applications automatically based on given criteria such as former employers, years of experience and schools attended. This has caused many to adapt techniques similar to those used in Search engine optimization when creating and formatting their résumé.

Resources:

Jobbee   **www.staffingrobot.com/2013/10/welcome-to-jobbee-v2-0.html#**
                      www.staffingrobot.com/job-board-applicant-tracking#

A web based service that enables staffing companies, recruiting firms and employers to sync jobs and candidate applications from their internal ATS with their website. Jobbee pulls jobs from any source (ATS, VMS, Job board, etc) and syncs them with the user's website, creating their very own job board. The jobs posted on the user's website then match their site design and improve their SEO.

Our clients will be primarily obtained through word-of-mouth referrals, but we will also advertise introductory offers to introduce people to our frequent buyer and preferred club membership programs. The combination of the perception of higher quality, exceptional customer service, innovative staffing services and the recognition of superior value should turn referral leads into satisfied clients.

The company's sales strategy will be based on the following elements:
> Advertising in the Yellow Pages - two inch by three inch ads describing our services will be placed in the local Yellow Pages.
> Placing classified advertisements in the regional editions of trade magazines.
> Word of mouth referrals - generating sales leads in the local community through customer referrals.

Our basic sales strategy is to:
> Develop a website for lead generation by _____ (date).
> Provide exceptional customer service.
> Accept payment by all major credit cards, cash, PayPal and check.
> Survey our clients regarding staffing services they would like to see added.
> Sponsor charitable and other community events.
> Provide tours of the agency so clients can learning how to be discriminating clients and build a trust bond with our operations.
> Motivate employees with a pay-for-performance component to their straight salary compensation package, based on profits and customer satisfaction rates.
> Build long-term customer relationships by putting the interests of clients first.
> Establish mutually beneficial relationship with local businesses serving the child caring and socializing needs of local residents.

6.5.1   Customer Retention Strategy

We will use the following post-purchase techniques to improve customer retention, foster referrals and improve the profitability of our business:
1.   Keep the office sparkling clean and well-organized.
2.   Use only well-trained sales associates.
3.   Actively solicit customer feedback and promptly act upon their inputs.
4.   Tell clients how much you appreciate their business.
5.   Call regular clients by their first names.
6.   Send thank you notes.
7.   Offer free new product and service samples.

8. Change displays and sales presentations on a regular basis.
9. Practice good phone etiquette
10. Respond to complaints promptly.
11. Reward referrals.
12. Publish a monthly opt-in direct response newsletter with customized content, dependent on recipient stated information preferences .
13. Develop and publish a list of frequently asked questions.
14. Issue Preferred Customer Membership Cards.
15. Hold informational seminars and workshops.
16. Provide an emergency hotline number.
17. Publish code of ethics and our service guarantees.
18. Help clients to make accurate competitor comparisons.
19. Build a stay-in-touch (drip marketing) communications calendar.
20. Keep marketing communications focused on our competitive advantages.
21. Offer repeat user discounts and incentives.
22. Be supportive and encouraging, and not judgmental.
23. Measure customer retention and look at recurring revenue and customer surveys.
24. Build a community of shared interests by offering a website forum or discussion group for professionals and patients to allow sharing of knowledge.
25. Offer benefits above and beyond those of our competitors.
26. Issue reminder emails and holiday gift cards.

We will also consider the following Customer Retention Programs:

Type of Program	Customer Rewards
Frequency Purchase Loyalty Program	Special Discounts
	Free Product or Services
'Best Customer' Program	Special Recognition/Treatment/Offers
Affinity Programs	Sharing of Common Interests
	Accumulate Credit Card Points
Customer Community Programs	Special Event Participation
Auto-Knowledge Building Programs	Purchase Recommendations based
	On Past Transaction History
Profile Building Programs	Recommendations Based on Stated
	Customer Profile Information.

6.5.2   Sales Forecast

Our sales projections are based on the following:
1. Actual sales volumes of local competitors
2. Interviews with other Health Care Staffing Agency owners and managers
3. Observations of office sales and traffic at competitor establishments.
4. Government and industry trade statistics
5. Local demographics and projections.

With _____ (community name) growing from a base of ____ (#) to _____ (#) residents, we expect Medical staffing revenue from Medical organizations in a range of

$_____ to $_____ over the course of the next _____ (#) years.

The balance of our forecasted staffing sales, representing some _____ (20)% of total sales, will come from sources external to _____ (community name), including corporate HR consulting services.

Our sales forecast is an estimated projection of expected sales over the next three years, based on our chosen marketing strategy, economic conditions and assumed competitive environment.

Sales are expected to be below average during the first year, until a regular customer base has been established. It has been estimated that it takes the average Health Care Staffing Agency a minimum of two years to establish a significant customer base. After the customer base is built, sales will grow at an accelerated rate from word-of-mouth referrals and continued networking efforts. We expect sales to steadily increase as our marketing campaign, employee training programs and contact management system are executed.

By using advertising, especially discounted introductory coupons, as a catalyst for this prolonged process, _____(company name) plans to attract more clients sooner. Throughout the first year, it is forecasted that sales will incrementally grow until profitability is reached toward the end of year ___(one?). Year two reflects a conservative growth rate of _____ (20?) percent. Year three reflects a growth rate of _____ (25?) percent. We expect to be open for business on _____ (date), and start with an initial enrollment of _____ (#) parents. With our unique household staffing service offerings, along with our thorough and aggressive marketing strategies, we believe that sales forecasts are actually on the conservative side.

Table: Sales Forecast

	Annual Sales		
Sales	**2017**	**2018**	**2019**
Temp Contract Fees			
Percentage Commissions			
Hourly Recruiting Fees			
Permanent Placement Fees			
Tutoring Services			
Consulting/Seminars			
Misc.			
Total Unit Sales			
Direct Cost of Sales:			
Temp Contract Fees			
Percentage Commissions			
Hourly Recruiting Fees			
Permanent Placement Fees			
Tutoring Services			
Consulting/Seminars			

Misc. _____
Subtotal Direct Cost of Sales _____

6.6 Merchandising Strategy

Merchandising is that part of our marketing strategy that is involved with promoting the sales of our merchandise, as by consideration of the most effective means of selecting, pricing, displaying, and advertising items for sale in our Health Care Staffing Agency business. Through proper product placement, space allocation, and in-store promotion, sales space will be geared towards high profit margin products.

The décor of the merchandising area is extremely important to sales. Display units are primary, but lighting, furniture, wall surfaces, window treatments, carpeting, accessories and countertops will all play important supporting roles.

We will monitor our sales figures and data to confirm that products in demand are well-stocked and slow moving software products are phased-out. We will   improve telephone skills of employees to boost phone orders. We will attach our own additional business labels to all products to promote our line of services and location.

6.7 Pricing Strategy

When setting prices, we will consider the following factors:
1. Direct Costs: labor, time and supplies
2. Indirect Costs: rent, utilities, taxes and expenses.
3. Demand: economic conditions, demographics, consumer behavior, etc.
4. Marketing Promotions
5. Level of Competition
6. Positioning Image
7. Goals: profit objectives, return on investment, growth objectives.

Pricing Guidelines for Service:
Associates will be paid by the hour, and the agency will cover its costs by charging a premium to the amount billed to the client. The exact amount of the premium differs from case to case and can vary from 5% to 50% or more. Some associates are willing to work for less and some clients are willing to pay more, which when properly matched can result in very decent profits for our temporary staffing agency. The contract will also spell out a flat fee to be paid to the agency in the event that a client decides to permanently hire an associate.

Medical Profession	Client Hourly Rate	(-)	Employee Pay	= Agency Profit
Ex: Pharmacist	40.00		30.00	10.00

Pricing will be based on competitive parity guidelines. Prices will be consistent with those of the other Medical staffing agencies in the area, with the exception of very high-volume operations who have more powerful pricing leverage. Pricing will be monitored continuously against neighborhood and other competitive sources who we can readily research.

We are not interested in being the low price leader, as our pricing strategy plays a major role in whether we will be able to create and maintain clients for a profit. Our revenue structure must support our cost structure, so the salaries we pay to our staff are balanced by the revenue we collect.

The number of competitors in the area largely determines what type of pricing we will have. We don't want to be known as the highest price agency in town but it is equally important not to be the cheapest. We will continuously try to expand our staffing service offerings.

Price List Comparison

Competitor	Service	Our Price	Competitor Price	B/(W) Competitor

We will adopt the following pricing guidelines:
1. We must insure that our price plus service equation is perceived to be an exceptional value proposition.
2. We must refrain from competing on price, but always be price competitive.
3. We must develop value-added services, and bundle those with our products to create offerings that cannot be easily price compared.
4. We must focus attention on our competitive advantages.
5. Development of a pricing strategy based on our market positioning strategy, which is ____ (mass market value leadership/exceptional premium niche value?)
6. Our pricing policy objective, which is to _____ (increase profit margins/   achieve revenue maximization to increase market share/lower unit costs).
7. We will use marketplace intelligence and gain insights from competitor pricing.
8. We will solicit pricing feedback from clients using surveys and   interviews.
9. We will utilize limited time pricing incentives to penetrate niche markets
10. We will conduct experiments at prices above and below the current price to determine the price elasticity of demand. (Inelastic demand or demand that does not decrease with a price increase, indicates that price increases may be feasible.)
11. We will keep our offerings and prices simple to understand and competitive,

based on market intelligence.

12. We will consider a price for volume strategy on certain items, and study the effects of price on volume and of volume on costs, as in a recession, trying to recover these costs through a price increase can be fatal.

Determining the costs of servicing business is the most important part of covering our expenses and earning profits. We will factor in the following pricing formula: Product Cost + Materials + Overhead + Labor + Profit + Tax = Price
Materials are those items consumed in the delivering of the service.
Overhead costs are the variable and fixed expenses that must be covered to stay in business. Variable costs are those expenses that fluctuate including vehicle expenses, rental expenses, utility bills and supplies. Fixed costs include the purchase of equipment, service ware, marketing and advertising, and insurance. After overhead costs are determined, the total overhead costs are divided among the total number of transactions forecasted for the year.
Labor costs include the costs of performing the services. Also included are Social Security taxes (FICA), vacation time, retirement and other benefits such as health or life insurance. To determine labor costs per hour, keep a time log. When placing a value on our time, we will consider the following: 1) skill and reputation; 2) wages paid by employers for similar skills and 3) where we live. Other pricing factors include image, inflation, supply and demand, and competition.
Profit is a desired percentage added to our total costs. We will need to determine the percentage of profit added to each service. It will be important to cover all our costs to stay in business. We will investigate available computer software programs to help us price our services and keep financial data for decision-making purposes. Close contact with clients will allow our company to react quickly to changes in demand.

We will develop a pricing strategy that will reinforce the perception of value to the customer and manage profitability, especially in the face of rising inflation. To ensure our success, we will use periodic competitor and customer research to continuously evaluate our pricing strategy. We intend to review our profit margins every six months.

6.8   Differentiation Strategies

We will use differentiation strategies to develop and market unique services for different customer segments. To differentiate ourselves from the competition, we will focus on the assets, creative ideas and competencies that we have that none of our competitors has. The goal of our differentiation strategies is to be able to charge a premium price for our unique products and services and/or to promote loyalty and assist in retaining our clients.

Differentiation in our health care staffing agency will be achieved in the following types of ways, including:

	Explanation
☐ Product features	

☐ Complementary services _____
☐ Technology embodied in design _____
☐ Location _____
☐ Service innovations _____
☐ Superior service _____
☐ Creative advertising _____
☐ Better supplier relationships _____
Source:
http://scholarship.sha.cornell.edu/cgi/viewcontent.cgi?article=1295&context=articles

Differentiating will mean defining who our perfect target market is and then catering to their needs, wants and interests better than everyone else. It will be about using surveys to determine what's most important to our targeted market and giving it to them consistently.   It will not be about being "everything to everybody"; but rather, "the absolute best to our chosen targeted group".

In developing our differentiation strategy will we use the following form to help define our differences:

1.	Targeted customer segments	_____
2.	Customer characteristics	_____
3.	Customer demographics	_____
4.	Customer behavior	_____
5.	Geographic focus	_____
6.	Ways of working	_____
7.	Service delivery approach	_____
8.	Customer problems/pain points	_____
9.	Complexity of customers' problems	_____
10.	Range of services	_____

We will use the following approaches to differentiate our products and services from those of our competitors to stand apart from standardised offerings:

1. Superior quality
2. Unusual or unique product features
3. More responsive customer service
4. Rapid product or service innovation
5. Advanced technological features
6. Engineering design or styling
7. Additional product features
8. An image of prestige or status

Specific Differentiators will include the following:
1. Being a Specialist in one procedure
2. Utilizing advanced/uncommon technology
3. Possessing extensive experience

4. Building an exceptional facility
5. Consistently achieving superior results
6. Having a caring and empathetic personality
7. Giving customer s WOW experience, including a professional customer welcome package.
8. Enabling convenience and 24/7 online accessibility
9. Calling customers to express interest in their challenges.
10. Keeping to the appointment schedule.
11. Remembering customer names and details like they were family
12. Assuring customer fears.
13. Building a visible reputation and recognition around our community
14. Acquiring special credentials or professional memberships
15. Providing added value services, such as taxi service, longer hours, financing plans, and post-sale services.

Primary Differentiation Strategies:

1. Beyond a marketing tool, we will use the web as a way to build an online community both among Medical professionals and between Medical organizations.
2. Technology will be a key differentiator, because being able to provide customized usage reports, sophisticated compliance systems, and real-time information on the contingent workforce are valuable services for today's Medical organizations.
3. We will utilize software systems that will enable us to personalize each customer's hiring experience, including easy access to customer transaction history, profile search criteria and information about all the services of interest to that particular client.
4. We will develop a referral program that turns our clients into referral agents.
5. We will use regular client satisfaction surveys to collect feedback, improvement ideas, referrals and testimonials.
6. We will promote our "green" practices, such as establishing a recycling program, purchasing recycled-content office goods and responsibly handling hazardous wastes.
7. We will customize our offerings according to the language, cultural influences, customs, interests and preferences of our local market to create loyalty and increase sales.
8. We will develop the expertise to satisfy the needs of targeted market segments with customized and exceptional staffing support services.
9. We take the time to understand our clients' aches and pains, as well as their cultures, business objectives and goals.
10. We take the time to assess not only our job candidates' competencies and backgrounds, but also their preferred work environments and styles.

6.9 Milestones   (select)

The Milestones Chart is a timeline that will guide our company in developing and growing our business. It will list chronologically the various critical actions and events that must occur to bring our business to life. We will make certain to assign real, attainable dates to each planned action or event.

_____ (company name) has identified several specific milestones which will function as goals for the company. The milestones will provide a target for achievement as well as a mechanism for tracking progress. The dates were chosen based on realistic delivery times and necessary construction times. All critical path milestones will be completed within their allotted time frames to ensure the success of contingent milestones. The following table will provide a timeframe for each milestone.

Table: Milestones

Milestones	Start Date	End Date	Budget	Responsibility
Business Plan Completion				
Secure Permits/Licenses				
Locate & Secure Space				
Obtain Insurance Coverage				
Secure Additional Financing				
Get Start-up Supplies Quotes				
Obtain County Certification				
Purchase Office Equipment				
Renovate Facilities				
Define Marketing Programs				
Install Equipment/Displays				
Technology Systems				
Set-up Accounting System				
Develop Office Policies				
Develop Procedures Manual				
Arrange Support Service Providers				
Finalize Media Plan				
Create Facebook Brand Page				
Conduct Blogger Outreach				
Develop Personnel Plan				
Develop Staff Training Programs				
Hire/Train Staff				
Implement Marketing Plan				
Get Website Live				
Conduct SEO Campaign				
Form Strategic Alliances				
Purchase Start-up Inventory/Supplies				
Press Release Announcements				
Advertise Grand Opening				
Kickoff Advertising Program				

Join Community Orgs./Network _____
Conduct Satisfaction Surveys _____
Evaluate/Revise Plan _____
Devise Growth Strategy _____
Monitor Social Media Networks _____
Respond to reviews _____
Measure Return on Marketing $$$ _____
Revenues Exceed $_____ _____
Reach Profitability _____
Totals: _____

7.0   Website Plan Summary

_____ (company name) is currently developing a website at the URL address www. (company name).com. We will focus on updating our website, adding new services, features and functions for our clients. We understand the special training, licensing and compliance requirements in Medical, as well as the need for skilled, motivated and productive employees and our website needs to reflect that knowledge and experience. Our site will also have enhanced search functions to assist physicians, nurses, laboratory technicians and other Medical professionals search for jobs in their local communities or in different areas of the country.

We will set up an online job board on our website to find candidates, and optimize it for the search engines so people looking for a job find our site, feel compelled to send their resume and come in for an interview. We will also post job openings on online sites such as Monster and CareerBuilder.com to find suitable candidates.

We will also provide multiple incentives to sign-up for various benefits, such as our newsletters and new job board notices. This will help us to build an email database, which will supply our automated customer follow-up system. We will create a personalized drip marketing campaign to stay in touch with our clients and recruits.

We will develop our website to be a resource for web visitors who are seeking knowledge and information about medical staffing alternatives, with a goal to service the knowledge needs of our clients and generate leads. Our home page will be designed to be a "welcome mat" that clearly presents our service benefits and offerings and provides links through which visitors can gain easy access to the information they seek. We will use our website to match the problems our clients face with the solutions we offer.

We will use the free tool, Google Analytics (http://www.google.com/analytics), to generate a history and measure our return on investment.

To improve the readability of our website, we will organize our website content in the following ways.

1.	Headlines	2.	Bullet points
3.	Callout text	4.	Top of page summaries

To improve search engine optimization, we will maximize the utilization of the following;

1.	Links	2.	Headers
3.	Bold text	4.	Bullets
5.	Keywords	6.	Meta tags

This website will serve the following purposes:

About Us	How We Work/Our Philosophy
Our Clients	
Service Team	

Personnel Benefits and Incentives

Contact Us	Customer service contact info
Our Services	Medical
Submit Staffing Needs	Form
Frequently Asked Questions	FAQs
Job Board	
Search Jobs	Job Listings
Submit Your Resume	Candidate Application
Candidate Resumes	
Articles	Interview Tips
Club Membership	Sign-up
Newsletter Sign-up	Join Mailing List
Newsletter Archives	Foot Care Articles
Upcoming Events	Wine Tasting Schedule
Testimonials	Letters w/photos
Referral Rewards Program	Details
Customer Satisfaction Survey	Feedback
Press Releases	Community Involvement
Strategic Alliance Partners	Links
Tradeshow Schedule	
Training Programs	Password Login
Resources	Professional Associations
Staffing Blog	Accept comments
Refer-a-Friend	Viral marketing
YouTube Video Clips	Seminar Presentation/Testimonials
Service Guarantees	
Code of Ethics	Compliance
Privacy Policy	
Customer Service Policy	
Report a Compliance Concern	Form
Join Our Staff	Career Opportunities
Client Access	Make a Payment
Social Networking Pages	MySpace/Facebook/Twitter
Heathcare News	
Classified Ads	

Classified Ads

By joining and incorporating a classified ad affiliate program into our website, we will create the ultimate win-win-win. We will provide our guests with a free benefit, increase our rankings with the search engines by incorporating keyword hyperlinks into our site, attract additional markets to expose to our product, create an additional income source as they upgrade their ads, and provide our prospects a reason to return to our web site again and again

Resources:

App Themes	www.appthemes.com/themes/classipress/
e-Classifieds	http://www.e-classifieds.net/

Noah's Classifieds   http://www.noahsclassifieds.org/
Joom Prod   http://www.joomprod.com/

7.1   Website Marketing Strategy

Our online marketing strategy will employ the following distinct mechanisms:

1.   Search Engine Submission

    This will be most useful to people who are unfamiliar with _____ (company name), but are looking for a local Health Care Staffing Agency. There will also be searches from clients who may know about us, but who are seeking additional information.

2.   Website Address (URL) on Marketing Materials

    Our URL will be printed on all marketing communications, business cards, letterheads, faxes, and invoices and product labels. This will encourage a visit to our website for additional information

3.   Online Directories Listings

    We will make an effort to list our website on relevant, free and paid online directories and manufacturer website product locators.

    The good online directories possess the following features:

    Free or paid listings that do not expire and do not require monthly renewal.

    Ample space to get your advertising message across.

    Navigation buttons that are easy for visitors to use.

    Optimization for top placement in the search engines based on keywords that people typically use to find Medical staffing agencies.

    Direct links to your website, if available.

    An ongoing directory promotion campaign to maintain high traffic volumes to the directory site. Ex: www.google.com/Top/Business/Medical/Employment/ Recruitment_and_Staffing/Staffing_Services/

4. Strategic Business Partners

    We will use a Business Partners page to cross-link to prominent _____ (city) area Medical web sites as well as the city Web sites and local recreational sites. We will also cross-link with brand name suppliers.

5.   YouTube Posting

    We will produce a video of testimonials from several of our satisfied clients and educate viewers as to the range of our services and products. Our research indicates that the YouTube video will also serve to significantly improve our ranking with the Google Search Engine.

6.   Exchange of links with strategic marketing partners.

    We will cross-link to non-profit businesses that accept our gift donations as in-house run contest prize awards.

7.   E-Newsletter

    Use the newsletter sign-up as a reason to collect email addresses and limited profiles, and use embedded links in the newsletter to return readers to website.

8. **Create an account for your photos on flickr.com**
Use the name of your site on flickr so you have the same keywords and your branded.

9. **Geo Target Pay Per Click (PPC) Campaign**
Available through Google Adwords program. Example keywords include Health Care Professionals, Health Care Staffing Agency, Temporary Staffing and _(city).

10. **Post messages on Internet user groups and forums.**
Get involved with Medical staffing related discussion groups and forums and develop a descriptive signature paragraph.
Ex: www.smallbusinessonlinecommunity.bankofamerica.com/message/97573

11. **Write up your own MySpace.com and Facebook.com bios.**
Highlight your background and professional interests.

12. **Facebook.com Brand-Building Applications:**
- Upload Videos of new seminars.   - Download wallpaper for cell phones.
- Sign-up for latest news and mailing list.   - Enter Contests
- Link to company website.   - Discussion Boards/ Solicit Feedback
- Post testimonials

13. **Blog to share our success stories and solicit comments**
Blogging will be a great way for us to share information, expertise, and news, and start a conversation with our clients, the media, suppliers, and any other target audiences. Blogging will be a great online marketing strategy because it keeps our content fresh, engages our audience to leave comments on specific posts, improves search engine rankings and attracts links. In the blog we will share Medical Professional screening tips. We will also provide a link to our Facebook.com page. Resource: www.blogger.com www.blogspot.com

7.2 Development Requirements

A full development plan will be generated as documented in the milestones. Costs that ____ (company name) will expect to incur with development of its new website include:

Development Costs

User interface design	$_____ .
Site development and testing	$_____
Site Implementation	$._____

Ongoing Costs

Website name registration	$_____ per year.
Site Hosting	$_____ or less per month.

Site design changes, updates and maintenance are considered part of Marketing.

The site will be developed by _____ (company name), a local start-up company. The user interface designer will use our existing graphic art to come up with the website logo and graphics. We have already secured hosting with a local provider, _____ (business name). Additionally, they will prepare a monthly statistical usage report to analyze and improve web usage and return on investment.

The plan is for the website to be live by ___(date). Basic website maintenance, including update and data entry will be handled by our staff. Site content, such as images and text will be maintained by _____ (owner name). In the future, we may need to contract with a technical resource to build the trackable article download and newsletter capabilities.

Resources:
www.staffingrobotonline.com/why-us-healthcare-staffing-web-design-marketing.html
www.proweaver.com/healthcare-staffing-web-design

7.3 Sample Frequently Asked Questions

We will use the following guidelines when developing the frequently asked questions for our the ecommerce section of the website:
1.   Use a Table of Contents: Offer subject headers at the top of the FAQ page with a hyperlink to that related section further down on the page for quick access.
2.   Group Questions in a Logical Way and group separate specific questions related to a subject together.
3.   Be Precise With the Question: Don't use open-ended questions.
4.   Avoid Too Many Questions: Publish only the popular questions and answers.
5.   Answer the Question with a direct answer.
6.   Link to Resources When Available: via hyperlinks so the customer can continue with self-service support.
7.   Use Bullet Points to list step-by-step instructions.
8.   Focus on Customer Support and Not Marketing.
9.   Use Real and Relevant Frequently Asked Questions from actual clients.
10.   Update Your FAQ Page as clients continue to communicate questions.

The following frequently asked questions will enable us to convey a lot of important information to our clients in a condensed format. We will post these questions and answers on our website and create a hardcopy version to be included on our sales presentation folder.

Who is _____ (company name)?
_____ (company name) is a Health Care Staffing Agency for Medical facilities. We offer Medical staffing services for a wide range of specialties, from nurses, Physicians, and Medical coders to allied health and administrative professionals. We offer opportunities and services to virtually every sector of the Medical industry.

Why should I use _____ (company name) for my Medical staffing needs?
We are a leading provider of high-quality Medical professionals for temporary, contract and permanent positions. Our nurse, physician and allied staffing capabilities enable us to

provide clients with a wide spectrum of assignment lengths in nearly every clinical discipline. _____ (company name) works as your single-source solution to simplify your staffing, cut down on vendor contacts and to improve staffing efficiencies. With ___ (#) years of staffing experience, an industry-leading quality assurance program and corporate certification by the Joint Commission, you can rest assured that ____ (company name) will place the best matched, most qualified candidates in your facility, while delivering the individualized service you need.

Can _____ (company name) provide me with staff quickly?

Our staffing consultants are on call 24 hours a day, 7 days a week to ensure that you are always able to reach someone to discuss your Medical staffing need. With our extensive network of Medical professionals, we are almost always able to provide the needed staff.

Are there cost benefits to using _____ (company name)?

_____ (company name) employs cost effective strategies that generate a return on investment for our clients. The Medical facilities that we staff have saved thousands of dollars every year by eliminating recruitment fees from their budget. These fees include placing ads and valuable time spent reviewing resumes and interviewing candidates. Contact us to learn more about our cost-effective staffing solutions.

How do you recruit Medical professionals?

_____ (company name) distinguishes itself from other Medical staffing companies by using a multi-media recruitment strategy that maximizes our outreach to Medical professionals through Internet, print and trade show channels. We reach out to thousands of Medical professionals every day through our recruitment Web sites and our portals dedicated to the needs of physicians, nurses and allied health professionals. We also advertise extensively on job boards, in the leading industry publications, as well as attend many national and regional trade shows and career fairs. Medical professionals are attracted to our staffing agency due to our long-standing reputation for high-level service, extensive assignment opportunities, a comprehensive benefits package and word-of-mouth referrals.

How do you screen your Medical professionals?

We prepare our Medical professionals to become part of your team, starting with our strict standards for job experience and education. Our quality management teams carefully screen all candidates for their skills, credentials, knowledge and experience, based on the criteria supplied by our clients. Our nurse candidates also undergo background and drug screening, and a personal interview. In addition, we focus on continuing education to provide the best patient care. We continue to evaluate our Medical professionals after they're placed to ensure satisfactory performance, and determine feasibility for future placements

What are the benefits I will be offered as an employee of ____ (company name)?

We offer competitive pay to all of our Medical professionals. Compensation reflects your clinical specialty, professional experience, and opportunity location. Other benefits include:

- Medical, Dental, and Vision coverage availability
- 401(k) Savings Plan
- 24/7 Personal Attention from our Staffing Consultants
- Weekly and/or Same-Day Pay
- Direct Deposit
- Flexible Scheduling
- Positive Work Environment and Friendly Internal Staff
- Bonuses and Incentives
- Continuing Education (CE) Program

What is the best way for me to apply to work at _____ (company name)?
We offer a wide range of Medical jobs and Medical staffing opportunities. If you are interested in a Medical job opportunity complete our online application.

Do you have travel nursing assignments?
Yes! We offer one-of-a-kind travel nursing opportunities from coast-to-coast. For more information, visit www._____.com.

Can _____ (company name) offer assistance with recruitment for permanent staff?
Yes. With our Recruitment Process Outsourcing (RPO) program, we can help you fill all of your permanent clinical staffing needs. RPO takes the entire process of recruitment, hiring and on-boarding and puts it in the hands of our skilled staffing experts who have a commitment to match your positions with the right candidates.

Can I pick up shifts to fit my schedule?
Yes. We place nurses, physicians, and other Medical professionals on contract, temp-to-perm, per-diem, travel, and direct hire assignments that vary in location, time, and responsibilities. Contact us today to find the right Medical job for your schedule.

Which nursing jobs does _____ (company name) staff?
We staff a broad range of nursing job opportunities. Registered Nurse (RN) jobs, License Practical Nurse (LPN) jobs, Certified Nurse Assistant (CNA) jobs, as well as a variety of therapy, and homecare jobs are available.

Do I have to sign a long-term contract?
No. You can choose a situation that fits you. We offer temp-to-perm, per diem, direct placement, and short- and long-term contracts.

What kind of job training does ____ (company name) provide?
The training you receive will vary based on the role you seek. We encourage ongoing education and job training of our employees. Be sure to contact one of our recruiters to discuss what job training options are available.

What type of requirements exist to become a nurse with _____ (company name)?
The requirements for nurses vary based on the assignment. It is best to touch base with the recruiters in the office with which you are seeking employment.

How will I learn about where I will be placed?

Assignments are scheduled through the recruiters in our offices. Applicants may call to learn about current Medical job openings and are always welcome to come into the office to meet with one of our Medical staffing recruiters.

What makes ___ (company name) stand apart from other agencies?

Our commitment to not compromise on screening procedures, our professionalism, our ability to listen and respond to our clients and our availability is the best around. From the feedback we get from clients, they say that we are the most responsive agency with whom they have ever worked.

How do you screen your Medical professionals?

We screen the candidate over the telephone to qualify them for an interview. Then we schedule an in-depth interview, in person if they are local or over the telephone if they are from out of town. Thirdly, the candidate completes a comprehensive application form. We check the references that are comprised of a detailed conversation with employers and a verification of education and all other types of employment. We also pay a private security firm to do a criminal, DMV and social security number check.

Why would a physician or other healthcare professional choose a temporary assignment?

Independently contracted doctors, dentists, CRNAs, physician assistants, nurse practitioners, and allied health professionals practice on a temporary basis for several reasons. Physicians just out of residency and other healthcare professionals use locum tenens employment to 'test drive' a practice setting or location. More experienced healthcare providers appreciate the opportunity to focus on patient care, without reimbursement concerns or other paperwork hassles. By accepting locum tenens physician employment opportunities, physicians and providers can maintain their independent status and the clinical autonomy that comes with it.

Do I have to pay a fee?

There is no up-front fee for requesting locum tenens coverage. We operate on a contingent basis. Daily rates for locum tenens physician services vary according to region and specialty. To learn how we can help your healthcare organization, please submit your medical staffing needs today.

7.4   Website Performance Summary

We will use web analysis tools to monitor web traffic, such as identifying the number of site visits. We will analyze customer transactions and take actions to minimize problems, such as incomplete sales and abandoned shopping carts. We will use the following table to track the performance of our website:

Category	2017		2018		2019	
	Fcst	Act	Fcst	Act	Fcst	Act
No. of Clients						
New Newsletter Subscribers						
Unique Visitors						
Avg. Time on Site						
Pages per Visit						
Percent New Visits						
Bounce Rate						
No. of Products						
Product Categories						
Number of Incomplete Sales						
Conversion Rate						
Affiliate Sales						
Customer Satisfaction Score						

8.0 Operations Plan

Operations include the business aspects of running our business, such as conducting quality assessment and improvement activities, auditing functions, cost-management analysis, and customer service. Our operations plan will present an overview of the flow of the daily activities of the business and the strategies that support them. It will focus on the following critical operating factors that will make the business a success:

1. We will enjoy the following advantages in the sourcing of our inventory:
   _____

2. We will utilize the following technological innovations in the customer relationship management (CRM) process:
   _____

3. We will make use of the following advantages in our distribution process:
   _____

4. We will develop the following in-house training program to improve worker productivity: _____

5. We will utilize the following system to better control inventory carrying costs.
   _____

6. We will implement the following quality control plan:
   _____

Quality Control Plan

Our Quality Control Plan will include a review process that checks all factors involved in our operations. The main objectives of our quality control plan will be to uncover defects and bottlenecks, and reporting to management level to make the decisions on the improvement of the whole production process. Our review process will include the following activities:

Quality control checklist
Finished product/service review
Structured walkthroughs
Statistical sampling
Testing process

Operations Planning

We will use Microsoft Visio to develop visual maps, which will piece together the different activities in our organization and show how they contribute to the overall "value stream" of our business. We will rightfully treat operations as the lifeblood of our business. We will develop a combined sales and operations planning process where sales and operations managers will sit down every month to review sales, at the same time creating a forward-looking 12-month rolling plan to help guide the product development and manufacturing processes, which can become disconnected from sales. We will approach our operations planning using a three-step process that analyzes the company's current state, future state and the initiatives it will tackle next. For each initiative, such as launching a new product or service, the company will examine the related financials, talent and operations needs, as well as target customer profiles. Our management team will map out the cost of development and then calculate forecasted return on investment and revenue predictions.

The Operating Plan will focus on creating a retail infrastructure by establishing permanent offices and forging strategic alliances with key customer groups.

Assemble Database of Job Candidates:
1. Run classified ads in local newspapers, monster.com and Craigslist.com.
2. Collect resumes
3. Interview candidates to find out their specialties and experience
4. Make selections
5. Make available skills training tutorial programs.
6. Match selected candidates to client needs after landing a contract.

Steps to Getting Started:
1. Present staffing needs to a member of our client services department, who will review our practices and pricing with client and discuss how our service agreement can be customized to suit client staffing needs.
2. After client reviews and signs our service agreement, a Manager will be assigned to their facility. This person will manage all of staffing orders and requests.
3. Client open positions will be made available to our recruiters nationwide, who will use our computerized matching system to find the candidates who possess the clinical skills and experience required.
4. Assigned Account Manager will forward client the profiles of the candidates who fit client specified job description and who have expressed an interest in working at client's facility. The applications will be sent to client via email, and made available directly from our proprietary database.
5. Client decides which candidates they want to interview by phone. Based on the interview, client will make an assignment offer to the appropriate traveler
6. We will confirm the acceptance and handle all pre-arrival health and competency requirements.

Start-up Business Manuals
Our Operations Manuals will be a comprehensive blueprint for structuring our agency for efficiency, reliability, and profit maximization. They will also include 'how-to' guides and training programs, which contain the forms and procedures we can use to run our full-service Health Care Staffing Agency.

Our Screening Process
Each of our candidates will be reviewed using the following screening process:
1. Undergoes a prescreening qualifying telephone interview.
2. Participates in an extensive interview face-to-face.
3. Has each individual reference checked and verified.
4. Has all previous employment and education verified.
5. Is checked by a private security agency for any past criminal record, as well as for

driver's license status, driving record and Social Security number confirmation.
6. Licensure verification.
7. A review of appropriate skills for their clinical area.
8. Experience Verification Interviews to make sure they are a good fit and able to easily adapt to new environments.

Our Job Order Processing Steps

1. Determine if this is a new or existing client
2. Confirm job order forms set up
3. Ask the client about the job order
   - What shifts he/she needs   – Candidate requirements
   - Skills requirements   - Equipment at facility
   - Licensing requirements
4. Document data on job orders
5. Communicate to client follow-up time to confirm the shift
6. Enter job order and client information into the database and handle admin duties pertaining to the job.
7. Find the right candidates.
8. Follow up with client to confirm or get more info.
9. Make follow up calls to client to confirm arrival time, performance etc.
10. Plan a trip to client or send a thank you letter.

Staff Filing System

Our staffing agency will maintain files containing the following types of documents for all our employment candidates:
1. Driver's license copy
2. Social security card copy
3. Employment application
4. Resume
5. W-2 forms
6. Performance Appraisal
7. Employment Contract
8. Screening and Placement Tests
9. Background Check Reports
10. Proof of CPR Certification
11. Copy of State License
12. TB Skin Test Results
13. Annual Training Status Matrix
14. Updated Skills Checklist

We will conduct a quality improvement plan, which consists of an ongoing process of improvement activities and includes periodic samplings of activities not initiated solely in response to an identified problem. Our plan will be evaluated annually and revised as necessary. Our client satisfaction survey goal is a ___ (98.0)% satisfaction rating.

Operations include the business aspects of running our business, such as conducting quality assessment and improvement activities, auditing functions, cost-management analysis, and customer service. We plan to write and maintain an operations manual and a personnel policies handbook. The Operating Manual will be a comprehensive document outlining virtually every aspect of the business. The operating manual will include management and accounting procedures, hiring and personnel policies, and daily operations procedures, such as opening and closing the store, and how to _____. The manual will cover the following topics:

- Community Relations	- Customer Relations
- Media Relations	- Employee Relations
- Vendor Relations	- Government Relations
- Competition Relations	- Equipment Maintenance Checklist
- Environmental Concerns	- Screening Techniques
- Intra Company Procedures	- Accounting and Billing
- Banking and Credit Cards	- Financing
- Computer Procedures	- Scheduling Tips
- Quality Controls	- Safety Procedures
- Open/Close Procedures	- Security Procedures
- Software Documentation	- Skills Checklist

We will also develop a personnel manual. Its purpose is to set fair and equal guidelines in print for all to abide. It's the playbook detailing specific policies, as well as enforcement, thereby preventing any misinterpretation, miscommunication or ill feelings. This manual will reflect only the concerns that affect our personnel. A companion policy and procedure manual will cover everything else.

We plan to create the following business manuals:

	Manual Type	Key Elements
1.	Operations Manual	Process flowcharts
2.	Employee Manual	Benefits/Appraisals/Practices
3.	Managers Manual	Job Descriptions
4.	Customer Service Policies	Inquiry Handling Procedures

We plan to develop and install a computerized customer tracking system that will enable us to target clients who are likely to have an interest in a particular type of store promotional event.

Resources:	Nursing Staffing Software	www.NursingBizGuide.com
	Medical Staffing Software	www.microstaffer.com/

9.0   Management Summary

The Management Plan will reveal who will be responsible for the various management functions to keep the business running efficiently. It will further demonstrate how that individual has the experience and/or training to accomplish each function. It will address who will do the planning function, the organizing function, the directing function, and the controlling function.

At the present time _____ (owner name) will run all operations for _____ (company name). _____ (His/Her) background in _____ (business management?) indicates an understanding of the importance of financial control systems. There is not expected to be any shortage of qualified staff from local labor pools in the market area.

_____ (owner name) will be the owner and operations manager of _____ (company name). His/her general duties will include the following:
1.   Oversee the daily operations
2.   Ordering inventory and supplies.
3.   Develop and implementing the marketing strategy
4.   Purchasing equipment.
5.   Arranging for the routine maintenance and upkeep of the facility.
6.   Hiring, training and supervision of new recruiters.
7.   Scheduling and planning of seminars and other special events.
8.   Creating and pricing products and services.
9.   Managing the accounting/financial aspect of the business.
10.   Contract negotiation/vendor relations.

9.1 Owner Personal History

The owner has been working in the _____ industry for over ____ (#) years, gaining personal knowledge and experience in all phases of the industry. _____ (owner name) is the founder and operations manager of _____ (company name). The owner holds a degree from the University of _____ at _____ (city). He/she began his/her career as a _____ . Over the last _ (#) years, ___ (owner name) became quite proficient in a wide range of management activities and responsibilities, becoming an operations manager for ___ (former employer name) from __ to _ (dates). There he/she was able to achieve _____. For ____ years he/she has managed a business similar to _____ (company name). _____ (His/her) duties included ____. Specifically, the owner brings _____ (#) years of experience as a ____ , as well as certification as a _____ from the _____ (National _____ Association). He/she is an experienced entrepreneur with ____ years of small business accounting, finance, marketing and management experience. Education includes college course work in business administration, banking and finance, investments, and commercial credit management. The owner will draw an annual salary of $___ from the business although most of this goes to repay loans to finance business start-up costs. These loans will be paid-in-full by _____ (month) of _____ (year).

9.2   Management Team Gaps

Despite the owner's and manager's experience in the _____ (?) industry, the company will also retain the consulting services of _____ (consultant company name). This company has over _____ (#) years of experience in the _____ industry, and has successfully opened dozens of Medical staffing agencies across the country. The Consultants will be primarily used for certification approval, market research, customer satisfaction surveys and to provide additional input in the evaluation of new business opportunities. The company also expects to retain the services of a local CPA to help the owner manage cash flow. Additionally the business will make use of the following advisory board to provide support for strategic planning and human resource related issues.

The Board of Advisors will provide continuous mentoring support on business matters. Expertise gaps in legal, tax, marketing and personnel will be covered by the Board of Advisors. The owner will actively seek free business advice from SCORE, a national non-profit organization with a local office. This is a group of retired executives and business owners who donate their time to serve as business counselors to new business owners.

Advisory Resources Available to the Business Include:

	Name	Address	Phone
CPA/Accountant			
Attorney			
Insurance Broker			
Banker			
Business Consultant			
Wholesale Suppliers			
Trade Association			
Realtor			
SCORE.org			
Other			

9.2.1   Management Matrix

Note: See appendix for attached management resumes.

Name	Title	Credentials	Functions	Responsibilities

9.2.2   Outsourcing Matrix

Company Name	Functions	Responsibilities	Cost

9.2.3   Company Structure

Our company will be structured according to the following primary service offerings:
1.   The facility staffing division will recruit and staff nursing jobs, Allied Health jobs, travel nursing jobs, physicians, government, health information services and medical administration jobs, among others.
2.   Our homecare services division will place qualified health professionals in home healthcare jobs to work with families in need of home health care assistance to find qualified nurses for themselves or a loved one.
3.   Our wellness division will offer flu clinics, wellness screenings, travel immunizations, and other wellness education services nationwide.

9.3.0   Employee Requirements

1.   **Recruitment**
    Experience suggests that personal referrals are an excellent source for experienced associates We will also place newspaper ads, and use our Yellow Page Ad to indicate what types of staff we use and what types of clients we serve. We will also make effective use of our newsletter to post positions available and contact local trade schools for possible job candidates. We will target the following groups:
> - Skilled but yet-inexperienced workers looking to get a foot in the door at prestigious companies.
> - "Drifters" or those who tend to rapidly drift from job to job because they
have the opportunity to work on short-term projects and move on
without the negative repercussions.
> - Retirees seeking rewarding mental enjoyment and extra income.
> - Students looking to gain valuable experience working with a technical agency.

U.S. Boards of Nursing by State
www.medscape.com/viewarticle/482270

Possible Blog entry related to employee referrals:
If you know someone that has expressed an interest in traveling, used to travel, or travels with another company, and think they'd be a good fit for our ____ (company name) team, have them give us a call. We are offering up to a $___ (750?) referral bonus for anyone you send our way that we can put to work for at least ___ (#) weeks. Excellent pay, full benefits, paid housing, per diem and a chance to see the world are just some of the reasons to join the travel team of _____ (company name).
Resource: www.linkedin.com/jobs?viewJob=&jobId=4138630&srchIndex=3

2.   **Training and Supervision**

Training is largely accomplished through hands-on experience and by manufacturer product reps with supplemental instruction. Additional knowledge is gained through our policy and operations manuals, and attending manufacturer and trade association seminars. We will foster professional development and independence in all phases of our business. Supervision is task-oriented and the quantity is dependent on the complexity of the job assignment. Employees are called team members because they are part of Team _____ (company name). To help them succeed and confidently handle customer questions, employees will receive assistance with our internal certification program. They will also participate in our written training modules and receive regular samples to evaluate.

3.   **Salaries and Benefits**
Staff will be basically paid a salary plus commission basis on product sales. Good training and incentives, such as cash bonuses handed out monthly to everyone for reaching goals, will serve to retain good employees. An employee discount of __ percent on personal sales is offered. As business warrants, we hope to put together a benefit package that includes insurance, and paid vacations. The personnel plan also assumes a 5% annual increase in salaries.

9.4.0   Job Descriptions

Placement Counselor
The Placement Counselor combines sales and human resources in a customer service environment resulting in a rewarding career of helping clients hire a Medical Professional their practice. This position covers a number of roles directly relating to the referral process and the success of the agency. The Placement Counselor sells the service to inquiring clients, markets and refers Medical Professional candidates in permanent and temporary positions through the matching process, follows the clients and candidates throughout the referral process including advice and counsel during the employment term. The responsibility involves gathering and documenting information and disclosing information to clients. This position is a major player in a team who together keeps the business productive. A bachelor's degree is preferred or two to three years demonstrated work experience in a fast paced administrative capacity with deadline orientation.

Placement Assistant
The Placement Assistant has a number of roles relating to the different aspects of the referral process and the success of the agency. The Placement Assistant supports and assists the Placement Counselor and Executive Director as well as performs administrative and clerical tasks. Included in the daily workday are duties such as interviewing candidates, managing Medical Professional files, assisting in matching candidates with clients, filling temporary job orders and computer input. Requirements include demonstrated ability to work in a busy environment where several tasks were juggled at once and worked as part of a team in the capacity of an assistant.

Recruiter

The Recruiter combines human resources and marketing in a customer service environment resulting in a rewarding career of helping people in finding the right job in a very warm and fuzzy field of work. This position has a number of roles directly relating to the referral process and the success of the agency. The Recruiter builds a rapport with inquiring parties, markets and refers candidates to permanent and temporary positions through the matching process, follows up with candidates including advise and counsel throughout the employment term. The responsibility involves gathering and documenting information through the prescreening, interviewing, reference checking and background investigating process. This position is a major player in a team who together keeps the business productive. A bachelor's degree is preferred or two to three years demonstrated work experience in a fast paced administrative capacity with deadline orientation. A background in staffing or human resources is helpful. Our Medical Recruiters will work hard to accommodate career preferences, matching candidate skills, experience and schedule to find the long-term, short-term or travel assignments that fulfill those preferences. As a member of our dynamic Medical team, the candidate will also enjoy 24-hours a day, seven days a week access to our Recruiters for the assistance that they need to get the job done.

Recruiter Assistant
The Recruiter's Assistant has a number of roles relating to the different aspects of the placement process and the success of the agency. The Recruiter Assistant supports and assists the Recruiter and Executive Director managing Medical Professional files and recruiting efforts as well as performs administrative and clerical tasks. Included in the daily workday are duties such as interviewing candidates, reference checking, background verifications, profile building and computer input. Requirements include demonstrated ability to work in a busy environment where several tasks were juggled at once and worked as part of a team in the capacity of an assistant.

Job Description— Agency Director
This position plans, organizes, and directs the operations of the Health Care Staffing Agency. They order supplies, monitor and evaluate cost effectiveness and efficiency of operations, and prepare and balance daily reports and maintain. Incumbents provide customer service and specialized information regarding laws, policies, and procedures governing Medical Professional related issues. Incumbents utilize effective public relations to provide services to clients, respond to inquiries, handle complaints or resolve problems. This position is responsible for the efficient operations of the agency. Incumbents determine staffing needs, prepare work schedules, establish and implement work procedures and priorities, and recommend changes to policies. They supervise staff including recruiting and training employees, assigning work, preparing and conducting performance evaluations, and handling employee problem solving issues. The Director must possess proven management skills, and the ability to drive sales. Must have a passion for people development and delivering excellent customer service. Must be capable of delivering performance through their teams and drive customer service through high placement standards, availability and presentation.
Key Accountabilities:
Exceptional customer focus.

Excellent Interpersonal skills.
Effective planning and organizational skills.
Influencing and negotiation skills.
Budget management
Supportive and persuasive management style.
Tactical and strategic planning and implementation skills are a must.
Clear vision and a determination to succeed.

9.4.1   Job Description Format
Our job descriptions will adhere to the following format guidelines:

1.	Job Title	2.	Reports to:
3.	Pay Rate	4.	Job Responsibilities
5.	Travel Requirements	5.	Supervisory Responsibilities
6.	Qualifications	7.	Work Experience
8.	Required Skills	10.	Salary Range
11.	Benefits	12.	Opportunities

9.5   Personnel Plan
1.   We will develop a system for recruiting, screening and interviewing employees.
2.   Background checks will be performed as well as reference checks and drug tests.
3.   We will develop an assistant training course.
4.   We will keep track of staff scheduling.
5.   We will develop client satisfaction surveys to provide feedback and ideas.
6.   We will develop and perform semi-annual employee evaluations.
7.   We will "coach" all of our employees to improve their abilities and range of skills.
8.   We will employ temporary employees via a local staffing agency to assist with one-time special projects.
9.   Each employee will be provided an Employee Handbook, which will include detailed job descriptions and list of business policies, and be asked to sign these documents as a form of employment contract.
10. Incentives will be offered for reaching quarterly financial and enrollment goals, completing the probationary period, and passing county inspections.
11. Customer service awards will be presented to those employees who best exemplify our stated mission and exceed customer expectations.
12. We will utilize the following Recruiting Retention Techniques:

• Offer referral bonuses	Offer sign on bonuses
• Offer flexible schedules	Premium pay rates
• Guarantee pay	Travel opportunities
• Vacation/Holiday Pay	Insurance benefits
• 401K	Offer to pay for day care

13. We will use the following methods to retain our agency staff:
- The right job opportunities to get them sufficient hours.
- The funding to guarantee their paycheck will be there.
- Respect and care for them as individuals.

- Offer a wide range of benefits, including health, dental, and life insurance, 401(k) savings plans, direct deposit, bonuses and other types of incentives.

Our Employee Handbook will include the following sections:
1. Overview
2. Introduction to the Company
3. Organizational Structure
4. Employment and Hiring Policies
5. Performance Evaluation and Promotion Policies
6. Compensation Policies
7. Time Off Policies
8. Training Programs and Reimbursement Policies
9. General Rules and Policies
10. Termination Policies.

We will go to great lengths to conduct thorough background checks, competency assessments and evaluations of all our Associates, which is why the client can be completely confident all our Associates meet or exceed the highest standards and competencies in their respective fields.

Initial Competency Evaluation
____ (company name) is committed to professionalism, high standards and quality service. Our Medical professionals must meet employment and practice requirements set forth by applicable regulatory agencies.

Provide documented evidence to verify employment eligibility to work in the United States

Have a cleared employment criminal background check and drug screen

Have verification of professional and education references

Complete competency screenings for their experience and expertise

Provide health clearance in accordance with specific Federal. Local, and State regulatory guidelines

    o Hepatitis B

    Two Measles Mumps Rubella (MMR) inoculations if born after 1957: One MMR inoculation if born before 1957

    Tuberculin Skin Test (PPD) (current, within one year)

    Reliable history of Chicken Pox and Varicella titer

    Any other facility specific requirements set forth in the Statement of Work

Have a minimum of one year of recent experience within the last three years specific to the specialty area assigned

Associates are carefully screened to ensure that they are competent to perform their job, and meet specific certification or licensure requirements.

At a minimum, licensed nurses must meet the requirements as set forth by State of Boards of Nursing:

    Successfully completed curriculum requirements from an accredited school of nursing

Successfully passed the NCLEX
Possess an unrestricted and current license

During the orientation stage we will evaluate the candidate's knowledge of key competencies, such as:
Clinical/Technical proficiencies
Abuse and neglect
Blood borne pathogens and infectious diseases
Restraints
Patient confidentiality
Pain management
Patient safety
Medication administration and safety
Other pertinent information required by JCAHO, OSHA and other regulations/organizations

The final stage of competency assessment consists of the applicant's performance as it relates to the job requirements and the unit-specific job description provided by the client facility. Continuous evaluation assesses the following areas:
Communication, confidentiality, customer service
Adaptability, flexibility
Teamwork, cooperation
Reliability, attendance
Initiative, enthusiasm
Professionalism, continuing education

Continuing competency is assessed through a review of client evaluations, audits and continuing education. When appropriate, we also conduct interviews with nurse managers who work with our Medical professionals.

9.6   Staffing Plan

The following table summarizes our personnel expenditures for the first three years, with compensation costs increasing from $_____ in the first year to about $_____ in the third year, based on _____ (5?) % payroll increases each year. The payroll includes tuition reimbursement, pay increases, vacation pay, bonuses and state required certifications.

Note: Nurses working for temporary help services are usually designated as employees. Some agencies hire independent contractors. The agency, the Medical facilities, the nurse, or the contract between the nurse and the agency are not the final word on worker status for tax purposes; the IRS has the final word on worker status for tax purposes. You may be responsible for back employee taxes and penalties if the IRS determines that the nurse (worker) is employee status and not independent contractor status.

Regional Director of Client Services

Your personalized nurse staffing solution begins with your Regional Director of Client Services (RD). Your RD is responsible for the initial set-up and ongoing maintenance of the staffing agreement between your facility/health system and AMN Medical. The RD is also responsible for the executive management of our service for your Medical staffing requirements. Other job titles include:

Hospital Account Managers - These nurse staffing specialists work diligently to support and fulfill the daily staffing needs of our contracted facilities.

Quality Management Specialists - Working directly with our network of Medical professionals, Quality Management Specialists gather assignment requirements, such as vaccines, certifications and credentials, and ensure all assignment requirements are submitted prior to the Medical staffing professional's start date.

Clinical Liaisons - Our Clinical Liaisons are all registered nurses who perform initial reviews of all traveler applications. They are also responsible for any counseling or disciplinary actions relating to behavioral or clinical issues.

Billing Specialists - To help streamline your paperwork, our billing specialists manage client invoicing and the completion and quality assurance of all billing activity.

Business Development Representatives- These specialists field inquiries and provide information to help facilities get started with AMN Medical's staffing services.

Marketing Consultants - Through on-site analysis, Marketing Consultants help set timeframes and assemble the physician recruitment teams. Marketing Consultants also monitor progress during the recruiting process and act as a liaison for the client.

Recruiting Consultants - Recruiting Consultants execute the candidate sourcing strategy, conduct in-depth screenings of the candidates and spouses, arrange for the interview, act as a third-party mediator and help complete the search.

Research Consultants – These specialists obtain detailed information about physicians, including their practice preferences, community preferences and their personal and familial needs, in order to match candidates with appropriate opportunities.

Resource Development Specialists - Resource Development Specialists coordinate candidate-sourcing efforts, in conjunction with Recruiting Consultants.

Territory Sales Consultants - Territory Sales Consultants monitor progress on temporary staffing assignments and assist with quality assurance.

Recruiting Consultant - These consultants work on specialty-driven teams to assure that a pipeline of qualified providers is available to quickly fill assignments in a wide range of geographic areas.

Scheduling Consultants - Matching candidates secured by Recruiting Consultants, Scheduling Consultants foster the client and provider relationship while facilitating the presentation, confirmation and logistics of each assignment.

Logistics Coordinators - Logistics Coordinators ensure a successful match between providers and Staff Care clients is made seamlessly, minimizing the effort required by both providers and clients.

Licensing Assistants - By developing relationships with various state Medical licensing boards and by understanding each state's licensing requirements, Licensing Assistants are often able to significantly reduce licensure turnaround times.

Privileging Assistants - Experts in multiple privileging regulations and methods, Privileging Assistants reduce the time it takes to get a provider into practice.

Table: Personnel Plan

	Number of Employees	Hourly Rate	Annual Salaries		
			2017	2018	2019
Agency Director					
Assistant Director					
Division Manager					
Placement Counselor					
Placement Assistant					
Recruiter					
Recruiter Assistant					
Receptionist					
Marketing Coordinator					
Bookkeeper					
P/T Janitor					
Other					

Total People: Headcount

Total Annual Payroll

Payroll Burden (Fringe Benefits)   (+)

Total Payroll Expense   (=)

Salary Notes:

The average salary for medical receptionist professional temp staffing agency jobs is $32,000. Average medical receptionist professional temp staffing agency salaries can vary greatly due to company, location, industry, experience and benefits. The typical Hourly Rate for a Medical Receptionist in United States is $10.35 - $14.11.

The average salary for temporary nurse jobs is $46,000. Average temporary nurse salaries can vary greatly due to company, location, industry, experience and benefits.

10.0   Risk Factors

Risk management is the identification, assessment, and prioritization of risks, followed by the coordinated and economical application of resources to minimize, monitor, and control the probability and/or impact of unfortunate events or to maximize the realization of opportunities. For the most part, our risk management methods will consist of the following elements, performed, more or less, in the following order.
1.   Identify, characterize, and assess threats
2.   Assess the vulnerability of critical assets to specific threats
3.   Determine the risk (i.e. the expected consequences of specific types of attacks on specific assets)
4.   Identify ways to reduce those risks
5.   Prioritize risk reduction measures based on a strategy

Types of Risks:
_____ (company name) faces the following kinds of risks:
1.   **Financial Risks**
      Our quarterly revenues and operating results are difficult to predict and may fluctuate significantly from quarter to quarter as a result of a variety of factors. Among these factors are:
            -Changes in our own or competitors' pricing policies.
            - Recession pressures.
            - Fluctuations in expected revenues from advertisers, sponsors and
                  strategic relationships.
            - Timing of costs related to acquisitions or payments.

2.   **Legislative / Legal Landscape.**
      Our participation in the Health Care Staffing Agency arena presents unique risks:
            - Service and other related liability.
            - Federal and State regulations on licensing, privacy and insurance.

3.   **Operational Risks**
      For the past __ (#) years the owner has been dealing with computers so he is comfortable with technology and understands a wide array of software applications. However, the biggest potential problem will be equipment malfunction. To minimize the potential for problems, the owner will be taking equipment repair training from the manufacturer and will deal with basic troubleshooting and minor repairs. Beyond that, we have identified a service technician who is located close-by.

      To attract and retain client to the _____ (company name) community, we must continue to provide differentiated and quality services . This confers certain risks including the failure to:
            - Anticipate and respond to consumer preferences for partnerships and
                  service.
            - Attract, excite and retain a large audience of clients to our

community.
- Create and maintain successful strategic alliances with quality partners.
- Deliver high quality, customer service.
- Build our brand rapidly and cost-effectively.
- Compete effectively against better-established Medical Staffing agencies.

4. Human Resource Risks

The most serious human resource risk to our business, at least in the initial stages, would be my inability to operate the business due to illness or disability. The owner is currently in exceptional health and would eventually seek to replace himself on a day-to-day level by developing systems to support the growth of the business.

5. Marketing Risks

Advertising is our most expensive form of promotion and there will be a period of testing headlines and offers to find the one that works the best. The risk, of course, is that we will exhaust our advertising budget before we find an ad that works. Placing greater emphases on sunk-cost marketing, such as our storefront and on existing relationships through direct selling will minimize our initial reliance on advertising to bring in a large percentage of business in the first year.

6. Business Risks

A major risk to retail service businesses is the performance of the economy and the small business sector. Since economists are predicting this as the fastest growing sector of the economy, our risk of a downturn in the short-term is minimized. The entrance of one of the major chains into our marketplace is a risk. They offer more of the latest equipment, provide a wider array of products and services, competitive prices and 24-hour service. This situation would force us to lower our prices in the short-term until we could develop an offering of higher margin, value-added services not provided by the large chains. It does not seem likely that the relative size of our market today could support the overhead of one of those operations. Projections indicate that this will not be the case in the future and that leaves a window of opportunity for ___ (company name) to aggressively build a loyal client base. We will also not pursue big-leap, radical change misadventures, but rather strive to hit stepwise performance benchmarks, with a planned consistency over a long period of time.

To combat the usual start-up risks we will do the following:

1. Utilize our industry experience to quickly establish desired strategic relationships.
2. Pursue business outside of our immediate market area.
3. Diversify our range of product and service offerings.
4. Develop multiple distribution channels.
5. Monitor our competitor actions.
6. Stay in touch with our clients and suppliers.
7. Watch for trends which could potentially impact our business.

8. Continuously optimize and scrutinize all business processes.
9. Institute daily financial controls using Business Ratio Analysis.
10. Create pay-for-performance compensation and training programs to reduce employee turnover.

Further, to attract and retain clients the Company will need to continue to expand its market offerings, utilizing third party strategic relationships. This could lead to difficulties in the management of relationships, competition for specific services and products, and/or adverse market conditions affecting a particular partner.
The Company will take active steps to mitigate risks. In preparation of the Company's pricing, many factors will be considered. The Company will closely track the activities of all third parties, and will hold monthly review meetings to resolve issues and review and update the terms associated with strategic alliances.

Additionally, we will develop the following kinds of contingency plans:
Disaster Recovery Plan
Business Continuity Plan
Business Impact and Gap Analysis
Testing & Maintenance

The Company will utilize marketing and advertising campaigns to promote brand identity and will coordinate all expectations with internal and third party resources prior to release. This strategy should maximize customer satisfaction while minimizing potential costs associated with unplanned expenditures and quality control issues.

10.1   Business Risk Reduction Strategy

We plan to implement the following strategies to reduce our start-up business risk:
1. Implement our business plan based on go, no-go stage criteria.
2. Develop employee cross-training programs.
3. Regularly back-up all computer files/Install ant-virus software.
4. Arrange adequate insurance coverage with higher deductibles.
5. Develop a limited number of prototype samples.
6. Test market offerings to determine level of market demand and appropriate pricing strategy.
7. Thoroughly investigate and benchmark to competitor offerings.
8. Research similar franchised businesses for insights into successful prototype business/operations models.
9. Reduce operation risks and costs by flowcharting all structured systems & standardized manual processes.
10. Use market surveys to listen to customer needs and priorities.
11. Purchase used equipment to reduce capital outlays.
12. Use leasing to reduce financial risk.
13. Outsource manufacturing to job shops to reduce capital at risk.
14. Use subcontractors to limit fixed overhead salary expenses.

15. Ask manufacturers about profit sharing arrangements.
16. Pay advertisers with a percent of revenues generated.
17. Develop contingency plans for identified risks.
18. Set-up procedures to control employee theft.
19. Do criminal background checks on potential employees.
20. Take immediate action on delinquent accounts.
21. Only extend credit to established account with D&B rating
22. Get regular competitive bids from alternative suppliers.
23. Check that operating costs as a percent of rising sales are lower as a result of productivity improvements.
24. Request bulk rate pricing on fast moving supplies.
25. Don't tie up cash in slow moving inventory to qualify for bigger discounts.
26. Reduce financial risk by practicing cash flow policies.
27. Reduce hazard risk by installing safety procedures.
28. Use financial management ratios to monitor business vitals.
29. Make business decisions after brainstorming sessions.
30. Focus on the products with biggest return on investment.
31. Where possible, purchase off-the-shelf components.
32. Request manufacturer samples and assistance to build prototypes.
33. Design production facilities to be flexible and easy to change.
34. Develop a network of suppliers with outsourcing capabilities.
35. Analyze and shorten every cycle time, including product development.
36. Develop multiple sources for every important input.
37. Treat the business plan as a living document and update it frequently.
38. Conduct a SWOT analysis and use determined strengths to pursue opportunities.
39. Conduct regular customer satisfaction surveys to evaluate performance.

10.2   Reduce Customer Perceived Risk Tactics

We will utilize the following tactics to help reduce the new customer's perceived risk of starting to do business with our company.

Status

1. Publish a page of testimonials. _____
2. Secure Opinion Leader written endorsements. _____
3. Offer an Unconditional Satisfaction Money Back Guarantee. _____
4. Long-term Performance Guarantee (Financial Risk). _____
5. Guaranteed Buy Back (Obsolete time risk) _____
6. Offer free trials and samples. _____
7. Brand Image (consistent marketing image and performance) _____
8. Patents/Trademarks/Copyrights _____
9. Publish case studies _____
10. Share your expertise (Articles, Seminars, etc.) _____
11. Get recognized Certification _____
12. Conduct responsive customer service _____

13. Accept Installment Payments _____
14. Display product materials composition or ingredients. _____
15. Publish product test results. _____
16. Publish sales record milestones. _____
17. Foster word-of-mouth by offering an unexpected extra. _____
18. Distribute factual, pre-purchase information. _____
19. Reduce consumer search costs with online directories. _____
20. Reduce customer transaction costs. _____
21. Facilitate in-depth comparisons to alternative services. _____
22. Make available prior customer ratings and comments. _____
23. Provide customized info based on prior transactions. _____
24. Become a Better Business Bureau member. _____
25. Publish overall customer satisfaction survey results. _____
26. Offer plan options that match niche segment needs. _____
27. Require client sign-off before proceeding to next phase. _____
28. Document procedures for dispute resolution. _____
29. Offer the equivalent of open source code. _____
30. Stress your compatibility features (avoid lock-in fear). _____
31. Create detailed checklists & flowcharts to show processes _____
32. Publish a list of frequently asked questions/answers. _____
33. Create a community that enables clients to connect with
    each other and share common interests. _____
34. Inform clients as to your stay-in-touch methods. _____
35. Conduct and handover a detailed needs analysis worksheet. _____
36. Offer to pay all return shipping charges and/or refund all
    original shipping and handling fees. _____
37. Describe your product testing procedures prior to shipping. _____
38. Highlight your competitive advantages in all marketing materials. _____

11.0   Financial Plan

The over-all financial plan for growth allows for use of the significant cash flow generated by operations. We are basing projected sales on the market research, industry analysis and competitive environment. ___ (company name) expects a profit margin of over __ % starting with year one. By year two, that number should slowly increase as the law of diminishing costs takes hold, and the day-to-day activities of the business become less expensive. Sales are expected to grow at __% per year, and level off by year _____. Our financial statements will show consistent growth in earnings, which provides notice of the durability of our company's competitive advantage.

The initial investment in _____ (company name) will be provided by _____ (owner name) in the amount of $ _____. The owner will also seek a ___ (#) year bank loan in the amount of $ _____ to provide the remainder of the required initial funding. The funds will be used to renovate the space and to cover initial operating expenses. The owner financing will become a return on equity, paid in the form of dividends to the owner. We expect to finance steady growth through cash flow. The owners do not intend to take any profits out of the business until the long-term debt has been satisfied.

Our financial plan includes:
     Moderate growth rate with a steady cash flow.
     Investing residual profits into company expansion.
     Company expansion will be an option if sales projections are met.
     Marketing costs will remain below ___ (5?) % of sales.
     Repayment of our loan calculated at a high A.P.R. of ___ (10?) percent and at a
            5-year-payback on our $_____ loan.

11.1   Important Assumptions

Since this is a start-up operation, a steady increase in sales is forecast over three years, as consumer awareness and regular repeat business grows with a strong and consistent increase in the local population, from an initial ___(#) residents to about __ (#) residents upon completion. A solid business plan and the management skills and experience of the managing partners should be sufficient to orchestrate the necessary growth to make this a successful launch with steady increases in sales over the first three years.

Operating expenses are based on an assessment of operational needs for a agency of this size. Observations of ____ (city) Health Care Staffing Agency staffing, direct experience at _____ Medical agencies, and interviews with agency owners and suppliers are the basis for these projections. Rent is based on negotiated lease agreement with the landlord. Other estimates are based on experience in operating a _____ (#) square foot _____ (city) office space, and on vendor quotes and estimates. Collection days should remain fairly short, given the substantial cash revenues, and standard credit card collection periods.

Financial Plan Assumptions

1. All operating costs are based on the management's research of similar operating companies.
2. Automated informational systems will reduce the staff requirements.
3. Developmental start-up costs are amortized over a five-year period.
4. Home office or other apartment expenses are not included.
5. Overhead and operations costs are calculated on an annual basis.
6. The founders' salary is based on a fixed monthly salary expense basis.
7. All fixed and variable labor costs are scheduled to rise annually at __ (5?) percent.
8. All revenues are figured to rise annually at ___ (10?) percent.
9. Administrative and office expenses rise at an annual rate of 2.5 percent.
10. Operating costs increase at ___ (5) percent annually.
11. Loan amount interest rate at ____(10) percent.

Other Assumptions:

1. The economy will grow at a steady slow pace, without another major recession.
2. There will be no major changes in the industry, other than those discussed in the trends section of this document.
3. The State will not enact 'impact' legislation on our industry.
4. Sales are estimated at minimum to average values, while expenses are estimated at above average to maximum values..
5. Staffing and payroll expansions will be driven by increased sales.
6. Materials expenses will not increase dramatically over the next several years, but will grow at a rate that matches increasing consumption.
7. We assume access to equity capital and financing sufficient to maintain our financial plan as shown in the tables.
8. The amount of the financing needed from the bank will be approximately $_____ and this will be repaid over the next 10 years at $_____ per month.
9. We assume that the area will continue to grow at present rate of __ % per year.
10. Interest rates and tax rates are based on conservative assumptions.
11. The Health Care Staffing Agency will have an annual revenue growth rate of ___(15)% per year.

Revenue Assumptions:

	Year	Sales/Month	Growth Rate
1.			
2.			
3.			

Assumptions	FY2017	FY2018	FY2019
Short-term Interest Rate %	10.00%	10.00%	10.00%
Long-term Interest Rate %	10.00%	10.00%	10.00%

Payment Days Estimator	30	30	30
Collection Days Estimator	45	45	45
Tax Rate %	25.00%	25.00%	25.00%
Expenses in Cash %	10.00%	10.00%	10.00%
Sales on Credit %	15.00%	15.00%	15.00%
Personnel Burden %	15.00%	15.00%	15.00%

Resource:
www.score.org/resources/business-plans-financial-statements-template-gallery

11.1.1　Sensitivity Analysis

This technique will be used to determine how different values of an independent variable will impact a particular dependent variable under our given set of assumptions. This technique is used within specific boundaries that will depend on one or more input variables, such as the effect that changes in loan interest rates will have on business profitability. Sensitivity analysis will be a way to predict the outcome of a decision if a situation turns out to be different compared to key predictions. The Sensitivity Analysis will enable our company to examine different scenarios on the forecasts we have made in the Profit and Loss Forecast.

We will utilize Sensitivity Analysis to accomplish the following:
Identify the key variables affecting profitability and cash-flow.
Identify the levels of these variables (worst case, best case, expected).
Project profitability and cash-flow under various combinations of these variables.
Project profitability and cash-flow breakeven under various assumptions.

SENSITIVITY ANALYSIS FOR THE FORECASTED YEAR 2017

	20% Decrease	10% Decrease	2017 Original	10% Increase	20% Increase
Revenue:					
Sales					
Variable Costs:					
Cost of Goods Sold					
Fixed Costs:					
Operating Expenses					
Net income **Before** Taxes					

The Company's revenues are not sensitive to changes in the economy. The demand for nurses and associated Medical professionals has continued to rise, and will continue to do so regardless of the state of the economy. Medical businesses are fully insulated from changes in the general economy as people will continue to require Medical care. As such, there is very little risk that the Company will have any issues with generation.

Conclusions:

_____
_____

11.2   Break-even Analysis

Break-Even Analysis will be performed to determine the point at which revenue received equals the costs associated with generating the revenue. Break-even analysis calculates what is known as a margin of safety, the amount that revenues exceed the break-even point. This is the amount that revenues can fall while still staying above the break-even point. The two main purposes of using the break-even analysis for marketing is to (1) determine the minimum number of sales that is required to avoid a loss at a designated sales price and (2) it is an exercise tool so that you can tweak the sales price to determine the minimum volume of sales you can reasonably expect to sell in order to avoid a loss.

Definition: Break-Even Is the Volume Where All Fixed Expenses Are Covered.

Three important definitions used in break-even analysis are:
·   **Variable Costs** (Expenses) are costs that change directly in proportion to changes in activity (volume), such as raw materials, labor and packaging.

·   **Fixed Costs** (Expenses) are costs that remain constant (fixed) for a given time period despite wide fluctuations in activity (volume), such as rent, loan payments, insurance, payroll and utilities.

·   **Unit Contribution Margin** is the difference between your product's unit selling price and its unit variable cost.
Unit Contribution Margin = Unit Sales Price - Unit Variable Cost

For the purposes of this breakeven analysis, the assumed fixed operating costs will be approximately $ _____ per month, as shown in the following table.

Averaged Monthly Fixed Costs:		**Variable Costs:**	
Payroll	_____	Cost of Inventory Sold	_____
Rent	_____	Labor	_____
Insurance	_____	Supplies	_____
Utilities	_____	Direct Costs per Patient	_____
Security.	_____	Other	_____
Legal/Technical Help	_____		
Other	_____		
Total:	_____	Total	_____

A break-even analysis table has been completed on the basis of average costs/prices. With monthly fixed costs averaging $_____ , $_____ in average sales and $_____ in average variable costs, we need approximately $_____ in sales per month to break-even.

Based on our assumed ____ % variable cost, we estimate our breakeven sales volume at around $ ____ per month. We expect to reach that sales volume by our _____ month of operations. Our break-even analysis is shown in further detail in the following table.

Breakeven Formulas:

Break Even Units = Total Fixed Costs / (Unit Selling Price - Variable Unit Cost)

$\cdot$ _____ = _____ / (_____ - _____)
$\cdot$

·BE Dollars = (Total Fixed Costs / (Unit Price – Variable Unit Costs))/ Unit Price

_____ = (_____ / (_____ - _____)) / _____

·BE Sales = Annual Fixed Costs / (1- Unit Variable costs / Unit Sales Price)

_____ = _____ / (1 - _____ / _____)

Table: Break-even Analysis

Monthly Units Break-even	_____
Monthly Revenue Break-even	$ _____
Assumptions:	
Average Per-Unit Revenue	$ _____
Average Per-Unit Variable Cost	$ _____
Estimated monthly Fixed Cost	$ _____

Ways to Improve Breakeven Point:

1. Reduce Fixed Costs via Cost Controls
2. Raise unit sales prices.
3. Lower Variable Costs by improving employee productivity or getting lower competitive bids from suppliers.
4. Broaden product/service line to generate multiple revenue streams.

11.3   Projected Profit and Loss

Pro forma income statements are an important tool for planning our future business operations. If the projections predict a downturn in profitability, we can make operational changes such as increasing prices or decreasing costs before these projections become reality.

Our monthly profit for the first year varies significantly, as we aggressively seek improvements and begin to implement our marketing plan. However, after the first ___ months, profitability should be established.

We predict advertising costs will go down in the next three years as word-of-mouth about our agency gets out to the public and we are able to find what has worked well for us and concentrate on those advertising methods, and corporate affiliations generate sales without the need for extra advertising.

Our net profit/sales ratio will be low the first year. We expect this ratio to rise at least _____ (15?) percent the second year. Normally, a startup concern will operate with negative profits through the first two years. We will avoid that kind of operating loss on our second year by knowing our competitors and having a full understanding of our target markets.

Our projected profit and loss is indicated in the following table. From our research of the Medical staffing industry, our annual projections are quite realistic and conservative, and we prefer this approach so that we can ensure an adequate cash flow.

Key P & L Formulas:

Gross Profit Margin = Total Sales Revenue - Cost of Goods Sold

Gross Margin % = (Total Sales Revenue - Cost of Goods Sold) / Total Sales Revenue
This number represents the proportion of each dollar of revenue that the company retains as gross profit.

EBITDA =Revenue - Expenses (exclude interest, taxes, depreciation & amortization)

PBIT = Profit (Earnings) Before Interest and Taxes = EBIT
A profitability measure that looks at a company's profits before the company has to pay corporate income tax and interest expenses. This measure deducts all operating expenses from revenue, but it leaves out the payment of interest and tax. Also referred to as "earnings before interest and tax ".

Net Profit = Total Sales Revenues - Total Expenses

Pro Forma Profit and Loss

	Formula	2017	2018	2019
Gross Revenue:				
Temp Contract Fees				
Percentage Commissions				
Hourly Recruiting Fees				
Permanent Placement Fees				
Tutoring Services				
Consulting/Seminars				
Total Revenue	**A**			
Cost of Sales				
Cost of Goods Sold				
Other				
Total Costs of Sales	**D**			
Gross Margin	A−D=E			
Gross Margin %	E / A			
Operating Expenses:				
Payroll				
Payroll Taxes				
Sales & Marketing				
Conventions/Trade Shows				
Depreciation				
License/Permit Fees				
Dues and Subscriptions				
Rent				
Utilities				
Deposits				
Repairs and Maintenance				
Janitorial Supplies				
Office Supplies				
Classroom Supplies				
Leased Equipment				
Buildout Costs				
Insurance				
Location Rental				
Van Expenses				
Contracted Therapists				
Professional Development				
Resource Library				
Merchant Fees				
Bad Debts				
Miscellaneous				

Total Operating Expenses   F   _____

Profit Before Int. & Taxes   E - F = G   _____

Interest Expenses   H   _____
Taxes Incurred   I   _____

Net Profit   **G - H - I = J**   _____

Net Profit / Sales   **J / A = K**   _____

11.4 Projected Cash Flow

The Cash Flow Statement shows how the company is paying for its operations and future growth, by detailing the "flow" of cash between the company and the outside world. Positive numbers represent cash flowing in, negative numbers represent cash flowing out. We are positioning ourselves in the market as a medium-risk concern with steady cash flows. Accounts payable is paid at the end of each month while sales are in cash and short-term credit card collectibles. Cash balances will be used to reduce outstanding line of credit balances, or will be invested in a low-risk liquid money market fund to decrease the opportunity cost of cash held. Surplus cash balances during the critical first year of operations will function as protection against unforeseen changes in the timing of disbursements required to fund operations.

The first year's monthly cash flows are will vary significantly, but we do expect a solid cash balance from day one. We expect that the majority of our sales will be done in cash or by credit card and that will be good for our cash flow position. Additionally, we will stock only slightly more than one month's inventory at any time. Consequently, we do not anticipate any problems with cash flow, once we have obtained sufficient start-up funds.

A __ year commercial loan in the amount of $_____, sought by the owner will be used to cover our working capital requirement. Our projected cash flow is summarized in the following table, and is expected to meet our needs. In the following years, excess cash will be used to finance our growth plans.

Cash Flow Management:
We will use the following practices to improve our cash flow position:
1. Perform credit checks and become more selective when granting credit.
2. Seek deposits or multiple stage payments.
3. Reduce the amount/time of credit given to clients.
4. Reduce direct and indirect costs and overhead expenses.
5. Use the 80/20 rule to manage inventories, receivables and payables.
6. Invoice as soon as the project has been completed.
7. Generate regular reports on receivable ratios and aging.
8. Establish and adhere to sound credit practices.
9. Use more pro-active collection techniques.
10. Add late payment fees where possible.
11. Increase the credit taken from suppliers.
12. Negotiate purchase prices and extended credit terms from vendors.
13. Use some barter arrangements to acquire goods and service.
14. Use leasing to gain access to the use of productive assets.
15. Covert debt into equity.
16. Regularly update cash flow forecasts.
17. Defer projects which cannot achieve acceptable cash paybacks.
18. Require a 50% deposit upon the signing of the contract and the balance in full, due five days before the event.
19. Speed-up the completion of projects to get paid faster.

20.   Ask for extended credit terms from major suppliers.
21.   Put ideal bank balances into interest-bearing (sweep) accounts.
22.   Charge interest on client installment payments.
23.   Check the accuracy of invoices to avoid unnecessary rework delays.
24.   Include stop-work clauses in contracts to address delinquent payments.

Cash Flow Formulas:

Net Cash Flow = Incoming Cash Receipts - Outgoing Cash Payments
Equivalently, net profit plus amounts charged off for depreciation, depletion, and amortization. (also called cash flow).

Cash Balance = Opening Cash Balance + Net Cash Flow
We are positioning ourselves in the market as a medium risk concern with steady cash flows. Accounts payable is paid at the end of each month, while sales are in cash, giving our company an excellent cash structure.

Pro Forma Cash Flow

	Formula	2017	2018	2019
Cash Received				
Cash from Operations				
Cash Sales	A			
Cash from Receivables	B			
Subtotal Cash from Operations	A + B = C			
Additional Cash Received				
Non Operating (Other) Income				
Sales Tax, VAT, HST/GST Received				
New Current Borrowing				
New Other Liabilities (interest fee)				
New Long-term Liabilities				
Sales of Other Current Assets				
Sales of Long-term Assets				
New Investment Received				
Total Additional Cash Received	D			
Subtotal Cash Received	C + D = E			
Expenditures				
Expenditures from Operations				
Cash Spending	F			
Payment of Accounts Payable	G			
Subtotal Spent on Operations	F+G = H			
Additional Cash Spent				
Non Operating (Other) Expenses				
Sales Tax, VAT, HST/GST Paid Out				
Principal Repayment Current Borrowing				
Other Liabilities Principal Repayment				
Long-term Liabilities Principal Repayment				
Purchase Other Current Assets				
Dividends				
Total Additional Cash Spent	I			
Subtotal Cash Spent	H + I = J			
Net Cash Flow	**E - J = K**			
Cash Balance				

11.5   Projected Balance Sheet

Pro forma Balance Sheets are used to project how the business will be managing its assets in the future. As a pure start-up business, the opening balance sheet may contain no values.

As the business grows, our investment in inventory increases. This reflects sales volume increases and the commensurate ability to secure favorable volume discount terms with our distributors.

The projected accounts receivable position is relatively low and steady due to the nature of the business, in which up to 50% of our sales are cash, and the balance are consumer credit card purchases. No other consumer credit terms are envisioned or necessary for the operation of this business.

Capital assets of $_____ are comprised of a quoted $_____ for the build-out of the store (depreciating straight line over the 15 year term of the lease), $_____ for start-up costs (amortized over five years), and $_____ for the landlord's security deposit (about eight months rent).

Long-term liabilities are projected to decrease steadily, reflecting re-payment of the original seven year term loan required to finance the business. It is important to note that part of the retained earnings may become a distribution of capital to the owners, while the balance would be reinvested in the business to replenish depreciated assets and to support further growth.

Note: The projected balance sheets must link back into the projected income statements and cash flow projections.

_____ (company name) does not project any real trouble meeting its debt obligations, provided the revenue predictions are met. We are very confident that we will meet or exceed all of our objectives in the Business Plan and produce a slow but steady increase in net worth.

All of our tables will be updated monthly to reflect past performance and future assumptions. Future assumptions will not be based on past performance but rather on economic cycle activity, regional industry strength, and future cash flow possibilities. We expect a solid growth in net worth by the year _____.

The Balance Sheet table for fiscal years 2017, 2018, and 2019 follows. It shows managed but sufficient growth of net worth, and a sufficiently healthy financial position.

Excel Resource:
www.unioncity.org/ED/Finance%20Tools/Projected%20Balance%20Sheet.xls

Key Formulas:

Paid-in Capital = Capital contributed to the corporation by investors on top of the par value of the capital stock.

Retained Earnings = The portion of net income which is retained by the corporation and used to grow its net worth, rather than distributed to the owners as dividends.

Retained Earnings = After-tax net earnings - (Dividends + Stock Buybacks)

Earnings = Revenues - (Cost of Sales + Operating Expenses + Taxes)

Net Worth = Total Assets - Total Liabilities
    Also known as 'Owner's Equity'.

Pro Forma Balance Sheet

	Formulas	2017	2018	2019
Assets				
Current Assets				
Cash				
Accounts Receivable				
Inventory				
Other Current Assets				
Total Current Assets	A			
Long-term Assets				
Long-term Assets	B			
Accumulated Depreciation	C			
Total Long-term Assets	B - C = D			
Total Assets	**A + D = E**			
Liabilities and Capital				
Current Liabilities				
Accounts Payable				
Current Borrowing				
Other Current Liabilities				
Subtotal Current Liabilities	**F**			
Long-term Liabilities				
Notes Payable				
Other Long-term Liabilities				
Subtotal Long-term Liabilities	**G**			
Total Liabilities	**F + G = H**			
Capital				
Paid-in Capital	I			
Retained Earnings	J			
Earnings	K			
Total Capital	I - J + K = L			
Total Liabilities and Capital	**H + L = M**			
Net Worth	**E - H = N**			

11.6   Business Ratios

Our comparisons to the SIC Industry profile are very favorable and we expect to maintain healthy ratios for profitability , risk and return. Use Business Ratio Formulas provided to assist in calculations.

Key Business Ratio Formulas:

EBIT = Earnings Before Interest and Taxes
EBITA = Earnings Before Interest, Taxes & Amortization. (Operating Profit Margin)

Sales Growth Rate =((Current Year Sales - Last Year Sales)/(Last Year Sales)) x 100
Ex: Percent of Sales = (Advertising Expense / Sales) x 100

Net Worth = Total Assets - Total Liabilities

Acid Test Ratio = Liquid Assets / Current Liabilities
Measures how much money business has immediately available. A ratio of 2:1 is good.

Net Profit Margin = Net Profit / Net Revenues
The higher the net profit margin is, the more effective the company is at converting revenue into actual profit.

Return on Equity (ROE) = Net Income / Shareholder's Equity
The ROE is useful for comparing the profitability of a company to that of other firms in the same industry. Also known as "return on net worth" (RONW).

Debt to Shareholder's Equity = Total Liabilities / Shareholder's Equity
A ratio below 0.80 indicates there is a good chance the company has a durable competitive advantage, with the exception of financial institutions, which are highly leveraged institutions.

Current Ratio = Current Assets / Current Liabilities
The higher the current ratio, the more capable the company is of paying its obligations. A ratio under 1 suggests that the company would be unable to pay off its obligations if they came due at that point.

Quick Ratio = Current Assets - Inventories / Current Liabilities
The quick ratio is more conservative than the current ratio, because it excludes inventory from current assets.

Pre-Tax Return on Net Worth = Pre-Tax Income / Net Worth
Indicates stockholders' earnings before taxes for each dollar of investment.

Pre-Tax Return on Assets = (EBIT / Assets) x 100
Indicates much profit the firm is generating from the use of its assets.

Accounts Receivable Turnover = Net Credit Sales / Average Accounts Receivable
A low ratio implies the company should re-assess its credit policies in order to ensure the timely collection of imparted credit that is not earning interest for the firm.

Net Working Capital = Current Assets - Current Liabilities
Positive working capital means that the company is able to pay off its short-term liabilities. Negative working capital means that a company currently is unable to meet its short-term liabilities with its current assets (cash, accounts receivable and inventory).

Interest Coverage Ratio = Earnings Before Interest & Taxes /Total Interest Expense
The lower the ratio, the more the company is burdened by debt expense. When a company's interest coverage ratio is 1.5 or lower, its ability to meet interest expenses may be questionable. An interest coverage ratio below 1 indicates the company is not generating sufficient revenues to satisfy interest expenses.

Collection Days = Accounts Receivables / (Revenues/365)
A high ratio indicates that the company is having problems getting paid for services.

Accounts Payable Turnover = Total Supplier Purchases/Average Accounts Payable
If the turnover ratio is falling from one period to another, this is a sign that the company is taking longer to pay off its suppliers than previously. The opposite is true when the turnover ratio is increasing, which means the firm is paying of suppliers at a faster rate.

Payment Days = (Accounts Payable Balance x 360) / (No. of Accounts Payable x 12)
The average number of days between receiving an invoice and paying it off.

Total Asset Turnover = Revenue / Assets
Asset turnover measures a firm's efficiency at using its assets in generating sales or revenue - the higher the number the better.

Sales / Net Worth = Total Sales / Net Worth

Dividend Payout = Dividends / Net Profit

Assets to Sales = Assets / Sales

Current Debt / Totals Assets = Current Liabilities / Total Assets

Current Liabilities to Liabilities = Current Liabilities / Total Liabilities

Business Ratio Analysis

	2017	2018	2019
Sales Growth			

Percent of Total Assets

Accounts Receivable			
Inventory			
Other Current Assets			
Total Current Assets			
Long-term Assets			
Total Assets			
Current Liabilities			
Long-term Liabilities			
Total Liabilities			
Net Worth			

Percent of Sales

Sales			
Gross Margin			
Selling G& A Expenses			
Advertising Expenses			
Profit Before Interest & Taxes			

Main Ratios

Current			
Quick			
Total Debt to Total Assets			
Pre-tax Return on Net Worth			
Pre-tax Return on Assets			

Additional Ratios

Net Profit Margin			
Return on Equity			

Activity Ratios

Accounts Receivable Turnover			
Collection Days			
Inventory Turnover			
Accounts Payable Turnover			
Payment Days			
Total Asset Turnover			
Inventory Productivity			
Sales per sq/ft.			
Gross Margin Return on Inventory (GMROI)			

Debt Ratios
Debt to Net Worth   _____
Current Liabilities to Liabilities   _____

Liquidity Ratios
Net Working Capital   _____
Interest Coverage   _____

Additional Ratios
Assets to Sales   _____
Current Debt / Total Assets   _____
Acid Test   _____
Sales / Net Worth   _____
Dividend Payout   _____

Business Vitality Profile
Sales per Employee   _____
Survival Rate   _____

12.0   Summary

_____ (company name) will be successful. This business plan has documented that the establishment of _____ (company name) is feasible. All of the critical factors, such as industry trends, marketing analysis, competitive analysis, management expertise and financial analysis support this conclusion.

Project Description: (Give a brief summary of the product, service or program.)
_____

Description of Favorable Industry and Market Conditions.
_____

Summary of Earnings Projections and Potential Return to Investors:
_____

Summary of Capital Requirements:
_____

Security for Investors & Loaning Institutions:
_____

Summary of expected benefits for people in the community beyond the immediate business concern:
_____

Means of Financing:
A. Loan Requirements: $_____
B. Owner's Contribution: $ $_____
C. Other Sources of Income: $_____
Total Funds Available: $_____

13.0   Potential Exit Scenarios

Two potential exit strategies exist for the investor:
1.   **Initial Public Offering. (IPO)**
      We seek to go public within ___ (#) years of operations. The funds used will both help create liquidity for investors as well as allow for additional capital to develop our _____ (international/national?) roll out strategy.
2.   **Acquisition Merger with Private or Public Company.**
      Our most desirable option for exit is a merger or buyout by a large corporation. We believe with substantial cash flows and a loyal customer base our company will be attractive to potential corporate investors within five years. Real value has been created through the novel combination of staffing services as well as partnering with key referral groups. The value of this company will far exceed the amount of money invested into the start-up. By positioning ourselves in the market, as a special needs ___ (RN) staffing service, we will gain the interest of hospitals, physicians, not to mention larger staffing agencies. Either we will run the business to generate positive cash flow or our firm would be acquired by another firm for its value chain and client base.

APPENDIX

Purpose: Supporting documents used to enhance your business proposal.

Tax returns of principals for the last three years, if the plan is for new business

A personal financial statement, which should include life insurance and endowment policies, if applicable

A copy of the proposed lease or purchase agreement for building space, or zoning information for in-home businesses, with layouts, maps, and blueprints

A copy of licenses and other legal documents including partnership, association, or shareholders' agreements and copyrights, trademarks, and patents applications

A copy of résumés of all principals in a consistent format, if possible

Copies of letters of intent from suppliers, contracts, orders, and miscellaneous.

In the case of a franchised business, a copy of the franchise contract and all supporting documents provided by the franchisor

Newspaper clippings that support the business or the owner, including something about you, your achievements, business idea, or region

Promotional literature for your company or your competitors

Product/Service Brochures of your company or competitors

Photographs of your product. equipment, facilities, etc.

Market research to support the marketing section of the plan

Trade and industry publications when they support your intentions

Quotations or pro-forma invoices for capital items to be purchased, including a list of fixed assets, company vehicles, and proposed renovations

References/Letters of Recommendation

All insurance policies in place, both business and personal

Operation Schedules

Organizational Charts

Job Descriptions

Additional Financial Projections by Month

Customer Needs Analysis Worksheet

Sample Sales Letters

Copies of Software Management Reports

Copies of Standard Business Forms

Equipment List

Personal Survival Budget

Helpful Resources:

Associations:

American Staffing Association   www.americanstaffing.net/   www.staffingtoday.net
Promotes the interests of the industry through legal and legislative advocacy, public relations, education, and the establishment of high standards of ethical conduct. ASA was founded in 1966 to ensure the quality of temporary help services and to promote flexible employment opportunities.

National Association of Personnel Services   www.recruitinglife.com/
The National Association of Personnel Services has been the staffing industry educator since 1961 and enjoys its reputation as the oldest industry association. They offer a certification program, continuing education initiatives, eLearning and an annual conference.

American Academy of Ambulatory Care Nursing
American Association of Critical-Care Nurses
American Association of Nurse Anesthetists
American Holistic Nurses Association
American Psychiatric Nurses Association
American Society of PeriAnesthesia Nurses (ASPAN)
Association of periOperative Registered Nurses
Association of Rehabilitation Nurses
Association of Women's Health, Obstetric & Neonatal Nurses
Emergency Nurses Association
Intravenous Nurses Society
National Association of Orthopaedic Nurses
National Association of School Nurses, Inc.
Oncology Nursing Society
Society of Otorhinolaryngology and Head-Neck Nurses

Healthcare Publications, Journals and News

AHA News - bi-weekly from American Hospital Association
American Journal of Managed Care / AJMC - clinical, economic, policy, finance & delivery
American Journal of Maternal Child Nursing / MCN - perinatal, neonatal, midwifery, & pediatric specialties
American Journal of Nursing / AJN - award-winning, peer-reviewed, monthly journal
American Medical News / AMNews - news effecting medical practice, AMA
Anesthesia & Pain Management Coding Alert - Coding Institute, expert coding advice
Applied Clinical Trials - practical hands-on information
Business Insurance - for those who purchase insurance
Cardiology Coding Alert - Coding Institute, expert coding & compliance advice
CIN / Computers, Informatics, Nursing - dedicated to computers in nursing practice

Clinical Examples in Radiology - guide to CPT coding & billing, AMA
CodeManager - software, data, quarterly updates from AMA
CPT Changes - companion to CPT Assistant
Critical Care Nurse - cardiac care, pharmacology, nutrition, pulmonary care, neurology
ED Coding Alert - Coding Institute, expert coding advice
eHealthcare Strategies & Trends - internet strategies for healthcare
Family Practice Coding Alert - Coding Institute, expert compliance & coding advice
Gastroenterology Coding Alert - Coding Institute, expert coding & compliance tools
General Surgery Coding Alert - Coding Institute, compliance & coding advice
Group Practice Journal - AMGA, American Medical Group Association
Healthcare Design - medical building & facilities design
Health Care Management Review - by leading health care executives, peer-reviewed
Health Care Manager - for professionals in managerial or supervisory roles
Healthcare Marketing Report - HMR Publications Group
Health Facilities Management - from AHA, ASHE & ASHES, facility management
Health Information Compliance Alert - monthly guide, HIPAA mandates, compliance
HealthLeaders - coverage of industry problems, issues, trends
Health Management Technology - for CIOs, IT Managers and other medical executives
Home Care Week - reimbursement, industry trends, fraud & abuse, contracting
Home Health ICD-9 Alert - monthly newsletter
Hospitals & Health Networks / H&HN - from American Hospital Association
Internal Medicine Coding Alert - Coding Institute, expert compliance & reimbursement advice
JONA's Healthcare Law Ethics & Regulation - nursing care management
Journal for Nurses in Staff Development - issues & innovations impacting staff development
Journal of Ambulatory Care Management / JACM - issues in ambulatory care
Journal of Nursing Administration / JONA - geared to top-level nurse executives
Journal of Nursing Care Quality - quality principles & concepts in practice
Journal of Public Health Management & Practice - design, implementation, health programs
Lippincott's Case Management - managing the process of patient care
Long-Term Care Report - issues shaping the long-term industry
Long-Term Care Survey Alert - The Joint Commission & state survey guidance
Managed Care Report - regulatory updates, business strategies, litigation, etc.
Managed Healthcare Executive - insight & analysis, apply industry trends to operating strategies
Marketing Health Services / MHS - from American Marketing Association, healthcare strategies
Maternal Child Nursing / MCN - perinatal, neonatal, midwifery, & pediatric specialties
Medical Marketing & Media / MM&M - articles on marketing & promotion
Medical Office Billing & Collections Alert - Coding Institute, optimizing billing, collections, medical practices
Medicare Part B Insider - Coding Institute, newsletter, billing, reimbursement
Modern Healthcare - the only health care business news weekly
Neurology Coding Alert - Coding Institute, compliance advice from experts

Neurosurgery Coding Alert - Coding Institute, expert coding techniques
Nurse Educator - peer-reviewed, developments, innovations in nursing education
Nursing - comprehensive range of nursing topics
Nursing Home Law & Litigation Report - recent cases & settlements in long-term care
Nursing Management - success strategies for health care managers & leaders
Nursing Research - more depth, more detail, more of what today's nurses demand
OASIS Alert - requirements, strategies, home health billing
OB-GYN Coding Alert - Coding Institute, expert coding advice
Oncology & Hematology Coding Alert - Coding Institute, compliance guidance from experts
Ophthalmology Coding Alert - Coding Institute, expert up-to-date coding advice
Optometry Coding & Billing Alert - Coding Institute, compliance & reimbursement
Orthopedic Coding Alert - Coding Institute, tools to optimize reimbursement
Otolaryngology Coding Alert - Coding Institute, coding & compliance
Outpatient Physical Therapy Coding Alert - monthly coding guidance for PT, OT, rehab
Pain Management Coding Alert - Coding Institute, expert coding alerts
Part B Insider - Coding Institute, news, analysis, Medicare Part B, regulation, reimbursement
Pathology / Lab Coding Alert - Coding Institute, reimbursement & compliance strategies
Pediatric Coding Alert - Coding Institute, expert coding advice
Physical Medicine & Rehab Coding Alert - Coding Institute, compliance & reimbursement advice
Physician Referral & Telephone Triage Times - marketing, technology, protocols, legal issues
Podiatry Coding & Billing Alert - Coding Institute, reimbursement & compliance
Professional Case Management - managing the process of patient care
Psychiatric Times - widely read publication in behavioral health & psychiatry
Pulmonology Coding Alert - Coding Institute, reimbursement, coding, compliance
Quality Management in Health Care - peer-reviewed, quarterly
Radiology Coding Alert - Coding Institute, reimbursement & compliance
Rehab Report - mastering the business side of rehab
Strategic Health Care Marketing - marketing strategies & plans
Trustee - for governing boards of health care systems & hospitals
Urology Coding Alert - Coding Institute, reimbursement & compliance tips

SI Review Magazine
Staffing Industry SOURCEBOOK: http://www.staffingindustry.com
A Guide for Staffing Industry Executives (2009-10 Edition)

Online Publications
Many of these publications will only give access to abstracts of articles unless you purchase the full print subscription, which usually includes access to the online versions.
American Hospital Association News - online version of print publication
American Medical News - online version of print publication
British Medical Journal - full text online version of print publication
Business Journals - links to numerous city business journals

CNN - Health Page - health news, mostly for popular consumption
Harvard Business Review
Health Affairs - from Project Hope
Health Care/Hospitals News - compilation of headlines, by Yahoo
Health Facilities Management - for facilities and environmental managers
Health Services and Outcomes Research Methodology
Hospitals & Health Networks - from American Hospital Association
JAMA - Journal of the American Medical Association, online version
Journal of Health Politics, Policy & Law - by Duke Univ. Press, abstracts only
Journal of Health Services Research & Policy - Royal Society of Medicine, not full access
Journal of the National Medical Association - articles online
Journal of Public Health Policy
Materials Management in Health Care - for purchasing depts.
MEDLINE - published med info, by National Library of Medicine
Milbank Quarterly - abstracts only, health policy
MMWR - Morbidity and Mortality Weekly Report
New England Journal of Medicine - medical research papers primarily
New York Times - daily newspaper with business news
Nurse Week - magazine for nurses
The Informatics Review - journal of Assoc. of Med. Directors of Info. Systems
Wall Street Journal - daily newspaper with healthcare business news

Miscellaneous:

Vista Print Free Business Cards	www.vistaprint.com
Free Business Guides	www.smbtn.com/businessplanguides/
Open Office	http://download.openoffice.org/
US Census Bureau	www.census.gov
Federal Government	www.business.gov
US Patent & Trademark Office	www.uspto.gov
US Small Business Administration	www.sba.gov
National Association for the Self-Employed	www.nase.org
International Franchise Association	www.franchise.org
Center for Women's Business Research	www.cfwbr.org

Joint Commission Certification   **www.jointcommission.org**

Some sites for USA business:
http://sbinformation.about.com/
http://www.business.gov/
http://www.sba.gov/regions/states.html
http://freeadvice.com/
http://www.government-grants-101.com/
http://www.pueblo.gsa.gov/
http://www.smallbusinessnotes.com/sitemap.html

Advertising Plan Worksheet

Ad Campaign Title: _____
Ad Campaign Start Date: _____ End Date: _____

What are the features (what product has) and hidden benefits (what product does for consumer) of my products/services?

Who is the targeted audience?

What problems are faced by this targeted audience?

What solutions do you offer?

Who is the competition and how do they advertise?

What is your differentiation strategy?

What are your bullet point competitive advantages?

What are the objectives of this advertising campaign?

What are your general assumptions?

What positioning image do you want to project?
- ___ Exclusiveness
- ___ Speedy Service
- ___ Low Cost
- ___ Convenient
- ___ High Quality
- ___ Innovative

What is the ad headline?

What is the advertising budget for this advertising campaign?

What advertising methods will be used?
- ___ Radio
- ___ Coupons
- ___ Direct Mail
- ___ Press Release
- ___ Other
- ___ TV/Cable
- ___ Telemarketing
- ___ Magazines
- ___ Brochures
- ___ Yellow Pages
- ___ Flyers
- ___ Newspapers
- ___ Billboards

When will each advertising method start and what will it cost?

Method	Start Date	Frequency	Cost

Indicate how you will measure the cost-effectiveness of the advertising plan?
Formula: Return on Investment (ROI) = Generated Sales / Ad Costs.

Marketing Action Plan

Month: _____

Target Market: _____

Responsibilities: _____

Allocated Budget: _____

Objectives _____

Strategies _____

Implementation _____

Tactics _____

Results _____
Evaluation _____

_____
_____
_____
_____
_____
_____
_____
_____
_____
_____
_____
_____
_____
_____

Lessons Learned:

_____
_____
_____

Viral Marketing

Definition: Also known as word-of-mouth advertising.
Objective: To prompt your clients to deliver your sales message to others.
Strategy: Encourage and enable communication recipients to pass the offer or message along to others.
Benefit: Provides an excellent advertising return on investment and builds the trust factor.

Methodologies:
1. Encourage blog comments and two-way dialogue.
2. Use surveys to solicit feedback.
3. Use refer-a-friend forms or scripts.
4. Provide discount coupon or logo imprinted giveaway rewards for telling a friend.
5. Utilize pre-existing social networks.
6. Participate in message boards or forums.
7. Add a signature line with a refer-a-friend tagline to all posts and emails.
8. Enable unrestricted access.
9. Facilitate website content sharing.
10. Write articles and e-books, and encourage free reprints with byline mention.
11. Submit articles with 'about the author' box to article directories, such as www.articlecity.com.
12. Develop attention-grabbing product line extensions to stay connected.
13. Do the unexpected by offering a surprise benefit.
14. Deliver a remarkable offering that exceeds customer expectations.
15. Provoke a strong emotional response by getting involved with a cause that is important to your clients.
16. Provide referral incentives.
17. Get free samples into the hands of respected opinion leaders.
18. Educate clients, as to your product benefits and competitive advantages, to act as spokespersons for your company.

Explain Your Viral Marketing Program

Marketing on Social Networking Websites

1. Place banner ads or Pay-Per-Click ads on social networking sites.
2. Create an account on the website and add your company logo.
3. Encourage word-of-mouth exchanges by posting comments on friend's profiles.
4. Post surveys on your social networking pages to solicit feedback.
5. Create a profile that subtly and humbly tells everyone about you and your gift basket products and services.
6. Include links to your gift basket business website.
7. Make your profile keyword rich with keyword phases from your business specialty.
8. Use a soft sell approach, and focus on establishing your credibility and expertise as a gift basket marketing guru, to be trusted by prospective clients.
9. Name your social networking page exactly as your organization is named.
10. Have a strong presence in one channel rather than all of them.
11. Make sure you give visitors a strong call to action to supply their email address, so you can contact them later.
12. Include a signature line with your website contact info.
13. Blog often, but make certain that instead of selling, you are sharing your gift industry expertise.

Helpful Resources:
http://en.wikipedia.org/wiki/List_of_social_networking_websites

Examples:	Facebook.com	Myspace.com
	LinkedIn.com	Ryse.com

Explain Your Online Social Networking Strategy

_____
_____
_____
_____
_____

Integrate Marketing into Daily Operations

Objective: To seamlessly integrate marketing processes into daily, routine operations.

Strategies:
1. Develop form to ask for referrals upon new customer registration and annual renewal.
2. Present a sales presentation folder upon registration or contract sign-up with needs analysis worksheets, testimonials, new product introduction flyers, innovative application ideas, etc.
3. Develop a second sales presentation folder version for presentation upon job completion or sale, with referral program details, warranty service contract blank, and accessory suggestions.
4. Include business cards and coupons with all product deliverables.
5. Install company yard signs during job set-up.
6. Include a thank you note/comment card with all deliverables.
7. Include flyers and helpful articles in all customer correspondence, especially mailed invoices and statements.
8. Attach logo and contact info to all finished products.
9. Conduct customer satisfaction surveys while clients are waiting to be served.
10. Develop enclosed warranty card to build customer database and feed drip marketing program.
11. Provide competitor product/service comparisons that highlight your strengths.
12. Incorporate feedback cards into merchandise displays.
13. Train all employees to also be sales and customer service agents.
14. Print your Mission Statement or slogan on all forms and correspondence.
15._____
16._____

Indicate how you will incorporate marketing into daily operations.

Sales Stage	Business Processes	Opportunities to Incorporate Marketing Techniques
Pre-sale		
Transaction		
Post Sale		

Monthly Marketing Calendar

Instruction: Use to plan your monthly marketing events or activities and evaluate individual event results and marketing lessons learned for the month.

Month/Year: _____

Event/ Activity	Responsibility	Cost	Comments	Date	Results Evaluation

Monthly Evaluation of Lessons Learned:

_____
_____
_____

Form Strategic Marketing Alliances

Definition: A collaborative relationship between two or more non-competing firms with the intent of accomplishing mutually compatible and beneficial goals that would be difficult for each to accomplish alone. Also referred to as 'Collaboration Marketing'.

Note: Usually, potential alliance partners sell distinct or complementary products and/or services to the same target market audience.

Advantages: Improve marketing efficiency by achieving synergy in resource allocation with strategic partners.
Improve marketing effectiveness by creating a one-stop or wraparound shopping experience.
A way to inexpensively test the market for growth potential.

Types of Co-Ventures:
1. Informal Strategic Alliances
2. Contractual Relationships (Attorney review recommended)
3. New Business Entity (Set-up by attorney)

Informal Strategic Alliances
1. Most involve consultations regarding:
   a. Mutual Referrals
   b. Research for product improvements
   c. Promotion of products or services (affiliate programs).
   d. Creative product bundling arrangements.
2. May or may not require a written agreement.
3. May or may not require compensation.

Topics to be Covered:
1. The specific strategic goals and objectives of the alliance.
2. The performance expectations of the parties..
3. The scope of the alliance.
4. The period of performance.
5. Termination and renewal procedures.
6. Strategic marketing plan to promote the alliance.
7. Dispute resolution procedures.
8. Performance tracking methods.
9. Periodic evaluation of reciprocal benefits realized.
10. Website pages/links to promote alliance partners.

Example: The mutual referral relationship between a sports bar and a fitness club or physical fitness trainer.

Strategic Marketing Alliance Worksheet

Methodology:
1. Identify the assets and capabilities you can provide to the alliance.
2. Identify the assets and capabilities that the proposed partner will bring to the alliance.
3. Determine the benefits you are seeking from the alliance.
4. Determine the gaps in your offerings that the alliance partner can fill.
5. List any conflicting relationships with other businesses and benefits received.
6. Research the potential alliance for strategic fit and other opportunities.
7. List the ways in which your clients will benefit from this alliance.
8. Assess any alliance risks.
9. Determine the ongoing actions needed to maintain the alliance.
10. Design a marketing plan to promote the alliance.
11. Develop a Mission Statement for the alliance.
12. Develop the Management Plan for the alliance.
13. Design the alliance appraisal and renewal procedures.

Potential Alliance Partner	Partner Strengths Offered	Your Offering Gaps Filled	Customer Benefits	Alliance Risks

Referral Program Tips

Objective: To formalize your referral program so that it can be easily and consistently integrated into your operating processes.

1. Define the stages in the sales process when you will ask for a referral. Ex: Registration, Renewals, Annual Drive, etc.)

2. Document your referral asking script (include objection handling responses).

3. Include a request for referrals in your customer satisfaction survey and your registration forms.

4. Stress the dependence of your business on referrals in all your marketing communications.

5. Set-up a follow-up procedure and tracking form to convert referral leads into actual clients.

6. Publish your referral incentives, awards criteria and timetable for settlement.

7. Customize your referral program to the motivational needs of a select number of potential 'Bird Dogs' or 'Big Hitters'.

8. Educate potential referral agents as to the characteristics of your ideal prospect. (Develop Ideal Prospect Profile)

9. Set-up special, mutual referral arrangements with strategic business alliance partners and track the reciprocity of efforts.

10. Join or start a local lead group.

11. Set-up 'thank-you note' templates to facilitate your expression of gratitude.

12. Use logo imprinted giveaways, such as T-sheets, as referral thank you expressions.

Seminar Outline Worksheet

Objective: To establish your expertise on the subject matter, and produce future possible networking contacts by offering a newsletter sign-up and/or business card exchange.

Warning: Make seminar information rich and not a sales presentation.

1. Start with Attention-Grabbing Headline
   Ex: Hard-hitting Quotation, Thought Provoking Question, Startling Fact
   _____

2. Introduce Yourself and Establish Your Credentials
   _____

3. Present Seminar Overview
   _____

4. Discuss Attendee Participation Guidelines
   _____

5. Solicit a sampling of attendee interests, backgrounds and concerns.
   _____

6. Establish Learning Objectives
   _____

7. Preview the Bulleted Topics To be Covered
   _____
   _____

8. Share a Relevant Success Story (Case Study).
   _____

9. Use analogies and comparisons to create reference points.
   _____

10. Use statistics to support your position.
    _____
    _____

11. Conclusion: - Summarize Benefits for Attendees / Appeal to Action
    _____
    _____
    _____

12. Hold Question and Answer Session

13. Final Thoughts
        - Appreciation for Help Received
        - Indicate after-seminar availability

14. Handout A Remembrance
        - Business Cards   - Glossary of Terms
        - Seminar Outline   - Feedback Survey

YouTube Marketing Tips

Definition: An online video destination to watch and share original video clips. (World-wide approx. 55 million unique users/month)

1. Focus on something that is funny or humorous, so that people will feel compelled to share it with friends and family.
2. Make the video begin and end with a black screen and include the URL of your originating website to bring traffic to your site.
3. Put your URL at the bottom of the entire video.
4. Clearly demonstrate how your product works.
5. Create how-to videos to share your expertise and develop a following.
6. Build contests and events around special holidays and occasions.
7. Run a search on similar content by keyword, and use the info to choose the right category and tags for your video.
8. Make sure the video is real, with no gimmicks or tricks.
9. Add as many keywords as you can.
10. Make sure that your running time is five minutes or less.
11. Break longer videos into several clips, each with a clear title, so that they can be selectively viewed.
12. Encourage viewer participation and support.
13. Take advantage of YouTube tags, use adjectives to target people searching based on interests, and match your title and description to the tags.
14. Use the flexibility provided by the medium to experiment.
15. Use the 'Guru Account' sign-up designation to highlight info videos and how-to guides.
16. Create 'Playlists' to gather individual clips into niche-targeted context so viewers can easily find related content.
17. Use 'Bulletins' to broadcast short messages to the world via Your YouTube Channel.
18. Email 'The Robin Good YouTube Channel' to promote a new video release.
19. Join a 'YouTube Group' to post videos or comments to the group discussion area and build your network of contacts.
20. Use 'YouTube Streams' to join or create a room where videos are shared and discussed in real-time.
21. Use 'Active Sharing' to broadcast the videos that you are currently watching, and drive traffic to your profile.
22. Use the 'Share Video' link found under each video you submit and then check the box 'Friends' to send your video to all your friends.
23. Create your own YouTube Channel when you sign-up for a new YouTube account.

Basic Monthly Marketing Plan Checklist

1. Send birthday greetings to existing clients. _____
2. Contact referral sources and express appreciation for their referrals. _____
3. Implement program to develop new referral sources. _____
4. Research new ways to solve more problems of your target clients. _____
5. Research possible new target audience needs. _____
6. Make your friends/family/associates/social contacts aware of your expanding capabilities. _____
7. Train all employees to assist in marketing efforts. _____
8. Conduct selected client interviews to assess performance, changing needs and suggestions. _____
9. Forward copies of articles of interest to contacts. _____
10. Take contact to breakfast, lunch or dinner. _____
11. Invite contact to sporting or cultural event. _____
12. Distribute articles that demonstrate your expertise. _____
13. Invite contacts to an informative seminar. _____
14. Send personal notes of congratulation. _____
15. Join organizations important to your contacts. _____
16. Update your mailing list. _____
17. Issue a press release on a firm accomplishment or planned marketing event. _____
18. Update your firm's list of competitive advantages. _____
19. Attend a networking event. _____
20. Update the helpful content on your website. _____
21. Arrange to speak on your area of expertise. _____
22. Become actively involved in the community. _____
23. Track your ad results to determine resource focus. _____
24. Develop alliances with complementary businesses. _____
25. Conduct customer satisfaction surveys. _____
26. Implement client needs analysis checklist. _____
27. Distribute newsletter featuring clients. _____
28. _____ _____
29. _____ _____
30. _____ _____

Networking Insights

Definition: A reciprocal process in which you share ideas, leads, information, and advice to build mutually beneficial relationships.

Networking Tips:
1. Start your own local referral group with other business owners.
2. Understand your long-term networking goals.
3. Become a helpful resource to networking members.
4. Research people and companies to know their goals and interests.
5. Offer referrals, resources and recommendations to receive same in return.
6. Consistently try to meet new people and make new friends.
7. Develop good listening skills.
8. Frequently express your gratitude for assistance.
9. Know what interests, strengths and availability you bring to the table.
10. Stay in touch with a newsletter, blog, postcards or email messages.
11. Keep asking questions to get others to tell you more about themselves.
12. Show warmth, display confidence, smile and shake hands firmly.
13. Explore organizations that offer accreditation and directory listings.

Entrepreneur Networking Possibilities

1. Meet Up — www.meetup.com
2. FaceBook, Friendster, Myspace — www.facebook.com
3. LinkedIn — www.linkedIn.com
4. Ryze — www.ryze.com
5. Int'l Virtual Women's Chamber of Commerce — www.ivwcc.org
6. Business Network International — www.BNI.com
7. Club E Network — www.clubENetwork.com
8. Local Chamber of Commerce
9. Rotary Club — www.rotary.org
10. Lion's Club — www.lionsclubs.org
11. Jaycees
12. Toastmasters — www.toastmasters.com
13. Woman Owned Network — wwwwomanowned.com
14. Alumni Associations
15. Parent Teacher Associations (PTA)
16. Trade Shows — www.tsnn.com
17. Trade Associations — www.associationscentral.com
18. EONetwork — www.eonetwork.org
19. Prof. Organizations, Economic Clubs, Charities, Churches, Museums, etc.

Perfect Your Elevator Pitch

A brief, focused message aimed at a particular person or niche segment that summarizes why they should be interested in your products and/or services.

am a/we are _____(profession) and we help _____ (target market description) to_____(primary problem solved).

Press Release Cover Letter Worksheet

Instructions: Use this form to build a ready-to-use cover letter.

Your Letterhead.

Date

Dear _____,

As a company located in your coverage area, we thought the attached Press Release would be of special concern to your readers/viewers, as it touches upon something that we all have in common, an interest in

_____.

Brief overview purpose of the press release.

_____

I have also enclosed a media kit to give you background information on _____ Company and myself. I hope to follow-up with you shortly.

I also possess expertise in the following related areas:

- _____
- _____
- _____

Should you wish to speak to me or require additional information, I can be reached at _____ or via email at _____.
Additional assistance with company supplied photos can be requested at the same number. This Press Release can also be downloaded from my company website at www. _____.

Thank you for your time and attention,

Contact Name
Company Title
Phone Number
Email Address

New Release Template

News Release

For Immediate Release
(Or Hold For Release Until …(date)….)

Contact:
Contact Person   _____
Contact Title   _____
Company Name   _____
Phone Number   _____
Fax Number   _____
Email Address   _____
Website Address   _____

Date: _____
Attention: _____ (Target Type of Editor)

Headline: Summarize Your Key Message:

Sub-Headline: Optional: _____

Location of the Firm and Date.

_____

Lead Paragraph: A summary of the newsworthy content.

_____
Answers the questions:
Who: _____
What: _____
Where: _____
When: _____

Second Paragraph:
Expand upon the first paragraph and elaborate on the purpose of the Press Release.

_____
_____

Third Paragraph:
Further details with additional quotes from staff, industry experts or satisfied clients.

_____
_____

For Additional Information Contact:

_____
_____

About Your Expertise:
Presentation of your expert credentials

_____
_____

About Your Business:
Background company history on the firm and central offerings.

_____
_____

Enclosures: Photographs, charts, brochures, etc.

Special Event Release Format   Notes

1.   Type of Event   _____
2.   Sponsoring Organization   _____
3.   Contact Person Before the Event   _____
4.   Contact Person At the Event   _____
5.   Date and Time of the Event   _____
6.   Location of the Event   _____
7.   Length of Presentation Remarks   _____
8.   Presentation Topic   _____
9.   Question Session (Y/N)   _____
10.   Speaker or Panel   _____
11.   Event Background   _____
12.   Noteworthy Expected Attendees   _____
13.   Estimated Number of Attendees   _____
14.   Why readers s/b interested in event.   _____
15.   Specifics of the Event.   _____
16.   Biographies   _____

Track Ad Return on Investment (ROI)

Objective: To invest in those marketing activities that generate the greatest return on invested funds.

Medium	Cost	Calls Received	Cost/Call	No. Act. New Clients	Cost/New Client
Formula:	A	B	A/B=C	D	A/D=E
Newspaper					
Classified Ads					
Yellow Pages					
Billboards					
Cable TV					
Magazine					
Flyers					
Posters					
Coupons					
Direct Mail					
Brochures					
Business Cards					
Seminars					
Demonstrations					
Sponsored Events					
Sign					
Radio					
Trade Shows					
Specialties					
Cold Calling					
Door Hangers					
T-shirts					
Coupon Books					
Transit Ads					
Press Releases					
Word-of-Mouth					
Totals:					

Advertising Tracking Form

Date	Customer	Phone/ Email	Advertising Source	Job?	Notes

Sample Thank-you and Referral Letter

Dear _____ (client name)

I wanted to take this opportunity to thank you for your business once again. If I can be of service to you in the future, I hope you will not hesitate to call.

In the meantime, I have enclosed a few business cards and referral cards. I would very much appreciate your passing them along to anyone in need of interior design services. As usual, I will mail you a referral fee for any business that comes my way from your efforts.

I have also enclosed a 'Customer Satisfaction Survey' with a self-addressed and stamped return envelope. Your feedback is invaluable in helping us to improve the services that we offer and we very much appreciate the time you will spend in completing the survey.

I hope you are enjoying your new surroundings and we look forward to serving you and your family in the future.

Please call me if I can be of any help. Thanks again.

Sincerely,

Sample Press Release Template

American Traveler Staffing Professionals Once Again Awarded Joint Commission Certification

Boca Raton, FL (PRWEB) June 1, 2017 -- For the fourth consecutive year, American Traveler Staffing Professionals has earned the Gold Seal of Approval from the Joint Commission on Accreditation of Medical Organizations. This prestigious award attests to American Traveler's status as a leading U.S. travel nursing company.

The Joint Commission certification is designed to identify the best Medical staffing agencies, through a painstaking process that incorporates an on-site review of a travel nursing agency's compliance with national standards. These standards include a rigorous set of performance measures for staffing services on how they determine the qualification and competency of their staff, as well as how staff is placed, monitored and supported. We are extremely proud of our achievements in Medical staffing sector," said Robert L. Bok, CEO of American Traveler Staffing Professionals. "Our continuing Joint Commission certification recognizes American Traveler's dedication to being the best travel nursing agency possible. Our goals are simple: first, to provide our client Medical facilities with nursing and allied Medical professionals that are qualified to deliver safe and high-quality care to patients; and second, to ensure that our client travel nurses enjoy a rewarding career by offering them the services and support they need to excel at their jobs."

"Our goals are simple: first, to provide our client Medical facilities with nursing and allied Medical professionals that are qualified to deliver safe and high-quality care to patients; and second, to ensure that our client travel nurses enjoy a rewarding career by offering them the services and support they need to excel at their jobs."

The independent, not-for-profit Joint Commission was founded in 1951 to ensure the safety and quality of care provided to the public, through accreditation programs and related services that support continuous performance improvement in Medical organizations. The Joint Commission evaluates and accredits more than 15,000 Medical organizations and programs in the United States, including more than 7,800 hospitals and home-care organizations, and more than 7,300 other Medical operations.

About American Traveler
The Joint Commission-certified American Traveler specializes in short-term, per diem, travel nursing and permanent positions for RNs, Physical Therapists, OTs, SLPs and other allied health professionals. American Traveler places these professionals in rewarding positions across the country, from world-renowned university teaching hospitals to rural Medical facilities. American Traveler is proud to offer a full array of workforce management software to hospitals that includes Internal Staffing, Vendor Staffing, and Contingent Workforce Management. Our solutions encompass all aspects of supplemental staffing that optimize hospitals' valuable human resources, savings of significant capital, and ease the burdens of maintaining adequate staffing levels.
# # #

Applicant Information:

Last Name First Name Middle Name
Current Address City State Zip
Permanent Address City State Zip
Telephone: Home Cellular Email Address
Social Security Number

Emergency Contact:

Name Relationship Phone
Permanent Address City State Zip

Credentials:

Professional Designation
Primary Specialty Other Specialty Other Specialty Other Specialty

Original State of Licensure

License # State Expiration Date Date Issued Active/Inactive?

Additional Licensure

License # State Expiration Date Active/Inactive?
License # State Expiration Date Active/Inactive?
License # State Expiration Date Active/Inactive?

Certifications

Certification Cert. # Cert. Date Exp. Date
Certification Cert. # Cert. Date Exp. Date
Certification Cert. # Cert. Date Exp. Date
Certification Cert. # Cert. Date Exp. Date

Employee Application

Background Questions:
Have you ever plead guilty to or been convicted of a DUI?
Have you ever been investigated by state or federal authorities for an alleged violation of a Medical law?
Have you ever been a defendant in a professional liability action?

Education:

High School

Graduate

Other

College

School

Education

Facility/Employer # of Beds (Hospital)
Address
Position Held Unit/Area # of Beds (Unit)
Charge Experience?
# of Cases / Patients Shift Travel Assignment? Agency:
Name and Title of Supervisor Phone Number Fax Number
From: To:
Employment Dates (mm/yyyy) Reason for Leaving
City State Zip
Diplomas/Degrees Received
Name, City and State Month/Year of Graduation
Has your professional license or certification ever been under investigation, subject to disciplinary action, suspension or
revocation?
Have you ever plead guilty to or been convicted of a crime other than a misdemeanor?
Application (page 2)
ADN/BSN/Certificate

Employment History: Provide employment history beginning with your most recent employer.
If more entries are needed, please provide on additional sheets.
Facility/Employer # of Beds (Hospital)
Address
Position Held Unit/Area # of Beds (Unit)
Charge Experience?
# of Shift Travel Cases Assignm/e nt?Agency: Patients
Name and Title of Supervisor Phone Number Fax Number
From: To:
Employment Dates (mm/yyyy) Reason for Leaving
Facility/Employer # of Beds (Hospital)
Address
Position Held Unit/Area # of Beds (Unit)
Charge Experience?
# of Shift Travel Cases Assignment? Agency: Patients

Name and Title of Supervisor Phone Number Fax Number
From: To:
Employment Dates (mm/yyyy) Reason for Leaving
Facility/Employer # of Beds (Hospital)
Address
Position Held Unit/Area # of Beds (Unit)
Charge Experience?
# of Shift Travel Cases Assignment? Agency: Patients
Name and Title of Supervisor Phone Number Fax Number
From: To:
Employment Dates (mm/yyyy) Reason for Leaving
City State Zip

Employment History
Facility/Employer # of Beds (Hospital)
Address
Position Held Unit/Area # of Beds (Unit)
Charge Experience?
# of Shift Travel Cases Assignment? Agency: Patients
Name and Title of Supervisor Phone Number Fax Number
From: To:
Employment Dates (mm/yyyy) Reason for Leaving
Facility/Employer Contact Name Title
Address City State Zip Phone
Facility/Employer Contact Name Title
Address City State Zip Phone
Facility/Employer Contact Name Title
Address City State Zip Phone

Signature   Date
Upon submitting and signing this employment application, I certify all of the foregoing
information to be true, accurate and complete. I understand and acknowledge that any
misrepresentation or omission of fact on this application may result in disqualification
from employment with _____ Staffing, Inc. I authorize _____ Staffing and its agents to
conduct any investigation concerning my background, civil and criminal records,
educational records and any other such records or information related to my potential
employment with _____ Staffing. If employed by _____ Staffing, I agree to abide by all
rules and regulations adopted by _____ Staffing and understand that those rules and
regulations are subject to change from time to time. I understand that, if employed by
_____ Staffing, I may be required to undergo a physical examination, including drug
screening, in order to determine my ability to perform the duties required in my position.
I hereby authorize my former employers to release to _____ Staffing and its agents any
and all information concerning my past employment.
Professional References:
City State Zip
References must be a Charge Nurse, Supervisor or Manager in a Medical setting.

Made in the USA
Las Vegas, NV
23 September 2024